Ultimate Pocket

WORLD
FACTFILE

A DORLING KINDERSLEY BOOK

Project Editor Debra Clapson
Project Cartographer Julia Lunn
Project Art Editor Yahya El-Droubie

Designer Katy Wall
Cartographic Research Michael Martin
Database Editor Ruth Duxbury

Art Director Chez Picthall
Editorial Direction Andrew Heritage, Louise Cavanagh
Production Controller David Proffit

Editorial Contributors
Kevin & Melanie McRae,
Louisa Somerville, Sean Connolly

Copyright © 1996 Dorling Kindersley Limited, London

*First published in Canada in 1996
by élan press,
an imprint of General Publishing Co. Ltd.,
30 Lesmill Road, Toronto, Canada, M3B 2T6*

Canadian Cataloguing in Publication Data
Ultimate Pocket World Factfile

ISBN 1-55144-123-3

1. Geography - Handbooks, manuals, etc.

G123.U57 1996   910   C95-933270-7

*Film output in England, by Euroscan
Printed and bound in Italy, by L.E.G.O.*

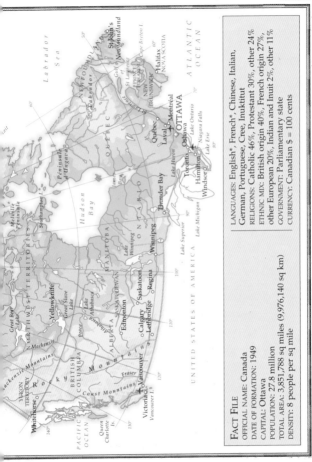

FACT FILE

OFFICIAL NAME: Canada
DATE OF FORMATION: 1949
CAPITAL: Ottawa
POPULATION: 27.8 million
TOTAL AREA: 3,851,788 sq miles (9,976,140 sq km)
DENSITY: 8 people per sq mile

LANGUAGES: English*, French*, Chinese, Italian, German, Portuguese, Cree, Inuktitut
RELIGIONS: Catholic 46%, Protestant 30%, other 24%
ETHNIC MIX: British origin 40%, French origin 27%, other European 20%, Indian and Inuit 2%, other 11%
GOVERNMENT: Parliamentary state
CURRENCY: Canadian $ = 100 cents

17

UNITED STATES OF AMERICA

STRETCHING ACROSS the most temperate part of North America, and with many natural resources, the USA is the world's leading economic power.

 GEOGRAPHY
Central plain, mountains in west, hills and low mountains in east. Forested north and east, southwestern deserts. Volcanic islands in Hawaii. Forest, tundra in Alaska.

CLIMATE
Wide variety. Continental in north, hot summers and mild winters in southeast, desert climate in southwest. Arctic climate in Alaska; Florida and Hawaii tropical.

PEOPLE AND SOCIETY
Multiracial population, established through successive waves of immigration, initially from Europe and Africa, with more recent influxes from Latin America and Asia. Strong sense of nationhood, despite cultural diversity. Conservative, usually Christian consensus, is increasingly challenged by liberal, secular values of US popular culture.

FACT FILE

OFFICIAL NAME: United States of America
DATE OF FORMATION: 1959
CAPITAL: Washington D.C.
POPULATION: 257.8 million
TOTAL AREA: 3,681,760 sq miles (9,372,610 sq km)

DENSITY: 73 people per sq mile
LANGUAGES: English*, Spanish, other
RELIGIONS: Protestant 56%, Catholic 28%, Muslim 3%, other 13%
ETHNIC MIX: White (inc. Hispanic) 83%, Black 13%, other 4%
GOVERNMENT: Multiparty republic
CURRENCY: US $ = 100 cents

THE ECONOMY

Traditions of innovation, skilled labor, and venture capital help high-tech industries replace outdated manufacturing. Global dominance of US culture boosts services, manufactures. Vast agriculture, mining sectors.

◆ INSIGHT: *The United States of America has the world's oldest constitution. Devised in 1787, it has been operated continuously ever since*

3000m/9843ft
2000m/6562ft
1000m/3281ft
500m/1640ft
200m/656ft
Sea Level

0   400 km

0   400 miles

MEXICO

LOCATED BETWEEN the southern end of North America and the Central American states, Mexico was a Spanish colony for 300 years, until 1836.

GEOGRAPHY
Coastal plains along Pacific and Atlantic seaboards rise to a high arid central plateau. To the east and west are Sierra Madre mountain ranges. Limestone lowlands in the Yucatan peninsula.

CLIMATE
Plateau and high mountains are warm for much of year. Pacific coast is tropical: storms occur mostly March–December. Northwest is dry.

THE ECONOMY
One of the world's largest oil producers, with large reserves. Tropical fruits, vegetables grown as cash crops. Population growth outstripping job creation. North American Free Trade Agreement, signed with USA and Canada, came into force in 1994. US companies poised to move into Mexico and enter competition with Mexican industry.

3000m/9843ft	
2000m/6562ft	
1000m/3281ft	
500m/1640ft	
200m/656ft	
Sea Level	

0   200 km
0   200 miles

FACT FILE
OFFICIAL NAME: United Mexican State
DATE OF FORMATION: 1836
CAPITAL: Mexico City
POPULATION: 90 million
TOTAL AREA: 756,061 sq miles (1,958,200 sq km)

DENSITY: 120 people per sq mile
LANGUAGES: Spanish*, Mayan dialects
RELIGIONS: Roman Catholic 89%, Protestant 6%, other 5%
ETHNIC MIX: *mestizo* 55%, Indian 30%, White 6%, other 9%
GOVERNMENT: Multiparty republic
CURRENCY: Peso = 100 centavos

Ultimate Pocket

WORLD

FACTFILE

CONTENTS

 NORTH & CENTRAL AMERICA 14-15

SOUTH AMERICA 42-43

 AFRICA 58-59

EUROPE 114-115

ASIA   160-161

AUSTRALASIA & OCEANIA   212-213

PHYSICAL WORLD

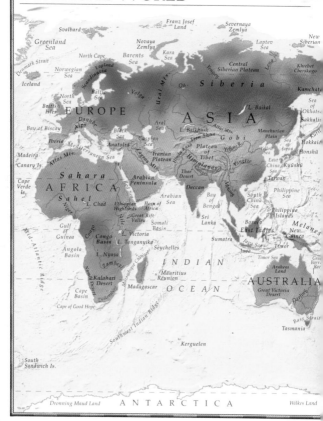

ARCTIC OCEAN

Limit of permanent pack ice

Queen
Elizabeth
Islands
Ellesmere I.
Greenland
Chukchi
Sea
Beaufort
Sea
Baffin
Bay
Baffin I.
Davis Strait
Arctic Circle
Brooks Range
Great Bear
Lake
Mackenzie
Iceland
Bering Strait
Yukon
Rocky Mountains
Great Slave
Lake
Hudson
Bay
Labrador
Sea
Bering
Sea
Gulf
of
Alaska
NORTH
Labrador
Aleutian Islands
Vancouver I.
AMERICA
Great
Lakes
St Lawrence
Grand
Banks
Mid-Atlantic Ridge
Missouri
North American
Basin
ATLANTIC
Hawaiian Is.
Mississippi
Baja
California
Sierra Madre
Gulf of
Mexico
West Indies
Tropic of Cancer
PACIFIC
Caribbean
Sea
OCEAN
Polynesia
OCEAN
Guiana
Highlands
Micronesia
Galápagos
Is.
Amazon
Amazon Basin
Equator
Andes
SOUTH
Brazil
Basin
Fiji
Tahiti
AMERICA
Mato
Grosso
New
Caledonia
Peru Basin
Tropic of Capricorn
Kermadec Trench
Patagonia
Pampas
North I.
Southwest Pacific
Basin
Argentine
Basin
New Zealand
Falkland Is.
South Georgia
South I.
Tierra
del Fuego
Cape Horn
Drake Passage
Antarctic
Peninsula
Antarctic Circle
Southeast Pacific
Basin
ANTARCTICA
Weddell
Sea
Ross Sea

9

POLITICAL WORLD

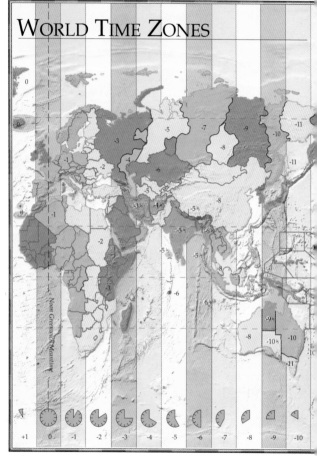

WORLD TIME ZONES

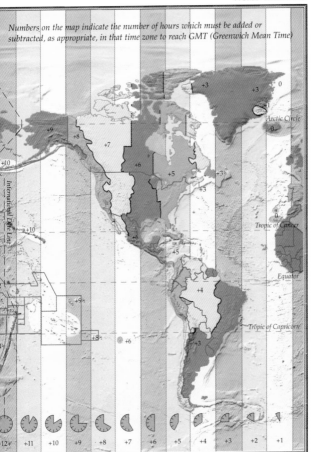

Numbers on the map indicate the number of hours which must be added or subtracted, as appropriate, in that time zone to reach GMT (Greenwich Mean Time)

13

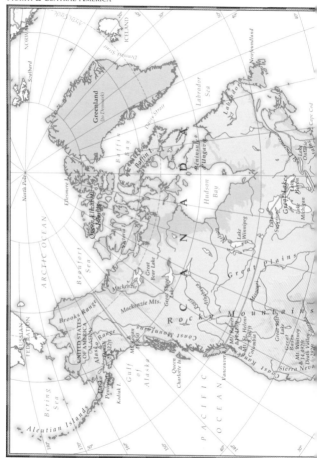

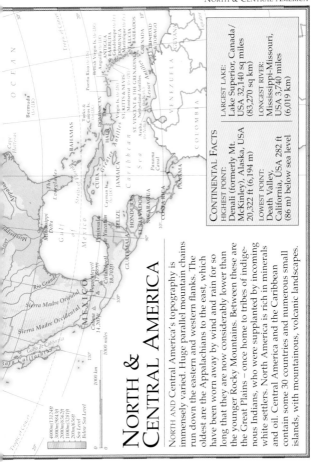

CONTINENTAL FACTS

HIGHEST POINT:
Denali (formerly Mt.
McKinley), Alaska, USA
20,322 ft (6,194 m)

LOWEST POINT:
Death Valley,
California, USA 282 ft
(86 m) below sea level

LARGEST LAKE:
Lake Superior, Canada/
USA 32,140 sq miles
(83,270 sq km)

LONGEST RIVER:
Mississippi-Missouri,
USA 3,740 miles
(6,019 km)

NORTH & CENTRAL AMERICA

NORTH AND Central America's topography is
immensely varied. Huge parallel mountain chains
run down the eastern and western flanks. The
oldest are the Appalachians to the east, which
have been worn away by wind and rain for so
long that they are now considerably lower than
the younger Rocky Mountains. Between these are
the Great Plains – once home to tribes of indigenous Indians, who were supplanted by incoming
white settlers. North America is rich in minerals
and oil. Central America and the Caribbean
contain some 30 countries and numerous small
islands, with mountainous, volcanic landscapes.

CANADA

CANADA EXTENDS from its long border with the USA northward to the Arctic Ocean. In recent years, the continued political relationship of French-speaking Québec with the rest of the country has been the key constitutional issue.

GEOGRAPHY

Arctic tundra and islands give way southward to forests, interspersed with lakes and rivers, and then central plains, with vast prairies. Rocky Mountains lie in the west, beyond which are the Coast Mountains, islands and fjords. Fertile lowlands in the east.

CLIMATE

Ranges from polar and subpolar in the north to cool in the south. Winters in the interior are colder and longer than on the coasts, with temperatures well below freezing and deep snow; summers are hotter. The Pacific coast has the warmest winters.

PEOPLE AND SOCIETY

Most people live along narrow strip near the US border, fostering shared cultural values. Social differences, however, include wider welfare provision and Commonwealth membership. Government welcomes ethnic diversity among immigrants. Land claims by indigenous peoples settled in recent years.

THE ECONOMY

Wide-ranging resources, providing cheap energy and raw materials for manufacturing, underpin high standard of living. Better productivity and rise of high-tech industries have increased unemployment. Concern over primary export prices.

◆ INSIGHT: The magnetic north pole, where the trembling needle of a compass stands still, is located just off Bathurst Island in northern Canada

◆ INSIGHT: *More people emigrate from Mexico than any other state in the world. Hundreds of thousands of Mexicans cross into the US each year, many of them staying as illegal immigrants*

PEOPLE AND SOCIETY

Most Mexicans are *mestizos* of mixed Spanish and Indian descent. Rural Indians are largely segregated from Hispanic society and most live in poverty. The situation leads to intermittent rebellion by landless Indians. Men remain dominant in business and few women take part in the political process. Mexico is a multiparty democracy in name; in practice, the PRI (Institutional Revolutionary Party) has retained power since 1929. Rural depopulation and high unemployment are major problems. Mexico has a faster-growing population than any other large country. Between 1960 and 1980, its population doubled.

RICA

Rio Grande

huahua

Rio Grande

Sierra Madre Oriental

Nuevo Laredo

Monclova

Torreón   Monterrey   Reynosa
           Saltillo   Matamoros

Durango

Ciudad Victoria

Caribbean Sea

Zacatecas   Ciudad
San Luis Potosí   de Valles   Tampico

Yucatán Channel

Tepic   Aguascalientes
         León
dalajara   Irapuato   Querétaro   Poza Rica
            Salamanca   Gulf
                      Pachuca   of
                                   Mexico

Mérida

Península
de
Yucatán

Colima   Morelia   ✦ MEXICO CITY
          Toluca   Puebla   Orizaba   Veracruz

Bahía
de
Campeche

Chetumal

Villahermosa

Coatzacoalcos   BELIZE

Oaxaca   Istmo de
          Tehuantepec   Tuxtla Gutiérrez

Acapulco

Rio Balsas

Sierra Madre del Sur

100°

Sierra Madre

GUATEMALA

95°   Tapachula   90°

PACIFIC

OCEAN

GUATEMALA

THE LARGEST state on the Central American isthmus, Guatemala returned to civilian rule in 1986, after 32 years of repressive military rule.

GEOGRAPHY
Narrow Pacific coastal plain. Central highlands with volcanoes. Short, swampy Caribbean coast. Tropical rain forests in the north.

CLIMATE
Tropical, hot, and humid in coastal regions and north. More temperate in central highlands.

PEOPLE AND SOCIETY
Indians form a majority, but power, wealth, and land controlled by *Ladino* elite. Highland Indians were main victims of the military's indiscriminate campaign against guerrilla groups 1978–1984. Since civilian rule, the level of violence has diminished, but extreme poverty is still widespread.

◆ INSIGHT: *Guatemala, which means "land of trees," was the center of the ancient Maya civilization*

THE ECONOMY
Agriculture is key sector. Sugar, coffee, beef, bananas, and cardamom top exports. Political stability has revived tourism.

| 3000m/9843ft |
| 2000m/6562ft |
| 1000m/3281ft |
| 500m/1640ft |
| 200m/656ft |
| Sea Level |

FACT FILE	
OFFICIAL NAME: Republic of Guatemala	DENSITY: 231 people per sq mile
DATE OF FORMATION: 1838	LANGUAGES: Spanish*, Quiché, Mam, Kekchí, Cakchiquel
CAPITAL: Guatemala City	RELIGIONS: Christian 99%, other 1%
POPULATION: 10 million	ETHNIC MIX: Maya Indian 55%, *Ladino* (Euro-Indian, White) 45%
TOTAL AREA: 42,043 sq miles (108,890 sq km)	GOVERNMENT: Multiparty republic
	CURRENCY: Quetzal = 100 centavos

BELIZE

BELIZE LIES on the eastern shore of the Yucatan Peninsula in Central America. A former British colony, it became fully independent in 1981.

GEOGRAPHY
Almost half the land area is forested. Low mountains in southeast. Flat swampy coastal plains.

CLIMATE
Tropical. Very hot and humid, with May–December rainy season.

PEOPLE AND SOCIETY
Spanish-speaking *mestizos* now outnumber black Creoles for the first time. The huge influx of migrants from other countries in the region in the past decade has caused some tension. Newcomers have provided labor for agriculture, but have put pressure on social services. Traditional Creole dominance has been weakened by emigration to the United States.

THE ECONOMY
Agriculture, tourism, and remittances from Belizeans living abroad are economic mainstays. Citrus fruit concentrates, lobsters, shrimp, and textiles are exported.

◆ INSIGHT: Belize's barrier reef is the second largest in the world

FACT FILE

OFFICIAL NAME: Belize
DATE OF FORMATION: 1981
CAPITAL: Belmopan
POPULATION: 200,000
TOTAL AREA: 8,865 sq miles (22,960 sq km)
DENSITY: 23 people per sq mile

LANGUAGES: English*, English Creole, Spanish, Maya, Garifuna
RELIGIONS: Christian 87%, other 13%
ETHNIC MIX: *mestizo* 44%, Creole 30%, Indian 11%, Garifuna 8%, other 7%
GOVERNMENT: Parliamentary democracy
CURRENCY: Belizean $ =100 cents

EL SALVADOR

EL SAVADOR IS Central America's smallest state. A 12-year war between US-backed government troops and left-wing guerrillas ended in 1992.

GEOGRAPHY

Narrow coastal belt backed by mountain ranges with over 20 volcanic peaks. Central plateau.

CLIMATE
Tropical coastal belt is very hot, with seasonal rains. Cooler, temperate climate in highlands.

PEOPLE AND SOCIETY

Population is largely *mestizo*; ethnic tensions are few. The civil war was fought over economic disparities, which still exist, despite some reform. 75,000 people died during the war, many were unarmed civilians. Around 500,000 more were displaced – mainly rural peasant families. In 1992, left-wing movement gave up its arms and joined formal political process.

THE ECONOMY
Civil war caused $2 billion-worth of damage. Huge amounts of foreign aid needed for survival. Overdependence on coffee, which accounts for 90% of exports.

◆ INSIGHT: Named for the Savior, Jesus Christ, El Salvador is the most densely populated state in the region

FACT FILE

OFFICIAL NAME: Republic of El Salvador
DATE OF FORMATION: 1856
CAPITAL: San Salvador
POPULATION: 5.4 million
TOTAL AREA: 8,124 sq miles (21,040 sq km)

DENSITY: 665 people per sq mile
LANGUAGES: Spanish*, Nahua
RELIGIONS: Roman Catholic 75%, other (inc. Protestant) 25%
ETHNIC MIX: *mestizo* (Euro-Indian) 89%, Indian 10%, White 1%
GOVERNMENT: Multiparty republic
CURRENCY: Colón = 100 centavos

HONDURAS

STRADDLING THE Central American isthmus, Honduras returned to democratic civilian rule in 1981 after a succession of military regimes.

GEOGRAPHY
Narrow plains along both coasts. Mountainous interior, cut by river valleys. Tropical forests, swamps, and lagoons in the east.

CLIMATE
Tropical coastal lowlands are hot and humid, with May–October rains. Interior is cooler and drier.

PEOPLE AND SOCIETY
Majority of population is *mestizo*. Garifunas on Caribbean coast maintain their own language and culture. Indians inhabit the east, and remote mountain areas; their land rights are often violated. Most of the rural population live in poverty. Land reform and high unemployment are main issues facing the government.

THE ECONOMY
Second poorest country in the region. Bananas are the traditional cash crop – production is dominated by two US companies. Coffee, timber, livestock are also exported.

◆ INSIGHT: *Honduran currency is named after a Lenca Indian chief who was the main leader of resistance to the Spanish conquest in the 16th century*

FACT FILE	DENSITY: 127 people per sq mile
OFFICIAL NAME: Republic of Honduras	LANGUAGES: Spanish*, English Creole, Garifuna, Indian languages
DATE OF FORMATION: 1821	RELIGIONS: Catholic 97%, other 3%
CAPITAL: Tegucigalpa	ETHNIC MIX: *mestizo* 90%, Indian 7%,
POPULATION: 5.6 million	Garifuna (Black Carib) 2%, White 1%
TOTAL AREA: 43,278 sq miles (112,090 sq km)	GOVERNMENT: Multiparty republic
	CURRENCY: Lempira = 100 centavos

NICARAGUA

NICARAGUA LIES at the heart of Central America. An 11-year war between left-wing Sandinistas and right-wing US-backed Contras ended in 1989.

GEOGRAPHY
Extensive forested plains in the east. Central mountain region with many active volcanoes. Pacific coastlands are dominated by lakes.

CLIMATE
Tropical. Hot all year round in the lowlands. Cooler in the mountains. Occasional hurricanes.

PEOPLE AND SOCIETY
The isolated Atlantic regions, populated by Miskito Indians and blacks, gained limited independence in 1987. Elections in 1990 brought a right-wing pro-US party to power, but the Sandinistas remain a major political force in a country where poverty and unrest are rising.

THE ECONOMY
Coffee, sugar, and cotton exports are affected by low world prices. Economy is dependent on foreign aid; the United States is the largest donor.

◆ INSIGHT: Lake Nicaragua is the only freshwater lake to contain ocean animals

1000m/3281ft
500m/1640ft
200m/656ft
Sea Level

HONDURAS

Ocotal
Estelí   Jinotega
        Matagalpa
Chinandega   Telica   Matiguas
Corinto
León
Nagarote   ✛ MANAGUA
San Rafael del Sur   Granada   Juigalpa   Bluefields
        Nandaime
Diriamba   Lago de
Jinotepe   Rivas   Nicaragua

Coco

La Mosquitia

Caribbean Sea

COSTA RICA   San Juan

0   100 km
0   100 miles

FACT FILE

OFFICIAL NAME: Republic of Nicaragua
DATE OF FORMATION: 1838
CAPITAL: Managua
POPULATION: 4.1 million
TOTAL AREA: 50,193 sq miles (130,000 sq km)

DENSITY: 82 people per sq mile
LANGUAGES: Spanish*, English Creole, Miskito
RELIGIONS: Catholic 95%, other 5%
ETHNIC MIX: mestizo 69%, White 17%, Black 9%, Indian 5%
GOVERNMENT: Multiparty republic
CURRENCY: Córdoba = 100 pence

COSTA RICA

COSTA RICA is the most stable country in Central America. Its neutrality in foreign affairs is long-standing, but it has very strong US ties.

GEOGRAPHY
Coastal plains of swamp and savanna rise to a fertile central plateau, which leads to a mountain range with active volcanic peaks.

CLIMATE
Hot and humid in coastal regions. Temperate uplands. High annual rainfall.

PEOPLE AND SOCIETY
Population has a mixture of Spanish, African, and native Indian ancestry. Costa Rica's long democratic tradition, developed public health system, and high literacy rates are unrivaled in the region. Landowners and the United States influence politics.

◆ INSIGHT: *Costa Rica's constitution is the only one in the world to forbid national armies*

THE ECONOMY
Traditionally agricultural, but mining and manufacturing are developing rapidly. Bananas, beef, and coffee are the leading exports. Tourism and travel have increased considerably in recent years.

FACT FILE

OFFICIAL NAME: Republic of Costa Rica
DATE OF FORMATION: 1821
CAPITAL: San José
POPULATION: 3.3 million
TOTAL AREA: 19,730 sq miles (51,100 sq km)

DENSITY: 166 people per sq mile
LANGUAGES: Spanish*, English Creole, Bribri, Cabecar
RELIGIONS: Catholic 95%, other 5%
ETHNIC MIX: White/*mestizo* (Euro-Indian) 96%, Black 2%, Indian 2%
GOVERNMENT: Multiparty republic
CURRENCY: Colón = 100 centimos

PANAMA

PANAMA IS the southernmost country in Central America. The Panama Canal (under US-control until 2000) links the Pacific and Atlantic oceans.

GEOGRAPHY
Lowlands along both coasts, with savanna-covered plains and rolling hills. Mountainous interior. Swamps and rain forests in the east.

CLIMATE
Hot and humid, with heavy rainfall in May–December wet season. Cooler at high altitudes.

PEOPLE AND SOCIETY
Multiethnic society, dominated by people of Spanish origin. Indians live in remote areas. The Canal and US military bases have given society a cosmopolitan outlook, but the Catholic extended family remains strong. In 1989, US troops invaded to arrest its dictator General Noriega on drug charges and to restore civilian rule.

THE ECONOMY
Important banking sector, plus related financial and insurance services. Earnings from merchant ships sailing under Panamanian flag. Banana and shrimp exports.

◆ INSIGHT: *The Panama Canal extends for 50 miles (80 km). Around 12,000 ships pass through it each year*

FACT FILE
OFFICIAL NAME: Republic of Panama
DATE OF FORMATION: 1903
CAPITAL: Panama City
POPULATION: 2.6 million
TOTAL AREA: 29,761 sq miles (77,080 sq km)

DENSITY: 87 people per sq mile
LANGUAGES: Spanish*, English Creole, Indian languages
RELIGIONS: Catholic 93%, other 7%
ETHNIC MIX: *mestizo* 70%, Black 14%, White 10%, Indian 6%
GOVERNMENT: Multiparty republic
CURRENCY: Balboa = 100 centesimos

JAMAICA

FIRST COLONIZED by the Spanish and then, from 1655, by the English, the Caribbean island of Jamaica achieved independence in 1962.

GEOGRAPHY
Mainly mountainous, with lush tropical vegetation. Inaccessible limestone area in the northwest. Low, irregular coastal plains are broken by hills and plateaus.

CLIMATE
Tropical. Hot and humid, with temperate interior. Hurricanes are likely June–November.

PEOPLE AND SOCIETY
Ethnically diverse, but tensions result from the gulf between rich and poor, rather than race. Economic and political life dominated by a few wealthy, long-established families. Armed crime, much of it drug-related, is a problem. Large areas of Kingston are ruled by *Dons*, gang leaders who administer their own violent justice.

THE ECONOMY
Major producer of bauxite (aluminum ore). Tourism well developed. Light industry and data processing for US companies. Sugar, coffee, and rum are exported.

◆ INSIGHT: *Jamaica's Rastafarians look to the late emperor of Ethiopia, Haile Selassie, as their spiritual leader, and Africa as their spiritual home*

FACT FILE
OFFICIAL NAME: Jamaica
DATE OF FORMATION: 1962
CAPITAL: Kingston
POPULATION: 2.5 million
TOTAL AREA: 4,243 sq miles (10,990 sq km)
DENSITY: 590 people per sq mile

LANGUAGES: English*, English Creole, Hindi, Spanish, Chinese
RELIGIONS: Christian 60%, other 40%
ETHNIC MIX: Black 75%, mixed 15%, South Asian 5%, other 5%
GOVERNMENT: Parliamentary democracy
CURRENCY: Jamaican $ = 100 cents

CUBA

CUBA IS the largest island in the Caribbean and the only Communist country in the Americas. It has been led by Fidel Castro since 1959.

GEOGRAPHY
Mostly fertile plains and basins. Three mountainous areas. Forests of pine and mahogany cover one quarter of the country.

CLIMATE
Subtropical. Hot all year round, and very hot in summer. Heaviest rainfall in the mountains. Hurricanes can strike in autumn.

PEOPLE AND SOCIETY
Castro's regime has reduced once extreme wealth disparities, given education a high priority, and established an efficient health service. Political dissent, however, is not tolerated. Recent fall in living standards has led 30,000 Cubans to flee by boat, to seek asylum in the United States.

THE ECONOMY
Main product is sugar. Cuba's economy is in crisis following the loss of its patron and supplier, the former USSR. Recent reforms have allowed small-scale enterprise and use of US dollar. The 30-year-old US trade embargo continues.

◆ INSIGHT: To combat fuel shortages, over half a million traditional black bicycles have been imported from China

HAVANA
(La Habana)
Marianao ○ ✈ ○ Matanzas
○ Colón
Pinar
del Río Cienfuegos ○ Santa Clara
Ciego de Avila ○
Archipiélago de los
Canarreos
Las Tunas ○ Holguín
Bayamo ○
Santiago ○ Guantánamo
de Cuba

ATLANTIC
OCEAN

Straits of Florida

Camagüey

Caribbean
Sea

GUANTÁNAMO BAY
(to USA)

1000m/3281
500m/1640ft
200m/656ft
Sea Level

0   100 km
0   100 miles

FACT FILE
OFFICIAL NAME: Republic of Cuba
DATE OF FORMATION: 1902
CAPITAL: Havana
POPULATION: 10.9 million
TOTAL AREA: 42,803 sq miles
(110,860 sq km)
DENSITY: 255 people per sq mile

LANGUAGES: Spanish*, English, French, Chinese
RELIGIONS: Roman Catholic 40%, other 60% (inc. unaffiliated)
ETHNIC MIX: White 66%, Afro-European 22%, other 12%
GOVERNMENT: Socialist republic
CURRENCY: Peso = 100 centavos

BAHAMAS

LOCATED IN the western Atlantic, off the Florida coast, the Bahamas comprises some 700 islands and 2,400 keys, 30 of which are inhabited.

GEOGRAPHY
Long, mainly flat coral formations with a few low hills. Some islands have pine forests, lagoons, and mangrove swamps.

CLIMATE
Subtropical. Hot summers and mild winters. Heavy rainfall, especially in summer. Hurricanes can strike July–December.

PEOPLE AND SOCIETY
Over half the population live on New Providence. Tourist industry employs 40% of the work force. Remainder are engaged in traditional fishing and agriculture, or in administration. Close US ties were strained in 1980s, with senior government members implicated in narcotics corruption. In 1993, tough policies instituted to deter settling of Haitian refugees.

THE ECONOMY
Tourism accounts for half of all revenues. Major international financial services sector, including banking and insurance.

◆ INSIGHT: Six tourists per inhabitant visit the Bahamas every year

FACT FILE

OFFICIAL NAME: The Commonwealth of the Bahamas
DATE OF FORMATION: 1973
CAPITAL: Nassau
POPULATION: 300,000
TOTAL AREA: 5,359 sq miles (13,880 sq km)

DENSITY: 55 people per sq mile
LANGUAGES: English*, English Creole
RELIGIONS: Protestant 76%, Roman Catholic 19%, other 5%
ETHNIC MIX: Black 85%, White 15%
GOVERNMENT: Parliamentary democracy
CURRENCY: Bahamian $ = 100 cents

HAITI

SHARES THE Caribbean island of Hispaniola with the Dominican Republic. At independence in 1804, it became the world's first black republic.

 GEOGRAPHY
Predominantly mountainous, with forests and fertile plains.

 CLIMATE
Tropical, with rain throughout the year. Humid in coastal areas, much cooler in the mountains.

PEOPLE AND SOCIETY
Majority of population is of African descent. A few have European roots, primarily French. Rigid class structure maintains vast disparities of wealth. Most Haitians live in extreme poverty. In recent years, political oppression and a collapsing economy led thousands to seek US asylum. In 1994, US-led troops reinstated the elected president, who was ousted by the military in 1991.

THE ECONOMY
Few natural resources. In 1994, after three years of UN sanctions, the country's economic links were restored and foreign aid resumed.

◆ INSIGHT: *Haiti's independence was achieved after Toussaint l'Ouverture led a slave rebellion in 1791*

1000m/3281ft	
500m/1640ft	
200m/656ft	0 50 km
Sea Level	0 50 miles

FACT FILE

OFFICIAL NAME: Republic of Haiti
DATE OF FORMATION: 1804
CAPITAL: Port-au-Prince
POPULATION: 6.9 million
TOTAL AREA: 10,714 sq miles
(27,750 sq km)
DENSITY: 644 people per sq mile

LANGUAGES: French*, French Creole*, English
RELIGIONS: Roman Catholic 80%, Protestant 16%, Voodoo 4%
ETHNIC MIX: Black 95%, Afro-European 5%
GOVERNMENT: Multiparty republic
CURRENCY: Gourde = 100 centimes

DOMINICAN REPUBLIC

OCCUPIES THE eastern two thirds of the island of Hispaniola in the Caribbean. Frequent coups and a strong US influence mark its recent past.

GEOGRAPHY
Highlands and rainforested mountains – including highest peak in Caribbean, Pico Duarte – interspersed with fertile valleys. Extensive coastal plain in the east.

CLIMATE
Hot and humid close to sea level, cooler at altitude. Heavy rainfall, especially in the northeast.

PEOPLE AND SOCIETY
White landowners and the military hold political power. Mixed-race majority control commerce and form bulk of middle classes. Many of the poor are black. White and mixed-race women are starting to enter the professions. Poverty and unemployment have led some Dominicans to emigrate to the United States, or become drug-traffickers.

THE ECONOMY
Mining – mainly of nickel and gold – and sugar are major sectors. Hidden economy based on transshipment of narcotics to the United States. Recent growth in tourism.

◆ INSIGHT: *Santo Domingo is the oldest city in the Americas. It was founded in 1496 by the brother of Christopher Columbus*

FACT FILE

OFFICIAL NAME: Dominican Republic
DATE OF FORMATION: 1865
CAPITAL: Santo Domingo
POPULATION: 7.6 million
TOTAL AREA: 18,815 sq miles (48,730 sq km)

DENSITY: 403 people per sq mile
LANGUAGES: Spanish*, French Creole
RELIGIONS: Roman Catholic 95%, other (Protestant, Jewish) 5%
ETHNIC MIX: Afro-European 73%, White 16%, Black 11%
GOVERNMENT: Multiparty republic
CURRENCY: Peso = 100 centavos

ST. KITTS & NEVIS

ST. KITTS and Nevis lies in the northern part of the Leeward Islands chain in the Caribbean. Nevis is the less developed of the two islands.

GEOGRAPHY
Volcanic in origin, with forested, mountainous interiors. Nevis has hot and cold springs.

CLIMATE
Tropical, tempered by trade winds. Little seasonal variation in temperature. Moderate rainfall.

PEOPLE AND SOCIETY
Majority of the population is of African descent. Intermarriage has blurred other racial lines and eliminated ethnic tensions. For most people, the extended family is the norm. Wealth disparities are not great, but urban professionals enjoy a higher standard of living than rural sugarcane farmers. Politics is based on the British system; funds are provided by professionals and the trade unions. The proposed Leeward Islands union is the main political issue.

THE ECONOMY
Sugar industry, currently UK-managed, has preferential access to EU and US markets. Successful and still expanding tourist industry.

◆ INSIGHT: *Nevis, renowned as a spa since the 18th century, is known as the "Queen of the Caribbean"*

FACT FILE

OFFICIAL NAME: Federation of Saint Christopher and Nevis
DATE OF FORMATION: 1983
CAPITAL: Basseterre
POPULATION: 44,000
TOTAL AREA: 139 sq miles (360 sq km)

DENSITY: 316 people per sq mile
LANGUAGES: English*, English Creole
RELIGIONS: Protestant 85%, Roman Catholic 10%, other Christian 5%
ETHNIC MIX: Black 95%, mixed 5%
GOVERNMENT: Parliamentary democracy
CURRENCY: E. Caribbean $ = 100 cents

ANTIGUA & BARBUDA

LYING AT the outer edge of the Leeward Islands group in the Caribbean, Antigua and Barbuda's area includes the uninhabited islet of Redonda.

GEOGRAPHY
Mainly low-lying limestone and coral islands with some higher volcanic areas. Antigua's coast is indented with bays and harbors.

CLIMATE
Tropical, moderated by trade winds and sea breezes. Humidity and rainfall are low for the region.

PEOPLE AND SOCIETY
Population almost entirely of African origin, with small communities of Europeans and South Asians. Women's status has risen as a result of greater access to education. Wealth disparities are small and unemployment is low. Politics dominated for past 30 years by the Bird family.

THE ECONOMY
Tourism is the main source of revenue and the biggest provider of jobs. Fishing and sea-island cotton industries are expanding.

◆ INSIGHT: In 1865, Redonda was "claimed" by an eccentric Englishman as a kingdom for his son

| 200m/656ft Sea Level |

0   5 km
0   5 miles

ATLANTIC OCEAN

17°40'

Codrington
Codrington Lagoon

The Highlands

Barbuda

17°35'

V.C. Bird Intl. Airport   Palmetto Point
Long I.   61°50'
Guiana I.   Spanish Point
61°45'

ST. JOHN'S

Antigua

Bolans   17°05'
Freetown   Green I.
61°40'
61°55'   Falmouth

61°50'   61°45'   17°00'   Guadeloupe Passage

Caribbean Sea

FACT FILE

OFFICIAL NAME: Antigua and Barbuda
DATE OF FORMATION: 1981
CAPITAL: St. John's
POPULATION: 200,000
TOTAL AREA: 170 sq miles (440 sq km)

DENSITY: 479 people per sq mile
LANGUAGES: English*, English Creole
RELIGIONS: Protestant 87%, Roman Catholic 10%, other 3%
ETHNIC MIX: Black 98%, other 2%
GOVERNMENT: Parliamentary democracy
CURRENCY: E. Caribbean $ = 100 cents

DOMINICA

DOMINICA RESISTED European colonization until the 18th century, when it was controlled first by the French, and then, until 1978, by the British.

GEOGRAPHY
Mountainous and densely forested. Volcanic activity has given it very fertile soils, hot springs, geysers, and black sand beaches.

CLIMATE
Tropical, cooled by constant trade winds. Heavy annual rainfall. Tropical depressions and hurricanes are likely June–November.

PEOPLE AND SOCIETY
Population mainly of African origin. Small community of Carib Indians – the last remaining in the Caribbean – on the east coast. Most people live in extended families. Electoral system based on British model; politicians tend to come from professional classes, usually doctors or lawyers. For 15 years until 1995, Dominica was governed by Eugenia Charles, the first female prime minister in the Caribbean.

THE ECONOMY
Bananas and tourism are the economic mainstays. Current preferential access to EU and US markets now threatened by moves to deregulate the banana trade.

◆ INSIGHT: *Dominica is known as the "Nature Island" due to its spectacular flora and fauna*

FACT FILE	
OFFICIAL NAME: Commonwealth of Dominica	DENSITY: 250 people per sq mile
	LANGUAGES: English*, French Creole, Carib, Cocoy
DATE OF FORMATION: 1978	RELIGIONS: Roman Catholic 77%, Protestant 15%, other 8%
CAPITAL: Roseau	
POPULATION: 72,000	ETHNIC MIX: Black 98%, Indian 2%
TOTAL AREA: 290 sq miles (750 sq km)	GOVERNMENT: Multiparty republic
	CURRENCY: E. Caribbean $ = 100 cents

ST. LUCIA

AMONG THE most beautiful of the Caribbean Windward Islands, St. Lucia retains both French and British influences from its colonial history.

GEOGRAPHY
Volcanic and mountainous, with some broad fertile valleys. The Pitons, ancient lava cones, rise from the sea on the forested west coast.

CLIMATE
Tropical, moderated by trade winds. May–October wet season brings daily warm showers. Rainfall is highest in the mountains.

PEOPLE AND SOCIETY
Population is a tension-free mixture of descendants of Africans, Europeans, and South Asians. Family and religious life are important to most St. Lucians. In rural areas women often head the households, and run much of the farming. There is growing local resistance to overdevelopment of the island by tourism. A proposed union with the other Windward Islands is the main political issue.

THE ECONOMY
Mainly agricultural, with some light industry. Bananas are biggest export. Successful tourist industry, but most resorts are foreign-owned.

◆ *INSIGHT: St. Lucia has the most Nobel laureates per capita in the world*

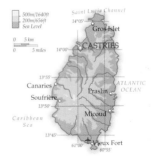

FACT FILE
OFFICIAL NAME: Saint Lucia
DATE OF FORMATION: 1979
CAPITAL: Castries
POPULATION: 156,000
TOTAL AREA: 239 sq miles
(620 sq km)
DENSITY: 653 people per sq mile

LANGUAGES: English*, French Creole, Hindi, Urdu
RELIGIONS: Catholic 90%, other 10%
ETHNIC MIX: Black 90%, Afro-European 6%, South Asian 4%
GOVERNMENT: Parliamentary democracy
CURRENCY: E. Caribbean $ = 100 cents

St. Vincent & the Grenadines

INDEPENDENT FROM Britain in 1979, the volcanic islands of St. Vincent and the Grenadines form part of the Windward group in the Caribbean.

GEOGRAPHY
St. Vincent is mountainous and forested, with one of two active volcanoes in the Caribbean, La Soufrière. The Grenadines are 32 islands and keys fringed by beaches.

CLIMATE
Tropical, with constant trade winds. Hurricanes are likely during July–November wet season.

PEOPLE AND SOCIETY
Population is racially diverse, but intermarriage has reduced tensions. Society is informal and relaxed, but family life is strongly influenced by the Anglican Church. Locals fear that their traditional lifestyle is being threatened by the expanding tourist industry.

◆ INSIGHT: The islands' precolonial inhabitants, the Carib Indians, named them "Harioun" – home of the blessed

THE ECONOMY
Dependent on agriculture and tourism. Bananas are the main cash crop. Tourism, targeted at the jet-set and cruise-ship markets, is concentrated on the Grenadines.

La Soufrière 4,049 ft
Chateaubelain
13°20'
Georgetown
St. Vincent
KINGSTOWN
Amos Vale Airport
13°10'

1000m/3281ft
500m/1640ft
200m/656ft
Sea Level

0   10 km
0   10 miles

Caribbean Sea

Bequia
13°00'
Isle à Quatre
Baliceaux
Mustique
12°50'
Canouan
61°10'
The Grenadines
Mayreau
12°40'
Union I.
61°20'
ATLANTIC OCEAN

FACT FILE
OFFICIAL NAME: St. Vincent and the Grenadines
DATE OF FORMATION: 1979
CAPITAL: Kingstown
POPULATION: 109,000
TOTAL AREA: 131 sq miles (340 sq km)

DENSITY: 832 people per sq mile
LANGUAGES: English*, English Creole
RELIGIONS: Protestant 62% Roman Catholic 19%, other 19%
ETHNIC MIX: Black 82%, mixed 14%, White 3%, South Asian 1%
GOVERNMENT: Parliamentary democracy
CURRENCY: E. Caribbean $ = 100 cents

BARBADOS

BARBADOS IS the most easterly of the Caribbean Windward Islands. Under British rule for 339 years, it became fully independent in 1966.

GEOGRAPHY
Encircled by coral reefs. Fertile and predominantly flat, with a few gentle hills to the north.

CLIMATE
Moderate tropical climate. Sunnier and drier than its more mountainous neighbors.

PEOPLE AND SOCIETY
Some latent tension between white community, which controls politics and much of the economy, and majority black population, but violence is rare. Increasing social mobility has enabled black Bajans to enter the professions. Despite political stability and good social services, emigration is high, notably to the United States and the UK.

◆ INSIGHT: Barbados retains a strong British influence and is referred to by its neighbors as "Little England"

THE ECONOMY
Sugar is the traditional cash crop. Well-developed tourist industry employs almost 40% of the work force. Financial services and information processing are important new growth sectors.

FACT FILE
OFFICIAL NAME: Barbados
DATE OF FORMATION: 1966
CAPITAL: Bridgetown
POPULATION: 260,000
TOTAL AREA: 166 sq miles (430 sq km)
DENSITY: 1,566 people per sq mile

LANGUAGES: English*, English Creole
RELIGIONS: Protestant 94%, Roman Catholic 5%, other 1%
ETHNIC MIX: Black 80%, mixed 15%, White 4%, other 1%
GOVERNMENT: Parliamentary democracy
CURRENCY: Barbados $ = 100 cents

GRENADA

THE WINDWARD island of Grenada became a focus of attention in 1983, when a US-led invasion severed the growing links with Cuba.

 GEOGRAPHY
Volcanic in origin, with densely forested central mountains. Its territory includes the islands of Carriacou and Petite Martinique.

CLIMATE
Tropical, tempered by trade winds. Hurricanes are a hazard in the July–November wet season.

PEOPLE AND SOCIETY
Grenadians are mainly of African origin; their traditions remain strong, especially on Carriacou. Interethnic marriage has reduced tensions between the groups. Extended families, often headed by women, are the norm. The invasion ousted the Marxist regime and restored democracy.

◆ *INSIGHT: Known as "the spice island of the Caribbean," it is the world's second largest nutmeg producer*

THE ECONOMY
Nutmeg, the most important crop, is currently affected by low world prices. Mace, cocoa, saffron, and cloves are also grown. Tourism has developed in the past decade.

	500m/1640ft
	200m/656ft
	Sea Level

| 0 | 8 km |
| 0 | 8 miles |

FACT FILE

OFFICIAL NAME: Grenada
DATE OF FORMATION: 1974
CAPITAL: St. George's
POPULATION: 91,000
TOTAL AREA: 131 sq miles
(340 sq km)
DENSITY: 695 people per sq mile

LANGUAGES: English*, English Creole
RELIGIONS: Roman Catholic
68%, Protestant 32%
ETHNIC MIX: Black 84%, Afro-European 13%, South Asian 3%
GOVERNMENT: Parliamentary democracy
CURRENCY: E. Caribbean $ = 100 cents

TRINIDAD & TOBAGO

THE FORMER British colony of Trinidad and Tobago is the most southerly of the West Indies, lying just 9 miles (15 km) off the coast of Venezuela.

GEOGRAPHY
Both islands are hilly and wooded. Trinidad has a rugged mountain range in the north, and swamps on its east and west coasts.

CLIMATE
Tropical, with July–December wet season. Escapes the region's hurricanes, which pass to the north.

PEOPLE AND SOCIETY
Blacks and South Asians are the biggest groups. Minorities of Chinese and Europeans. Politics has recently become fragmented, and dominated by the race issue. An attempted coup by a Muslim sect in 1990 strengthened black opposition to the possibility of a South Asian prime minister.

◆ INSIGHT: *Trinidad and Tobago is the birthplace of steel bands and Calypso*

THE ECONOMY
Oil accounts for 70% of export earnings. Gas is increasingly being exploited to support new industries. Tourism, particularly on Tobago, is being developed.

FACT FILE

OFFICIAL NAME: Republic of Trinidad and Tobago
DATE OF FORMATION: 1962
CAPITAL: Port-of-Spain
POPULATION: 1.3 million
TOTAL AREA: 1,981 sq miles (5,130 sq km)

DENSITY: 656 people per sq mile
LANGUAGES: English*, other
RELIGIONS: Christian 58%, Hindu 30%, Muslim 8%, other 4%
ETHNIC MIX: Black 43%, South Asian 40%, mixed 14%, other 3%
GOVERNMENT: Multiparty republic
CURRENCY: Trin. & Tob. $ = 100 cents

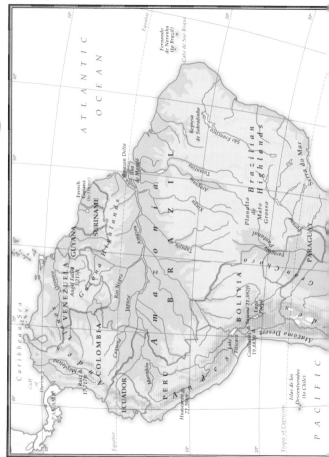

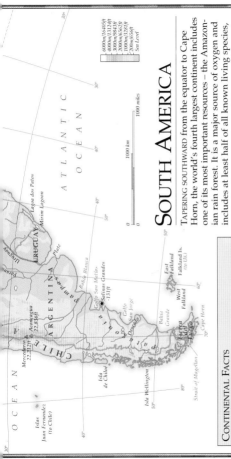

6000m/19685ft
4000m/13124ft
3000m/9843ft
2000m/6562ft
1000m/3281ft
200m/656ft
Sea Level

1000 km

1000 miles

SOUTH AMERICA

TAPERING SOUTHWARD from the equator to Cape Horn, the world's fourth largest continent includes one of its most important resources – the Amazonian rain forest. It is a major source of oxygen and includes at least half of all known living species, while the Amazon – the world's second longest river – contains one fifth of the world's fresh water. The Andes mountain chain reaches down South America's western flank, sheltering Amazonia, the prairies of the Gran Chaco, the grasslands of the Pampas, and the wastelands of the far south. The continent has massive mineral resources, many exploited by US and European multinationals.

CONTINENTAL FACTS

HIGHEST POINT:
Aconcagua, Argentina
22,833 ft
(6,959 m)

LOWEST POINT:
Salinas Grandes,
Argentina 131 ft (40 m)
below sea level

LARGEST LAKE:
Lake Titicaca,
Bolivia/Peru 3,220 sq
miles (8,340 sq km)

LONGEST RIVER:
Amazon, Brazil
4,050 miles
(6,516 km)

43

COLOMBIA

LYING IN northwest South America, Colombia is one of the world's most violent countries, with powerful drugs cartels and guerrilla activity.

GEOGRAPHY
The densely forested and almost uninhabited east is separated from the western coastal plains by the Andes, which divide into three ranges with intervening valleys.

CLIMATE
Coastal plains are hot and wet. The highlands are cooler. The equatorial east has two wet seasons.

PEOPLE AND SOCIETY
Most Colombians are of mixed blood. Native Indians are concentrated in the southwest and Amazonia. Recent constitutional reform has given them a greater political voice. Blacks are the least represented group.The government, with US help, is engaged in an all-out war against the drug barons.

THE ECONOMY
Healthy and diversified export sector – especially coffee and coal. Considerable growth potential, but drug-related violence and corruption deter foreign investors.

◆ INSIGHT: Colombia is the world's leading producer of emeralds

FACT FILE	
OFFICIAL NAME: Republic of Colombia	DENSITY: 78 people per sq mile
	LANGUAGES: Spanish*, Indian languages, English Creole
DATE OF FORMATION: 1903	RELIGIONS: Catholic 95%, other 5%
CAPITAL: Bogotá	ETHNIC MIX: mestizo 58%, White 20%, mixed 14%, other 8%
POPULATION: 34 million	
TOTAL AREA: 439,733 sq miles (1,138,910 sq km)	GOVERNMENT: Multiparty republic
	CURRENCY: Peso = 100 centavos

VENEZUELA

LOCATED ON the north coast of South America, Venezuela has the continent's most urbanized society. Most people live in the northern cities.

GEOGRAPHY
Andes mountains and the Maracaíbo lowlands in the north-west. Central grassy plains drained by Orinoco river system. Forested Guiana Highlands in the southeast.

CLIMATE
Tropical. Hot and humid. Uplands are cooler. Orinoco plains are alternately parched or flooded.

PEOPLE AND SOCIETY
Latin America's "melting pot" with immigrants from Europe and all over South America. The few indigenous Indians live in remote areas and maintain their traditional lifestyle. Oil wealth has brought prosperity, but many people still live in poverty. 1991 food riots forced government to initiate poverty programs. Corruption is a feature of Venezuelan political life.

THE ECONOMY
In addition to oil, Venezuela has vast reserves of coal, bauxite, iron, and gold. Government revenues dented by overstaffed and often inefficient state sector, plus widespread tax evasion.

◆ INSIGHT: Venezuela's Angel Falls (3,212 ft) is the world's highest waterfall

FACT FILE

OFFICIAL NAME: Republic of Venezuela
DATE OF FORMATION: 1830
CAPITAL: Caracas
POPULATION: 20.6 million
TOTAL AREA: 352,143 sq miles (912,050 sq km)

DENSITY: 57 people per sq mile
LANGUAGES: Spanish*, Indian languages
RELIGIONS: Roman Catholic 96%, Protestant 2%, other 2%
ETHNIC MIX: mestizo 67%, White 21%, Black 10%, Indian 2%
GOVERNMENT: Multiparty republic
CURRENCY: Bolívar = 100 centimos

GUYANA

THE ONLY English-speaking country in South America, Guyana gained independence from Britain in 1966 and became a republic in 1970.

GEOGRAPHY
Mainly artificial coast, re-claimed by dikes and dams from swamps and tidal marshes. Forests cover 85% of the interior, rising to savanna uplands and mountains.

CLIMATE
Tropical. Coast cooled by sea breezes. Lowlands are hot, wet and humid. Highlands are a little cooler.

PEOPLE AND SOCIETY
Population largely descended from Africans brought over during slave trade or from South Asian laborers who arrived after slavery was abolished. Racial rivalry exists between the two groups. Small numbers of Chinese and native Indians. Government was once characterized by favoritism toward Afro-Guyanese. This was reversed with the election in 1992 of a South Asian-dominated party.

THE ECONOMY
Free-market economics have improved prospects. Bauxite, gold, rice, and diamonds are produced.

◆ *INSIGHT: Guyana means "land of many waters" – it has 1,000 mi. of rivers*

FACT FILE
OFFICIAL NAME: Republic of Guyana
DATE OF FORMATION: 1966
CAPITAL: Georgetown
POPULATION: 800,000
TOTAL AREA: 83,000 sq miles (214,970 sq km)
DENSITY: 10 people per sq mile

LANGUAGES: English*, English Creole, Hindi, Urdu, Indian languages
RELIGIONS: Christian 57%, Hindu 33%, Muslim 9%, other 1%
ETHNIC MIX: South Asian 51%, Black and mixed 43%, other 6%
GOVERNMENT: Multiparty republic
CURRENCY: Guyana $ =100 cents

SURINAME

A FORMER Dutch colony on the north coast of
South America. Democracy was restored in 1991
after almost 11 years of military rule.

GEOGRAPHY
Mostly covered by tropical
rain forest. Coastal plain, central
plateaus, and the Guiana Highlands.

CLIMATE
Tropical. Hot and humid,
cooled by trade winds. High
rainfall, especially in the interior.

PEOPLE AND SOCIETY
About 200,000 people have
emigrated to the Netherlands since
independence. Of those left, 90%
live near the coast, the rest live in
scattered rain forest communities.
Around 7,000 are indigenous
Indians. Also *bosnegers* – descendants
of runaway African slaves. They
fought the Creole-dominated
government in the 1980s. Many
South Asians and Javanese work
in farming. Since return to civilian
rule, each group has a political
party representing its interests.

THE ECONOMY
Aluminum and bauxite are
the leading exports. Rice and fruit
are main cash crops. Oil reserves.

◆ *INSIGHT: Suriname was ceded to
Holland by the British, in exchange for
New Amsterdam (New York), in 1667*

FACT FILE

OFFICIAL NAME: Republic of Suriname
DATE OF FORMATION: 1975
CAPITAL: Paramaribo
POPULATION: 400,000
TOTAL AREA: 63,039 sq miles
(163,270 sq km)
DENSITY: 6 people per sq mile

LANGUAGES: Dutch*, Pidgin English
(Taki-Taki), Hindi, Javanese, Carib
RELIGIONS: Christian 48%, Hindu
27%, Muslim 20%, other 5%
ETHNIC MIX: South Asian 37%, Creole
31%, Javanese 15%, other 17%
GOVERNMENT: Multiparty republic
CURRENCY: Guilder = 100 cents

ECUADOR

ECUADOR SITS high on South America's western coast. Its territory includes the Galápagos Islands, 610 miles (970 km) to the west.

GEOGRAPHY
Broad coastal plain, inter-Andean central highlands, dense jungle in upper Amazon basin.

CLIMATE
Hot and moist on the coast, cool in the Andes, and hot equatorial in the Amazon basin.

PEOPLE AND SOCIETY
Most people live in coastal lowlands or Andean highlands. Many have migrated from over-farmed Andean valleys to main port and commercial center, Guayaquil. Strong and unified Indian movement backed by Catholic Church. Amazonian Indians are successfully pressing for recognition of land rights.

◆ INSIGHT: Darwin's study on the Galápagos Islands in 1856 played a major part in his theory of evolution

THE ECONOMY
World's biggest banana producer. Net oil exporter. Commercial agriculture is main employer. Fishing industry. Eco-tourism on Galápagos Islands.

FACT FILE

OFFICIAL NAME: Republic of Ecuador
DATE OF FORMATION: 1830
CAPITAL: Quito
POPULATION: 11.3 million
TOTAL AREA: 109,483 sq miles (283,560 sq km)
DENSITY: 104 people per sq mile

LANGUAGES: Spanish*, Quechua* and eight other Indian languages
RELIGIONS: Catholic 95%, other 5%
ETHNIC MIX: mestizo (Euro-Indian) 55%, Indian 25%, Black 10%, White 10%
GOVERNMENT: Multiparty republic
CURRENCY: Sucre = 100 centavos

PERU

ONCE THE heart of the Inca empire, before the Spanish conquest in the 16th century, Peru lies on the Pacific coast of South America.

GEOGRAPHY
Coastal plain rises to Andes mountains. Uplands, dissected by fertile valleys, lie east of Andes. Tropical forest in extreme east.

CLIMATE
Coast is mainly arid. Middle slopes of Andes are temperate; higher peaks are snow-covered. East is hot, humid, and very wet.

PEOPLE AND SOCIETY
Populated mainly by Indians or mixed-race *mestizos*, but society is dominated by a small group of Spanish descendants. Indians, together with the small black community, suffer discrimination in the towns. In 1980, *Sendero Luminoso* (Shining Path) guerrillas began armed struggle against the government. Since then, over 25,000 people have died as a result of guerrilla, and army, violence.

THE ECONOMY
Abundant mineral resources. Rich fish stocks. Illegal export of coca leaves for cocaine production.

◆ INSIGHT: *Lake Titicaca is the world's highest navigable lake*

FACT FILE

OFFICIAL NAME: Republic of Peru
DATE OF FORMATION: 1824
CAPITAL: Lima
POPULATION: 22.9 million
TOTAL AREA: 496,223 sq miles (1,285,220 sq km)
DENSITY: 47 people per sq mile

LANGUAGES: Spanish*, Quechua*, Aymará*, other Indian languages
RELIGIONS: Catholic 95%, other 5%
ETHNIC MIX: Indian 45%, *mestizo* 37%, White 15%, Black, Japanese, Chinese, and other 3%
GOVERNMENT: Multiparty republic
CURRENCY: New sol = 100 centimos

BRAZIL

COVERING ALMOST half of South America, Brazil is the site of the world's largest and ecologically most important rain forest. The country has immense natural and economic resources, but most of its people still live in poverty.

GEOGRAPHY

Vast, heavily wooded Amazon Basin covers northern half of the country. Semiarid scrubland in northeast mountains, fertile highlands in the south. Coastal plain with swampy areas in the southeast. Atlantic coastline is 1,240 miles (2,000 km) long.

CLIMATE

Constantly hot and humid in Amazon Basin. Frequent droughts in northeast. Greater range of temperature and rainfall on plateau. Hot summers and cool winters in south.

PEOPLE AND SOCIETY

Diverse population includes native Indians, blacks, and people of mixed race. Shanty towns in the cities attract poor migrants from the northeast. Urban crime, violent land disputes, and unchecked Amazonia development tarnish image as a modern nation. Catholicism and the family remain strong.

THE ECONOMY

Hyperinflation, poor planning, and corruption frustrate efforts to harness undoubted potential: vast mineral reserves, diverse industry and agriculture.

50

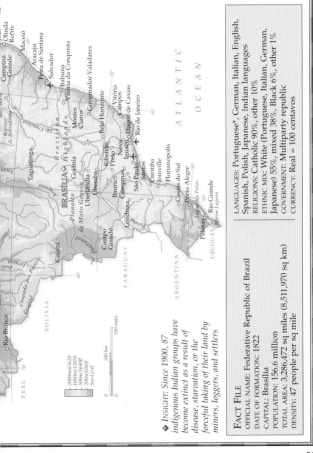

◆ INSIGHT: Since 1900, 87
indigenous Indian groups have
become extinct as a result of
disease, starvation, or the
forceful taking of their land by
miners, loggers, and settlers

LANGUAGES: Portuguese*, German, Italian, English,
Spanish, Polish, Japanese, Indian languages
RELIGIONS: Catholic 90%, other 10%
ETHNIC MIX: White (Portuguese, Italian, German,
Japanese) 55%, mixed 38%, Black 6%, other 1%
GOVERNMENT: Multiparty republic
CURRENCY: Real = 100 centavos

FACT FILE
OFFICIAL NAME: Federative Republic of Brazil
DATE OF FORMATION: 1822
CAPITAL: Brasilia
POPULATION: 156.6 million
TOTAL AREA: 3,286,472 sq miles (8,511,970 sq km)
DENSITY: 47 people per sq mile

51

CHILE

EXTENDS IN a ribbon down the west coast of South America. It returned to democracy in 1989 after a referendum rejected its military dictator.

GEOGRAPHY
Pampas (broad grassy plains) between coastal uplands and Andes. Atacama Desert in north. Deep sea channels, lakes, and fjords in south.

CLIMATE
Arid in the north. Hot, dry summers and mild winters in the center. Higher Andean peaks have glaciers and year round snow. Very wet and stormy in the south.

PEOPLE AND SOCIETY
Most people are of European descent, and are highly urbanized. Indigenous Indians live almost exclusively in the south. Poor housing, water and air pollution are problems in Santiago. General Pinochet's dictatorship was brutally repressive, but the business and middle classes prospered. Growth has continued under civilian rule, but many Chileans live in poverty.

THE ECONOMY
World's biggest copper producer. Growth in foreign investment due to political stability. Wine, fishmeal, fruit, and salmon are exported.

◆ INSIGHT: *Chile's Atacama Desert is the driest place on Earth*

4000m/13124
2000m/6562ft
1000m/3281ft
200m/656ft
Sea Level

0   300 km
0   300 miles

FACT FILE
OFFICIAL NAME: Republic of Chile
DATE OF FORMATION: 1818
CAPITAL: Santiago
POPULATION: 13.8 million
TOTAL AREA: 292,258 sq miles
(756,950 sq km)
DENSITY: 47 people per sq mile

LANGUAGES: Spanish*, Indian languages
RELIGIONS: Roman Catholic 89%, Protestant 11%
ETHNIC MIX: White and *mestizo* 92%, Indian 6%, other 2%
GOVERNMENT: Multiparty republic
CURRENCY: Peso = 100 centavos

BOLIVIA

BOLIVIA LIES landlocked high in central South America. Mineral riches once made it the region's wealthiest state. Today, it is the poorest.

GEOGRAPHY
A high windswept plateau, the *altiplano*, lies between two Andean mountain ranges. Semi-arid grasslands to the southeast; dense tropical forests to the north.

CLIMATE
Altiplano has extreme tropical climate, with night frost in winter. North and east are hot and humid.

PEOPLE AND SOCIETY
Indigenous majority is discriminated against at most levels of society. Political process and economy remain under the control of a few wealthy families of Spanish descent. Most Bolivians are poor subsistence farmers or miners. Women have low status.

◆ *INSIGHT: La Paz is the world's highest capital city, at 13,385 feet (3,631 meters) above sea level*

THE ECONOMY
Gold, silver, zinc, and tin are mined. Recently discovered oil and natural gas deposits. Overseas investors remain deterred by social problems of extreme poverty, and the influence of cocaine barons.

FACT FILE

OFFICIAL NAME: Republic of Bolivia
DATE OF FORMATION: 1903
CAPITAL: La Paz
POPULATION: 7.8 million
TOTAL AREA: 424,162 sq miles (1,098,580 sq km)

DENSITY: 18 people per sq mile
LANGUAGES: Spanish*, Quechua*, Aymará*, Tupi-Guaraní
RELIGIONS: Catholic 95%, other 5%
ETHNIC MIX: Indian 55%, *mestizo* 27%, White 10%, other 8%
GOVERNMENT: Multiparty republic
CURRENCY: Boliviano = 100 centavos

PARAGUAY

LANDLOCKED in central South America. Its post-independence history has included periods of military rule. Free elections were held in 1993.

GEOGRAPHY
The River Paraguay divides hilly and forested east from a flat alluvial plain with marsh and semidesert scrubland in the west.

CLIMATE
Subtropical. Gran Chaco is generally hotter and drier. All areas experience floods and droughts.

PEOPLE AND SOCIETY
Population mainly of mixed Spanish and native Indian origin. Most are bilingual, but Guaraní is spoken by preference outside the capital. Gran Chaco is home to small groups of pure Guaraní Indians, cattle ranchers, and Mennonites, a sect of German origin, who live by a cooperative farming system.

◆ INSIGHT: *The joint Paraguay-Brazil hydroelectric power project at Itaipú is the largest in the world*

THE ECONOMY
Agriculture employs 45% of the work force. Soybeans and cotton are main exports. Electricity exporter – earnings cover oil imports. Growth is slow due to remote, landlocked position.

FACT FILE

OFFICIAL NAME: Republic of Paraguay
DATE OF FORMATION: 1935
CAPITAL: Asunción
POPULATION: 4.5 million
TOTAL AREA: 157,046 sq miles (406,750 sq km)

DENSITY: 29 people per sq mile
LANGUAGES: Spanish*, Guaraní*, Plattdeutsch (Low German)
RELIGIONS: Catholic 90%, other 10%
ETHNIC MIX: *mestizo* (Euro-Indian) 95%, White 3%, Indian 2%
GOVERNMENT: Multiparty republic
CURRENCY: Guaraní = 100 centimos

URUGUAY

URUGUAY IS situated in southeastern South America. It returned to civilian government in 1985, after 12 years of military dictatorship.

GEOGRAPHY
Low, rolling grasslands cover 80% of the country. Narrow coastal plain. Alluvial flood plain in southwest. Five rivers flow westwards and drain into the River Uruguay.

CLIMATE
Temperate throughout the country. Warm summers, mild winters, and moderate rainfall.

PEOPLE AND SOCIETY
Uruguayans are largely second- or third-generation Italians or Spaniards. Wealth derived from cattle ranching enabled the country to become the first welfare state in South America. Economic decline since 1960s, but a large, if less prosperous, middle class remains. Although a Roman Catholic country, Uruguay is liberal in its attitude to religion and all forms are tolerated. Divorce is legal.

THE ECONOMY
Most land given over to crops and livestock. Wool, meat, and hides are exported. Earnings as offshore banking center. Buoyant tourism.

◆ INSIGHT: *Uruguay's literacy rates and life expectancy are the region's highest*

FACT FILE
OFFICIAL NAME: Republic of Uruguay
DATE OF FORMATION: 1828
CAPITAL: Montevideo
POPULATION: 3.1 million
TOTAL AREA: 68,498 sq miles (177,410 sq km)

DENSITY: 45 people per sq mile
LANGUAGES: Spanish*, other
RELIGIONS: Roman Catholic 77%, Protestant 3%, Jewish 2%, other 18%
ETHNIC MIX: White 88%, *mestizo* (Euro-Indian) 8%, Black 4%
GOVERNMENT: Multiparty republic
CURRENCY: Peso = 100 centesimos

ARGENTINA

OCCUPYING MOST of the southern half of South America, Argentina extends 2,145 miles (3,460 km) from Bolivia to Tierra del Fuego. It is beginning to realize its potential after decades of political and economic instability.

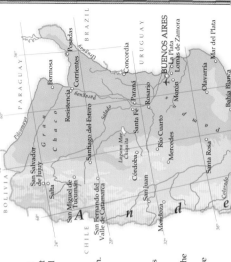

GEOGRAPHY

Andes Mountains in the west run north–south, forming a natural border with Chile. East of the Andes are heavily wooded plains (Gran Chaco) in the north, treeless but fertile Pampas plains in the center. Bleak and arid Patagonia in the far south.

CLIMATE

Northeast is subtropical. Andes are semiarid in the north and snowy in the south. Western lowlands are arid. Pampas have a mild climate with summer rains.

THE ECONOMY

Harsh economic recovery program and new stable currency have offset worst excesses of hyperinflation and inefficient nationalized industries. Rich and varied agricultural base. Powerful agribusiness – Argentina is among the world's leading exporters of beef, wheat, and fruit. Important known oil and gas reserves are still underexploited. Skilled labor force.

Falkland Islands
(to UN)

4000m/13124ft
3000m/9843ft
2000m/6562ft
1000m/3281ft
200m/656ft
Sea Level

ATLANTIC

OCEAN

CHILE

Neuquén
Negro

San Carlos
de Bariloche

Esquel

Chubut

Viedma

Golfo
San Matías

Trelew

Golfo
San Jorge

Comodoro Rivadavia
Caleta Olivia

Lago
Buenos
Aires

Bahía
Grande

Río Gallegos

Deseado

Tierra
del
Fuego

Ushuaia

0   100 km

0   100 miles

0   200 km

0   200 miles

PEOPLE AND SOCIETY

People are largely of European descent, mostly from recent 20th-century migrations; over one third are of Italian origin. Indigenous peoples are now in a minority, living mainly in Andean regions or in the Gran Chaco. Over 85% of Argentinians are urban dwellers, with 40% living in the capital. Paraguayan and Bolivian immigrants are the poorest groups. Catholicism and the extended family remain strong. Social and religious reunions are common. The family also forms the backbone of many successful businesses. Women have a higher profile than in most Latin American states. Many enter professional fields. Claim to the Falkland Islands remains an emotive issue.

◆ INSIGHT: *The Tango originated in the poorer quarters of Buenos Aires at the end of the 19th century. The name "Tango" predates the dance – it was given to the carnivals (and dances) of the country's black inhabitants in the early 1800s*

FACT FILE

OFFICIAL NAME: Argentine Republic
DATE OF FORMATION: 1850
CAPITAL: Buenos Aires
POPULATION: 33.5 million
TOTAL AREA: 1,068,296 sq miles (2,766,890 sq km)
DENSITY: 31 people per sq mile

LANGUAGES: Spanish*, Italian, English, German, French, Indian languages
RELIGIONS: Catholic 90%, Jewish 2%, other 8%
ETHNIC MIX: White 85%, other (including *mestizo* and Indian) 15%
GOVERNMENT: Multiparty republic
CURRENCY: Peso = 100 centavos

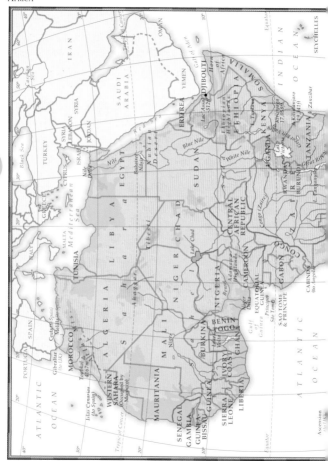

AFRICA

AFRICA is the second largest continent after Asia and the only one through which the equator and both tropics run. It is also contains the world's longest river, the Nile. Africa is dominated by the Sahara in the north and the Great Rift Valley in the east. A belt of tropical rain forest lies along the equator and Africa's vast tropical savanna grasslands provide grazing for herds of wild animals and domestic livestock. The center and south of the continent are rich in minerals. Almost one tenth of the planet's population live in Africa – a wide variety of peoples with their own distinctive languages and cultures.

CONTINENTAL FACTS

HIGHEST POINT:
Kilimanjaro,
Tanzania
19,341 ft (5,895 m)

LOWEST POINT:
Lac' Assal, Djibouti
512 ft (156 m)
below sea level

LARGEST LAKE:
Lake Victoria
26,560 sq miles
(68,880 sq km)

LONGEST RIVER: Nile,
Uganda/ Sudan/
Egypt 4,160 miles
(6,695 km)

4000m/13124ft
3000m/9843ft
2000m/6562ft
1000m/3281ft
200m/656ft
Sea Level
Below Sea Level

1000 km

100 miles

MOROCCO

A FORMER French colony in northwest Africa, independent in 1956. Morocco has occupied the disputed territory of Western Sahara since 1975.

GEOGRAPHY
Fertile coastal plain is interrupted in the east by the Rif Mountains. Atlas Mountain ranges to the south. Beyond lies the outer fringe of the Sahara.

CLIMATE
Ranges from temperate and warm in the north, to semiarid in the south. Cooler in the mountains.

PEOPLE AND SOCIETY
About 35% are descendants of original Berber inhabitants of northwest Africa, and live mainly in mountain villages. Arab majority inhabit lowlands. Large rural-urban gap in wealth. High birth rate. King Hassan heads a powerful monarchy. Government threatened by Islamic militants who fear country is losing its Islamic, Arab identity and becoming too influenced by Europe.

THE ECONOMY
World's main exporter of phosphates. Tourism and agriculture have great potential. Production of cannabis complicates closer EU links.

◆ INSIGHT: *Fès's Karueein University, founded in A.D. 859, is the world's oldest existing educational institution*

FACT FILE
OFFICIAL NAME: Kingdom of Morocco

DATE OF FORMATION: 1956

CAPITAL: Rabat

POPULATION: 27 million

TOTAL AREA: 269,757 sq miles (698,670 sq km)

DENSITY: 101 people per sq mile

LANGUAGES: Arabic*, Berber, French

RELIGIONS: Muslim 99%, other 1%

ETHNIC MIX: Arab and Berber 99%, European 1%

GOVERNMENT: Constitutional monarchy

CURRENCY: Dirham = 100 centimes

ALGERIA

ALGERIA ACHIEVED independence from France in 1962. Today, its military-dominated government faces a severe challenge from Islamic extremists.

GEOGRAPHY
85% of the country lies within the Sahara. Fertile coastal region with plains and hills rises in the southeast to the Atlas Mountains.

CLIMATE
Coastal areas are warm and temperate, with most rainfall during the mild winters. The south is very hot, with negligible rainfall.

PEOPLE AND SOCIETY
Algerians are predominantly Arab, under 30 years of age, and urban. Most indigenous Berbers consider the mountainous Kabylia region in the northeast to be their homeland. The Sahara sustains just 500,000 people, mainly oil workers and Tuareg nomads with goat and camel herds, who move between the irrigated oases. In recent years, political violence has claimed the lives of 3,000 people.

THE ECONOMY
Oil and gas exports. Political turmoil has led to exodus of skilled foreign labor. Limited agriculture.

◆ INSIGHT: The world's highest sand dunes are found in east central Algeria

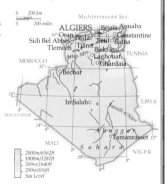

FACT FILE

OFFICIAL NAME: Democratic and Popular Republic of Algeria
DATE OF FORMATION: 1962
CAPITAL: Algiers
POPULATION: 200,000
TOTAL AREA: 919,590 sq miles (2,381,740 sq km)

DENSITY: 29 people per sq mile
LANGUAGES: Arabic*, Berber, French
RELIGIONS: Muslim 99%, Christian and Jewish 1%
ETHNIC MIX: Arab and Berber 99% European 1%
GOVERNMENT: Military regime
CURRENCY: Dinar = 100 centimes

TUNISIA

TUNISIA HAS traditionally been one of the more liberal Arab states, but its government is now facing a challenge from Islamic fundamentalists.

GEOGRAPHY
Mountains in the north are surrounded by plains. Vast, low-lying salt pans in the center. To the south lies the Sahara.

CLIMATE
Summer temperatures are high. The north is often wet and windy in winter. Far south is arid.

PEOPLE AND SOCIETY
Population almost entirely of Arab-Berber descent, with Jewish and Christian minorities. Many still live in extended families. Women have better rights than in any other Arab country and make up 25% of the total work force. Politics, however, remains a male preserve. Low birth rate is a result of a long-standing family planning policy.

◆ INSIGHT: Matmata – a Berber village – appeared in the movie "Star Wars"

THE ECONOMY
Well-diversified, despite limited resources. Oil and gas exports. Expanding manufacturing. Tourism. European investment.

FACT FILE	
OFFICIAL NAME: Republic of Tunisia	DENSITY: 136 people per sq mile
DATE OF FORMATION: 1956	LANGUAGES: Arabic*, French
CAPITAL: Tunis	RELIGIONS: Muslim 98%, Christian 1%, other 1%
POPULATION: 8.6 million	ETHNIC MIX: Arab and Berber 98%, European 1%, other 1%
TOTAL AREA: 63,170 sq miles (163,610 sq km)	GOVERNMENT: Multiparty republic
	CURRENCY: Dinar = 1,000 millimes

LIBYA

SITUATED ON the Mediterranean coast of North Africa, Libya is a Muslim dictatorship, politically marginalized by the West for its terrorist links.

GEOGRAPHY
Apart from the coastal strip and a mountain range in the south, Libya is desert or semidesert. Oases provide agricultural land.

CLIMATE
Hot and arid. Coastal area has temperate climate, with mild, wet winters and hot, dry summers.

PEOPLE AND SOCIETY
Most Libyans are of Arab and Berber origin. 1969 revolution brought Colonel Gadaffi to power. He represents independence, Islamic faith, belief in communal lifestyle, and hatred of urban rich. Revolution wiped out private enterprise and middle classes. Jews and European settlers were banished. Since then, Libya has changed from being largely a nation of nomads and livestock herders to 70% city-dwellers.

THE ECONOMY
90% of export earnings come from oil. Subject to fluctuating world prices. Dates, olives, peaches, and grapes are grown in the oases.

◆ INSIGHT: Libya's sulfur-free oil yields little pollution when burned

FACT FILE
OFFICIAL NAME: The Great Socialist People's Libyan Arab *Jamahiriya*
DATE OF FORMATION: 1951
CAPITAL: Tripoli
POPULATION: 5.5 million
TOTAL AREA: 679,358 sq miles (1,759,540 sq km)

DENSITY: 8 people per sq mile
LANGUAGES: Arabic*, Tuareg
RELIGIONS: Muslim 97%, other 3%
ETHNIC MIX: Arab and Berber 97%, other 3%
GOVERNMENT: Socialist *jamahiriya* (state of the masses)
CURRENCY: Dinar = 1,000 dirhams

EGYPT

EGYPT OCCUPIES the northeast corner of Africa. Its essentially pro-Western, military-backed regime is being challenged by Islamic fundamentalists.

GEOGRAPHY
Fertile Nile valley separates arid Libyan Desert from smaller semiarid eastern desert. Sinai peninsula has mountains in south.

CLIMATE
Summers are very hot, but winters are cooler. Rainfall is negligible, except on the coast.

PEOPLE AND SOCIETY
Continuously inhabited for over 8,000 years, with a tradition of religious and ethnic tolerance. Egyptians are mostly Arabs, Bedouins, and Nubians. Women play full part in education system, politics, and economy. Government is fighting Islamic terrorist groups, whose acts of violence have included attacks on politicians, police, and tourists.

THE ECONOMY
Oil and gas are main sources of revenue. Tolls from the Suez Canal. Successful tourist industry is threatened by security fears.

◆ INSIGHT: Egypt has been a major tourist destination since the 1880s

---

FACT FILE

OFFICIAL NAME: Arab Republic of Egypt
DATE OF FORMATION: 1936
CAPITAL: Cairo
POPULATION: 56.1 million
TOTAL AREA: 386,660 sq miles (1,001,450 sq km)

DENSITY: 145 people per sq mile
LANGUAGES: Arabic*, French, English, Berber, Greek, Armenian
RELIGIONS: Muslim 94%, other 6%
ETHNIC MIX: Eastern Hamitic 90%, other (inc. Greek, Armenian) 10%
GOVERNMENT: Multiparty republic
CURRENCY: Pound = 100 piastres

SUDAN

THE LARGEST country in Africa, Sudan borders the Red Sea. In 1989, an army coup installed a military Islamic fundamentalist regime.

GEOGRAPHY
Lies within the upper Nile basin. Mostly arid plains, with marshes in the south. Highlands border the Red Sea in the northeast.

CLIMATE
North is hot, arid desert with constant dry winds. Rainy season ranging from two months in the center, to eight in the south.

PEOPLE AND SOCIETY
Large number of ethnic and linguistic groups. Two million people are nomads, moving over ancient tribal areas in the south. Major social division is between Arabized Muslims in north, and mostly African, largely Christian or animist peoples in south. Attempts to impose Arab and Islamic values throughout Sudan have been the root cause of the civil war that has ravaged the south since 1983.

THE ECONOMY
Sudan is affected by drought and food shortages. Sesame seeds, cotton, gum arabic are cash crops.

◆INSIGHT: Sudan's Sudd plain contains the world's largest swamp

FACT FILE
OFFICIAL NAME: Republic of Sudan
DATE OF FORMATION: 1956
CAPITAL: Khartoum
POPULATION: 27.4 million
TOTAL AREA: 967,493 sq miles (2,505,815 sq km)

DENSITY: 29 people per sq mile
LANGUAGES: Arabic*, other
RELIGIONS: Muslim 70%, traditional beliefs 20%, Christian 5%, other 5%
ETHNIC MIX: Arab 51%, Dinka 13%, Nuba 9%, Beja 7%, other 20%
GOVERNMENT: Military regime
CURRENCY: Pound = 100 piastres

ERITREA

LYING ON the shores of the Red Sea, Eritrea effectively seceded from Ethiopia in 1991, following a 30-year war for independence.

GEOGRAPHY
Mostly rugged mountains, bush, and the Danakil Desert, which falls below sea level.

CLIMATE
Warm in the mountains; desert areas are hot. Droughts from July onward are common.

PEOPLE AND SOCIETY
Nine main ethnic groups. Tigrinya-speakers are the largest in number. Strong sense of nationhood forged by the war. Women played important role in the war, fighting alongside men. Over 80% of people are subsistence farmers. Few live beyond the age of 45. Transitional government will hold multiparty elections in 1997.

◆ INSIGHT: 75% of Eritreans are dependent upon aid for all, or part, of their annual food supply

THE ECONOMY
Legacy of disruption and destruction from war. Susceptible to drought and famine. Most of the population live at subsistence level. Potential for mining of gold, copper, silver, and zinc. Possible foreign earnings from oil exports.

FACT FILE

OFFICIAL NAME: State of Eritrea
DATE OF FORMATION: 1993
CAPITAL: Asmara
POPULATION: 3.5 million
TOTAL AREA: 36,170 sq miles
(93,680 sq km)
DENSITY: 96 people per sq mile

LANGUAGES: Tigrinya*, Arabic*, Tigre, Afar, Bilen, Kunama, Nara
RELIGIONS: Coptic Christian 45%, Muslim 45%, other 10%
ETHNIC MIX: Nine main ethnic groups
GOVERNMENT: Provisional military government
CURRENCY: Ethiopian birr = 100 cents

DJIBOUTI

A CITY state with a desert hinterland, Djibouti lies in northeast Africa. Once known as French Somaliland, it became independent in 1977.

GEOGRAPHY
Mainly low-lying desert and semidesert, with a volcanic mountain range in the north.

CLIMATE
Hot all year round, with June–August temperatures reaching 109°F (45°C). Scant rainfall.

PEOPLE AND SOCIETY
Dominant ethnic groups are the Issas in the south and the mainly nomadic Afars in the north. Tensions between them developed into a guerrilla war in 1991. Smaller tribal groups make up the rest of the population, together with French and other European expatriates, and Arabs. Population was swelled by 20,000 Somali refugees in 1992. France still exerts considerable influence in Djibouti, supporting it financially and maintaining a naval base and a military garrison.

THE ECONOMY
Djibouti's major asset is its port in a key Red Sea location.

◆ INSIGHT: Chewing the leaves of the mildly narcotic Qat shrub is an age-old social ritual in Djibouti

FACT FILE

OFFICIAL NAME: Republic of Djibouti
DATE OF FORMATION: 1977
CAPITAL: Djibouti
POPULATION: 500,000
TOTAL AREA: 8,958 sq miles
(23,200 sq km)
DENSITY: 55 people per sq mile

LANGUAGES: Arabic*, French*, Somali, Afar, other
RELIGIONS: Christian 87%, other 13%
ETHNIC MIX: Issa 35%, Afar 20%, Gadaboursis and Isaaks 28%, other (inc. Arab, European) 17%
GOVERNMENT: Single-party republic
CURRENCY: Franc = 100 centimes

ETHIOPIA

LOCATED IN northeast Africa, Ethiopia was a Marxist regime from 1974–1991. It has had a series of economic, civil, and natural crises.

GEOGRAPHY
Great Rift Valley divides mountainous northwest region from desert lowlands in northeast and southeast. Ethiopian Plateau is drained mainly by the Blue Nile.

CLIMATE
Generally moderate with summer rains. Highlands are warm, with night frost and snowfalls on the mountains.

PEOPLE AND SOCIETY
76 Ethiopian nationalities speak 286 languages. Oromo are largest group. In 1995, the first multiparty elections were held, ending four years of rule by transitional government, and beginning a new nine-state federation.

◆ INSIGHT: Solomon and the Queen of Sheba are said to have founded the Kingdom of Abyssinia (Ethiopia) c. 1000 B.C

THE ECONOMY
World's second poorest nation. Most people are subsistence farmers. Despite war-damaged infrastructure and periodic serious droughts, agricultural and industrial output are growing as it moves toward a market economy.

| 0 | 200 km |
| 0 | 200 miles |

4000m/13124ft
3000m/9843ft
2000m/6562ft
1000m/3281ft
500m/1640ft
200m/656ft
Sea Level
Below Sea Level

FACT FILE

OFFICIAL NAME: *Undetermined*
DATE OF FORMATION: 1993
CAPITAL: Addis Ababa
POPULATION: 51 million
TOTAL AREA: 435,605 sq miles (1,128,221 sq km)
DENSITY: 117 people per sq mile

LANGUAGES: Amharic*, English, Arabic, Tigrinya, Orominga
RELIGIONS: Muslim 43%, Christian 37%, traditional beliefs, other 20%
ETHNIC MIX: Oromo 40%, Amhara and Tigrean 32%, other 28%
GOVERNMENT: Multiparty republic
CURRENCY: Birr = 100 cents

SOMALIA

A SEMIARID state occupying the horn of Africa. Italian Somaliland and British Somaliland were united in 1960 to form an independent Somalia.

GEOGRAPHY
Highlands in the north, flatter scrub-covered land to the south. Coastal areas are more fertile.

CLIMATE
Very dry, except for the north coast, which is hot and humid. Interior has among world's highest average yearly temperatures.

PEOPLE AND SOCIETY
Clan system forms the basis of all commercial, political, and social activities. Most people are herders (Samaal) while the rest are farmers (Sab). Years of clan-based civil war have resulted in collapse of central government. US-led UN peacekeeping force was deployed, but it was withdrawn in 1994.

◆ INSIGHT: *Present-day Somalia was known to the Egyptians, Phoenicians, and Greeks as "the land of incense"*

THE ECONOMY
Somalia is heavily reliant on foreign aid, since all commodities except arms are in short supply. Formal economy has collapsed due to civil war and drought.

FACT FILE

OFFICIAL NAME: Somali Democratic Republic
DATE OF FORMATION: 1960
CAPITAL: Mogadishu
POPULATION: 9.5 million
TOTAL AREA: 246,200 sq miles (637,660 sq km)

DENSITY: 39 people per sq mile
LANGUAGES: Somali*, Arabic*, other
RELIGIONS: Sunni Muslim 99%, other (inc. Christian) 1%
ETHNIC MIX: Somali 98%, Bantu, Arab 1.5%, European, other 0.5%
GOVERNMENT: Transitional
CURRENCY: Shilling = 100 cents

UGANDA

UGANDA LIES landlocked in East Africa. It was ruled by one of Africa's more eccentric leaders, the dictator Idi Amin Dada, from 1971–1980.

GEOGRAPHY
Predominantly a large plateau with Ruwenzori mountain range and Great Rift Valley in the west. Lake Victoria in the southeast. Vegetation is of savanna type.

CLIMATE
Altitude and the influence of the lakes modify the equatorial climate. Rain falls throughout the year; spring is the wettest period.

PEOPLE AND SOCIETY
Predominantly rural population comprises 13 main ethnic groups. Since 1986, President Museveni has worked hard to break down traditional animosities. In 1993, he allowed the restoration of Uganda's four historical monarchies. New constitution will use a federal system with boundaries based on those of the old kingdoms.

THE ECONOMY
Coffee earns 93% of export income. Hydroelectric power is to be developed to replace 50% of oil imports. Reopening of mines should improve the economy.

◆ INSIGHT: *Lake Victoria is the world's third largest lake*

3000m/9843ft	
2000m/6562ft	
1000m/3281ft	
500m/1640ft	

FACT FILE

OFFICIAL NAME: Republic of Uganda
DATE OF FORMATION: 1962
CAPITAL: Kampala
POPULATION: 19.2 million
TOTAL AREA: 91,073 sq miles (235,880 sq km)
DENSITY: 245 people per sq mile

LANGUAGES: English*, Luganda, Nkole, Chiga, Lango, Acholi, Teso
RELIGIONS: Catholic/Protestant 66%, traditional beliefs 18%, Muslim 16%
ETHNIC MIX: Buganda 18%, Banyoro 14%, Teso 9%, other 59%
GOVERNMENT: Multiparty republic
CURRENCY: Shilling = 100 cents

KENYA

KENYA STRADDLES the equator on Africa's east coast. It became a multiparty democracy in 1992 and has been led by President Moi since 1978.

GEOGRAPHY
Central plateau divided by Great Rift Valley. North of the equator is mainly semidesert. To the east lies a fertile coastal belt.

CLIMATE
Coast and Great Rift Valley are hot and humid. Plateau interior is temperate. Northeastern desert is hot and dry. Rain generally falls April–May and October–November.

PEOPLE AND SOCIETY
Kenya's 70 ethnic groups speak about 40 languages. Rural majority has strong clan and family links. One of the world's highest population growth rates, together with poverty, has exacerbated the recent surge in ethnic violence.

◆ INSIGHT: Kenya has more than 40 game reserves and national parks, and two marine parks in the Indian Ocean

THE ECONOMY
Tourism is the leading foreign exchange earner. Tea and coffee grown as cash crops. Large and diversified manufacturing sector.

FACT FILE

OFFICIAL NAME: Republic of Kenya
DATE OF FORMATION: 1963
CAPITAL: Nairobi
POPULATION: 26.1 million
TOTAL AREA: 224,081 sq miles (580,370 sq km)
DENSITY: 114 people per sq mile

LANGUAGES: Swahili*, English, Kikuyu, Luo, Kamba, other
RELIGIONS: Catholic/Protestant 66%, animist 26%, Muslim 6%, other 2%
ETHNIC MIX: Kikuyu 21%, Luhya 14%, Kamba 11%, other 54%
GOVERNMENT: Multiparty republic
CURRENCY: Shilling = 100 cents

RWANDA

RWANDA LIES just south of the equator in east central Africa. Since independence from France in 1962, ethnic tensions have dominated politics.

GEOGRAPHY
Series of plateaus descends from ridge of volcanic peaks in the west to Akagera River on eastern border. Great Rift Valley also passes through this region.

CLIMATE
Tropical, tempered by the altitude. Two wet seasons are separated by a dry season, June–August. Heaviest rain in the west.

PEOPLE AND SOCIETY
Rwandans live a subsistence existence. Traditional family and clan structures are strong. For over 500 years the cattle-owning Tutsi were politically dominant over the land-owning Hutu. In 1959, violent revolt led to a reversal of the roles. The two groups have since been waging a spasmodic war. In the most recent outbreak of violence, in 1994, over 200,000 people died.

THE ECONOMY
All economic activity has been suspended due to ethnic conflict. Rwanda has few resources, but during peace, it produces coffee. Possible oil and gas reserves.

◆ INSIGHT: *Rwanda is Africa's most densely populated country*

FACT FILE

OFFICIAL NAME: Republic of Rwanda
DATE OF FORMATION: 1962
CAPITAL: Kigali
POPULATION: 7.5 million
TOTAL AREA: 10,170 sq miles
(26,340 sq km)
DENSITY: 737 people per sq mile

LANGUAGES: Kinyarwanda*, French*, Kiswahili
RELIGIONS: Catholic 65%, Protestant 9%, traditional beliefs 25%, other 1%
ETHNIC MIX: Hutu 90%, Tutsi 9%, Twa pygmy 1%
GOVERNMENT: Multiparty republic
CURRENCY: Franc = 100 centimes

BURUNDI

SMALL, DENSELY populated, and landlocked, Burundi lies just south of the equator, on the Nile–Congo watershed in Central Africa.

GEOGRAPHY
Hilly with high plateaus in center and savanna in the east. Great Rift Valley on western side.

CLIMATE
Temperate, with high humidity. Heavy and frequent rainfall, mostly October–May.

PEOPLE AND SOCIETY
Burundi's postindependence history has been dominated by ethnic conflict – with repeated large-scale massacres – between majority Hutu and the Tutsi, who control the army. Over 120,000 people, mostly Hutu, have been killed since 1992. Twa pygmies are not involved in the conflict. Most people are subsistence farmers.

◆ INSIGHT: Burundi's birth rate is one of the highest in Africa. On average, families have seven children

THE ECONOMY
Overwhelmingly agricultural economy. Small quantities of gold and tungsten. Potential of oil in Lake Tanganyika. Burundi has 5% of the world's nickel reserves.

FACT FILE

OFFICIAL NAME: Republic of Burundi
DATE OF FORMATION: 1962
CAPITAL: Bujumbura
POPULATION: 5.8 million
TOTAL AREA: 10,750 sq miles (27,830 sq km)
DENSITY: 539 people per sq mile

LANGUAGES: Kirundi*, French*, Swahili, other
RELIGIONS: Catholic 62%, traditional beliefs 32%, Protestant 6%
ETHNIC MIX: Hutu 85%, Tutsi 13%, Twa pygmy 1%, other 1%
GOVERNMENT: Multiparty republic
CURRENCY: Franc = 100 centimes

CENTRAL AFRICAN REPUBLIC

A LANDLOCKED country lying between the basins of the Chad and Congo rivers. Its arid north sustains less than 2% of the population.

GEOGRAPHY
Comprises a low plateau, covered by scrub or savanna. Rain forests in the south. One of Africa's great rivers, the Ubangi, forms the border with Zaire.

CLIMATE
The south is equatorial; the north is hot and dry. Rain occurs all year round, with heaviest falls between July and October.

PEOPLE AND SOCIETY
Baya and Banda are largest ethnic groups, but Sango, spoken by minority river peoples in the south, is the *lingua franca*. Most political leaders since independence have come from the south. Women, as in other non-Muslim African countries, have considerable power. Large number of ethnic groups helps limit disputes.

THE ECONOMY
Dominated by subsistence farming. Exports include gold, diamonds, cotton, and timber. Country is self-sufficient in food production. Poor infrastructure.

◆ *INSIGHT: The country was severely depopulated in previous centuries by the Arab and European slave trades*

FACT FILE

OFFICIAL NAME: Central African Republic
DATE OF FORMATION: 1960
CAPITAL: Bangui
POPULATION: 3.3 million
TOTAL AREA: 240,530 sq miles (622,980 sq km)

DENSITY: 13 people per sq mile
LANGUAGES: French*, Sangho, Banda
RELIGIONS: Christian 50%, traditional beliefs 27%, Muslim 15%, other 8%
ETHNIC MIX: Baya 34%, Banda 27%, Mandjia 21%, Sara 10%, other 8%
GOVERNMENT: Multiparty republic
CURRENCY: CFA franc = 100 centimes

ZAIRE

STRADDLING THE equator in east central Africa, Zaire is one of Africa's largest countries. It achieved independence from Belgium in 1960.

GEOGRAPHY
Rain forest basin of River Congo occupies 60% of the land. High mountain ranges stretch down the eastern border.

CLIMATE
Tropical and humid. Distinct wet and dry seasons south of the equator. The north is mainly wet.

PEOPLE AND SOCIETY
12 main groups and around 190 smaller ones. Original inhabitants, Forest Pygmies, are now a marginalized group. Ethnic tensions inherited from colonial period were contained until 1990, since when outbreaks of ethnic violence have occurred.

◆ INSIGHT: *Zaire's rain forests comprise almost 6% of the world's, and 50% of Africa's, remaining woodlands*

THE ECONOMY
25 years of mismanagement have brought economy near to collapse. Hyperinflation. Minerals, including copper and diamonds, provide 85% of export earnings.

2000m/6562ft
1000m/3281ft
500m/1640ft
200m/656ft
Sea Level

0   200 km
0   200 miles

FACT FILE

OFFICIAL NAME: Republic of Zaire
DATE OF FORMATION: 1960
CAPITAL: Kinshasa
POPULATION: 41.2 million
TOTAL AREA: 905,563 sq miles (2,345,410 sq km)
DENSITY: 45 people per sq mile

LANGUAGES: French*, Kiswahili, Tshiluba, Kikongo, Lingala
RELIGIONS: Christian 70%, traditional beliefs 20%, Muslim 10%
ETHNIC MIX: Bantu 23%, Hamitic 23%, other (inc. Pygmy) 54%
GOVERNMENT: Transitional
CURRENCY: New zaire = 100 makuta

AFRICA

NIGER

NIGER LIES landlocked in West Africa, but it is linked to the sea by its one permanent river, the Niger. It became independent of France in 1960.

GEOGRAPHY
North and northeast regions are part of Sahara and Sahel. Aïr mountains in center rise high above the desert. Savanna in the south.

CLIMATE
High temperatures for most of the year – around 95°F (35°C). The north is virtually rainless.

PEOPLE AND SOCIETY
A largely Islamic society. Women have limited rights and restricted access to education. Considerable tensions exist between Tuareg nomads in the north and groups in the south. Tuaregs have felt alienated from mainstream politics. They mounted a low-key revolt in 1990. Sense of community and egalitarianism among southern peoples helps to combat economic difficulties.

THE ECONOMY
Vast uranium deposits. Frequent droughts and southwest expansion of Sahara are problems.

◆ INSIGHT: Niger's name is derived from the Tuareg word n'eghirren, meaning "flowing water"

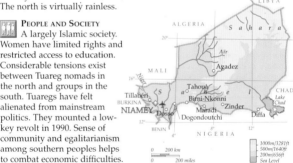

FACT FILE

OFFICIAL NAME: Republic of Niger
DATE OF FORMATION: 1960
CAPITAL: Niamey
POPULATION: 8.5 million
TOTAL AREA: 489,188 sq miles
(1,267,000 sq km)
DENSITY: 18 people per sq mile

LANGUAGES: French*, Hausa, Djerma, Fulani, Tuareg, Teda
RELIGIONS: Muslim 85%, traditional beliefs 14%, Christian 1%
ETHNIC MIX: Hausa 56%, Djerma 22%, Fulani 9%, other 13%
GOVERNMENT: Multiparty republic
CURRENCY: CFA franc = 100 centimes

76

CHAD

LANDLOCKED IN north central Africa, Chad has been torn by intermittent periods of civil war since independence from France in 1960.

GEOGRAPHY
Mostly plateaus sloping westward to Lake Chad. Northern third is Sahara. Tibesti Mountains in north rise to 10,826 ft (3,300 m).

CLIMATE
Three distinct zones: desert in north, semiarid region in center, and tropics in south.

PEOPLE AND SOCIETY
Half the population live in southern fifth of the country. Northern third has only 100,000 people, mainly Muslim Toubeu nomads. Political strife between Muslims in north and Christians in south. Recent attempts to introduce multiparty system, after 30 years of military and one-party rule.

◆ INSIGHT: Lake Chad is progressively drying up – it is now estimated to be just 20% of its size in 1970

THE ECONOMY
One of Africa's poorest states. Vast majority of people involved in subsistence agriculture, notably cotton and cattle herding. Recent discovery of large oil deposits.

FACT FILE
OFFICIAL NAME: Republic of Chad
DATE OF FORMATION: 1960
CAPITAL: N'Djamena
POPULATION: 6 million
TOTAL AREA: 495,752 sq miles (1,284,000 sq km)
DENSITY: 13 people per sq mile

LANGUAGES: French*, Sara, Maba
RELIGIONS: Muslim 44%, Christian 33%, traditional beliefs 23%
ETHNIC MIX: Bagirmi, Sara and Kreish 31%, Sudanic Arab 26%, Teda 7%, other 36%
GOVERNMENT: Transitional
CURRENCY: CFA franc = 100 centimes

MAURITANIA

SITUATED IN northwest Africa, two thirds of Mauritania's territory is desert. A former French colony, it achieved independence in 1960.

GEOGRAPHY
The Sahara, barren with scattered oases, covers the north. Savanna lands to the south.

CLIMATE
Generally hot and dry, aggravated by dusty *harmattan* wind. Summer rain in the south, virtually none in the north.

PEOPLE AND SOCIETY
The Maures control political life and dominate the minority black population. Ethnic tension centers on the oppression of blacks by Maures. Tens of thousands of blacks are estimated to be in slavery. Family solidarity among nomadic peoples is particularly strong.

◆ *INSIGHT: Slavery officially became illegal in Mauritania in 1980, but* de facto *slavery still persists*

THE ECONOMY
Agriculture and herding. Iron and copper mining. World's largest gypsum deposits. Rich fishing grounds. Large foreign debt.

FACT FILE
OFFICIAL NAME: Islamic Republic of Mauritania
DATE OF FORMATION: 1960
CAPITAL: Nouakchott
POPULATION: 2.2 million
TOTAL AREA: 395,953 sq miles (1,025,520 sq km)

DENSITY: 5 people per sq mile
LANGUAGES: French*, Hassaniyah Arabic, Wolof
RELIGIONS: Muslim 100%
ETHNIC MIX: Maure 80%, Wolof 7%, Tukulor 5%, other 8%
GOVERNMENT: Multiparty republic
CURRENCY: Ouguiya = 5 khoums

MALI

LANDLOCKED IN the heart of West Africa, Mali held its first free elections in 1992, more than 30 years after it gained independence from France.

GEOGRAPHY
Northern half lies in the Sahara. Inland delta of River Niger flows through grassy savanna region in the south.

CLIMATE
In the south, intensely hot, dry weather precedes the westerly rains. The north is almost rainless.

PEOPLE AND SOCIETY
Most people live in southern savanna region. Bambara are politically dominant. A few nomadic Fulani and Tuareg herders travel northern plains. Extended family provides social security. Tension between peoples of the south and Tuaregs in north.

◆ INSIGHT: Tombouctou was the center of the huge Malinke empire during the 14th century

THE ECONOMY
One of the poorest countries in the world. Less than 2% of land can be cultivated. Most people are farmers, herders, or river fishers. Gold deposits now being mined.

500m/1640ft
200m/656ft
Sea Level

FACT FILE

OFFICIAL NAME: Republic of Mali
DATE OF FORMATION: 1960
CAPITAL: Bamako
POPULATION: 10.1 million
TOTAL AREA: 478,837 sq miles
(1,240,190 sq km)
DENSITY: 21 people per sq mile

LANGUAGES: French*, Bambara, Fulani, Senufo, Soninké
RELIGIONS: Muslim 80%, traditional beliefs 18%, Christian 2%
ETHNIC MIX: Bambara 31%, Fulani 13%, Senufo 12%, other 44%
GOVERNMENT: Multiparty republic
CURRENCY: CFA franc = 100 centimes

SENEGAL

A FORMER French colony, Senegal achieved independence in 1960. Its capital, Dakar, stands on the westernmost cape of Africa.

 GEOGRAPHY
Arid semidesert in the north. The south is mainly savanna bushland. Plains in the southeast.

 CLIMATE
Tropical, with humid rainy conditions June–October, and drier season December–May. Coast is cooled by northern trade winds.

PEOPLE AND SOCIETY
Very little ethnic tension, due to considerable amount of interethnic marriage. Groups can be identified regionally. Dakar is a Wolof area, the Senegal River is dominated by the Toucouleur, and the Malinke mostly live in the east. The Diola in Casamance have felt politically excluded and this has led to unrest. A French-influenced class system is still prevalent and has become more apparent in recent years.

THE ECONOMY
70% of people are farmers – groundnuts are main export crop. Phosphate is mined. More industry than most West African countries.

◆ *INSIGHT: Senegal's name derives from the Zenega Berbers who invaded in the 1300s, bringing Islam with them*

FACT FILE

OFFICIAL NAME: Republic of Senegal
DATE OF FORMATION: 1960
CAPITAL: Dakar
POPULATION: 7.9 million
TOTAL AREA: 75,950 sq miles (196,720 sq km)
DENSITY: 104 people per sq mile

LANGUAGES: French*, Wolof, Fulani, Serer, Diola, Malinke, Soninke
RELIGIONS: Muslim 92%, traditional beliefs 6%, Christian 2%
ETHNIC MIX: Wolof 46%, Fulani 25%, Serer 16%, Diola 7%, Malinke 6%
GOVERNMENT: Multiparty republic
CURRENCY: CFA franc = 100 centimes

GAMBIA

A NARROW state on the west coast of Africa, Gambia was renowned for its stability until its government was overthrown in a coup in 1994.

GEOGRAPHY
Narrow strip of land which borders River Gambia. Long, sandy beaches backed by mangrove swamps along river. Savanna and tropical forests higher up.

CLIMATE
Subtropical, with wet, humid months July–October and warm, dry season November–May.

PEOPLE AND SOCIETY
Little tension between various ethnic groups. Creole community, known as the Aku, is small but socially prominent. People are increasingly leaving rural areas for the towns, where average incomes are four times higher. Each year seasonal immigrants from neighboring states come to farm groundnuts. Women are active as traders.

THE ECONOMY
80% of the labor force is involved in agriculture. Groundnuts are the principal crop. The fisheries sector is being improved. Growth in tourism now halted by political instability. Most donor aid has been suspended until civilian rule is restored.

◆ INSIGHT: *Banjul's airport was upgraded by NASA in 1989, for Space Shuttle emergency landings*

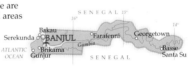

FACT FILE

OFFICIAL NAME: Republic of The Gambia
DATE OF FORMATION: 1965
CAPITAL: Banjul
POPULATION: 900,000
TOTAL AREA: 4,363 sq miles (11,300 sq km)

DENSITY: 206 people per sq mile
LANGUAGES: English*, other
RELIGIONS: Muslim 85%, Christian 9%, traditional beliefs 6%
ETHNIC MIX: Mandinka 41%, Fulani 14%, Wolof 13%, other 32%
GOVERNMENT: Military regime
CURRENCY: Dalasi = 100 butut

CAPE VERDE

OFF THE west coast of Africa, in the Atlantic Ocean, lies the group of islands that make up Cape Verde, a Portuguese colony until 1975.

GEOGRAPHY
Ten main islands and eight smaller islets, all of volcanic origin. Mostly mountainous, with steep cliffs and rocky headlands.

CLIMATE
Warm and very dry. Subject to droughts that may last for years at a time.

PEOPLE AND SOCIETY
Most people are of mixed Portuguese-African origin; rest are largely African, descended from slaves or from more recent immigrants from the mainland. 50% of the population live on Santiago. Roman Catholicism and the extended family are strong. Some ethnic tension between islands.

◆ INSIGHT: Poor soils and lack of surface water mean that Cape Verde must import 90% of its food

THE ECONOMY
Most people are subsistence farmers. Fish is the main export. Only minerals produced are salt, and volcanic rock for cement.

FACT FILE

OFFICIAL NAME: Republic of Cape Verde
DATE OF FORMATION: 1975
CAPITAL: Praia
POPULATION: 400,000
TOTAL AREA: 1,556 sq miles (4,030 sq km)

DENSITY: 258 people per sq mile
LANGUAGES: Portuguese*, Creole
RELIGIONS: Roman Catholic 98%, Protestant 2%
ETHNIC MIX: Creole (mestiço) 71%, Black 28%, White 1%
GOVERNMENT: Multiparty republic
CURRENCY: Escudo = 100 centavos

GUINEA-BISSAU

KNOWN AS Portuguese Guinea during its days as a colony, Guinea-Bissau is situated on Africa's west coast, bordered by Senegal and Guinea.

 GEOGRAPHY
Low-lying, apart from savanna highlands in northeast. Rain forests and swamps are found along coastal areas.

 CLIMATE
Tropical, with wet season May–November and dry season December–April. Hot *harmattan* wind blows during dry season.

PEOPLE AND SOCIETY
Largest ethnic group is Balante, who live in the south. Though less than 2% of the population, the mixed Portuguese-African *mestiços* dominate top ranks of government and bureaucracy. Most people live on small family farms in self-contained villages. After 20 years of single-party rule, the first multiparty elections were held in 1994.

THE ECONOMY
Mostly subsistence farming – corn, sweet potatoes, cassava. Main cash crops are cashews, groundnuts, and palm kernels. Offshore oil as yet untapped.

◆ *INSIGHT: In 1974, Guinea-Bissau became the first Portuguese colony to gain independence*

FACT FILE

OFFICIAL NAME: Republic of Guinea-Bissau
DATE OF FORMATION: 1974
CAPITAL: Bissau
POPULATION: 1 million
TOTAL AREA: 13,940 sq miles (36,120 sq km)

DENSITY: 71 people per sq mile
LANGUAGES: Portuguese*, other
RELIGIONS: Traditional beliefs 54%, Muslim 38%, Christian 8%
ETHNIC MIX: Balante 27%, Fulani 22%, Malinke 12%, other 39%
GOVERNMENT: Multiparty republic
CURRENCY: Peso = 100 centavos

GUINEA

FACING THE Atlantic Ocean, on the west coast of Africa, Guinea became the first French colony in Africa to gain independence, in 1958.

 GEOGRAPHY
Coastal plains and mangrove swamps in west rise to forested or savanna highlands in the south. Semidesert in the north.

 CLIMATE
Tropical, with wet season April–October. Heavy annual rainfall. Hot *harmattan* wind blows from Sahara during dry season.

PEOPLE AND SOCIETY
Malinke and Fulani make up most of the population, but traditional rivalries between them have allowed coastal peoples such as the Susu to dominate politics. Daily life revolves around the extended family. Women gained influence under Marxist party rule from 1958–1984, but Muslim revival since then has reversed the trend. First multiparty elections held in 1995.

THE ECONOMY
Two thirds of people are farmers. Cash crops are palm oil, bananas, pineapples, and rice. Gold, diamond, and bauxite reserves.

◆ INSIGHT: The colors of Guinea's flag represent the three words of the country's motto: work (red), justice (yellow), and solidarity (green)

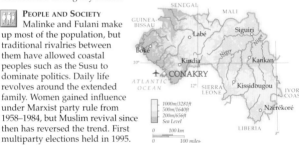

FACT FILE
OFFICIAL NAME: Republic of Guinea
DATE OF FORMATION: 1958
CAPITAL: Conakry
POPULATION: 6.3 million
TOTAL AREA: 94,926 sq miles (245,860 sq km)
DENSITY: 65 people per sq mile

LANGUAGES: French*, Fulani, Malinke, Susu, Kissi, other
RELIGIONS: Muslim 85%, Christian 8%, traditional beliefs 7%
ETHNIC MIX: Fulani 40%, Malinke 25%, Susu 12%, Kissi 7%, other 16%
GOVERNMENT: Multiparty republic
CURRENCY: Franc = 100 centimes

SIERRA LEONE

THE WEST African state of Sierra Leone achieved independence from the British in 1961. Today, it is one of the world's poorest nations.

GEOGRAPHY
Flat plain, running the length of the coast, stretches inland for 83 miles (133 km). Beyond, forests rise to highlands near neighboring Guinea in the northeast.

CLIMATE
Hot tropical weather, with very high rainfall and humidity. Dusty, northeastern *harmattan* wind blows November–April.

PEOPLE AND SOCIETY
Mende and Temne are major ethnic groups. Freetown's citizens are largely descended from slaves freed from Britain and the US, resulting in a strongly anglicized Creole culture. A military coup in 1992 halted plans to turn the government into a multiparty democracy. Rebel forces have been fighting the government since 1991; thousands have died in clashes.

THE ECONOMY
Vast majority of people are subsistance farmers. Cash crops include palm kernels, cocoa beans, and kola. Main export is diamonds.

◆ *INSIGHT: The British philanthropist Granville Sharp set up a settlement for freed slaves in Sierra Leone in 1787*

1000m/3281ft	
500m/1640ft	
200m/656ft	
Sea Level	

FACT FILE
OFFICIAL NAME: Republic of Sierra Leone
DATE OF FORMATION: 1961
CAPITAL: Freetown
POPULATION: 4.5 million
TOTAL AREA: 27,699 sq miles (71,740 sq km)

DENSITY: 162 people per sq mile
LANGUAGES: English*, Krio (Creole)
RELIGIONS: Traditional beliefs 52%, Muslim 40%, Christian 8%
ETHNIC MIX: Mende 34%, Temne 31%, Limba 9%, Kono 5%, other 21%
GOVERNMENT: Military regime
CURRENCY: Leone = 100 cents

LIBERIA

LIBERIA FACES the Atlantic Ocean in equatorial West Africa. Africa's oldest republic, it was established in 1847. Today it is torn by civil war.

GEOGRAPHY
Coastline of beaches and mangrove swamps rises to forested plateaus and highlands inland.

CLIMATE
High temperatures. Except in extreme southeast, there is only one wet season, May–October.

PEOPLE AND SOCIETY
Key social distinction has been between Americo-Liberians – descendants of freed slaves – and the indigenous tribal peoples. However, political assimilation and intermarriage have eased tensions. Inter-tribal tension is now a problem. A civil war has ravaged the country since 1990, with private armies competing for power.

◆ INSIGHT: *Liberia is named after the people liberated from US slavery who arrived in the 1800s*

THE ECONOMY
Civil war has led to collapse of economy – little commercial activity. Only 1% of land is arable. Estimated one billion tons of iron ore reserves at Mount Nimba.

1000m/3281ft
500m/1640ft
200m/656ft
Sea Level

0   50 km
0   50 miles

FACT FILE
OFFICIAL NAME: Republic of Liberia
DATE OF FORMATION: 1847
CAPITAL: Monrovia
POPULATION: 2.8 million
TOTAL AREA: 43,000 sq miles
(111,370 sq km)
DENSITY: 65 people per sq mile

LANGUAGES: English*, Kpelle, Bassa Vai, Grebo, Kru, Kissi, Gola
RELIGIONS: Traditional beliefs 70%, Muslim 20%, Christian 10%
ETHNIC MIX: Kpelle 20%, Bassa 14%, Americo-Liberians 5%, other 61%
GOVERNMENT: Transitional
CURRENCY: Liberian $ = 100 cents

IVORY COAST

ONE OF the larger nations along the coast of West Africa, the Ivory Coast remains under the influence of its former colonial ruler, France.

GEOGRAPHY
Sandy coastal strip backed by a largely rain forest interior, and savanna plateaus in the north.

CLIMATE
High temperatures all year round. South has two wet seasons; north has one, with lower rainfall.

PEOPLE AND SOCIETY
More than 60 ethnic groups. President Houphouët-Boigny, who ruled from independence until 1993, promoted his own group, the Baoule. Succession of Konan Bedic, another Baoule, has annoyed other tribes. The extended family keeps laborers who migrate to the cities in contact with their villages.

◆ INSIGHT: The Basilica of Our Lady of the Peace in Yamoussoukro is the second largest church in the world. It holds up to 100,000 people

THE ECONOMY
Cash crops include cocoa, coffee, palm oil, bananas, and rubber. Teak, mahogany, and ebony in rain forests. Oil reserves.

FACT FILE

OFFICIAL NAME: Republic of the Ivory Coast
DATE OF FORMATION: 1960
CAPITAL: Yamoussoukro
POPULATION: 13.4 million
TOTAL AREA: 124,503 sq miles (322,463 sq km)

DENSITY: 107 people per sq mile
LANGUAGES: French*, Akran, other
RELIGIONS: Traditional beliefs 63%, Muslim 25%, Christian 12%
ETHNIC MIX: Baoule 23%, Bété 18%, Kru 17%, Malinke 15%, other 27%
GOVERNMENT: Multiparty republic
CURRENCY: CFA franc = 100 centimes

BURKINA

KNOWN AS Upper Volta until 1984, the West African state of Burkina has had military rulers for most of its postindependence history.

GEOGRAPHY
North of country is covered by the Sahara. South is largely savanna. Three main rivers are Black, White, and Red Voltas.

CLIMATE
Tropical. Dry, cool weather November–February. Erratic rain March–April, mostly in southeast.

PEOPLE AND SOCIETY
No ethnic group is dominant, but the Mossi have always played an important part in government. Extreme poverty has led to a strong sense of egalitarianism. The extended family is important, and reaches from villages into towns and cities. Women wield considerable power and influence within this system, but most are still denied access to education.

THE ECONOMY
Based on agriculture – cotton is most valuable cash crop – but not self-sufficient in food. Gold is the leading nonagricultural export.

◆ INSIGHT: Poor soils and droughts mean that many men migrate seasonally to Ghana and the Ivory Coast for work

FACT FILE
OFFICIAL NAME: Burkina
DATE OF FORMATION: 1960
CAPITAL: Ouagadougou
POPULATION: 9.8 million
TOTAL AREA: 105,870 sq miles
(274,200 sq km)
DENSITY: 91 people per sq mile

LANGUAGES: French*, Mossi, Fulani, Tuareg, Dyula, Songhai
RELIGIONS: Traditional beliefs 65%, Muslim 25%, Christian 10%
ETHNIC MIX: Mossi 45%, Mande 10%, Fulani 10%, others 35%
GOVERNMENT: Multiparty republic
CURRENCY: CFA franc = 100 centimes

GHANA

ONCE KNOWN as the Gold Coast, Ghana in West Africa has experienced intermittent periods of military rule since independence in 1957.

GEOGRAPHY
Mostly low-lying. West is covered by rain forest. Lake Volta – the world's third largest artificial lake – was created by damming the White Volta River.

CLIMATE
Tropical. Two wet seasons in the south; one in the north.

PEOPLE AND SOCIETY
Around 75 ethnic groups. The largest is the Akan. Over 100 languages and dialects are spoken. Southern peoples are richer and more urban than those of the north. In recent years, tension between groups in the north has erupted into violence. Multiparty elections in 1992 confirmed former military leader Jerry Rawlings in power.

◆ INSIGHT: Ghana was the first British colony in Africa to gain independence

THE ECONOMY
Produces 15% of the world's cocoa. Hardwood trees such as maple and sapele are exploited. Gold, diamonds, bauxite, and manganese are major exports.

FACT FILE

OFFICIAL NAME: Republic of Ghana
DATE OF FORMATION: 1957
CAPITAL: Accra
POPULATION: 16.4 million
TOTAL AREA: 92,100 sq miles
(238,540 sq km)
DENSITY: 178 people per sq mile

LANGUAGES: English*, Akan, Mossi, Ewe, Ga, Twi, Fanti, Gurma, other
RELIGIONS: Traditional beliefs 38%, Muslim 30%, Christian 24%, other 8%
ETHNIC MIX: Akan 52%, Mossi 15%, Ewe 12%, Ga 8%, other 13%
GOVERNMENT: Multiparty republic
CURRENCY: Cedi = 100 pesewas

TOGO

TOGO LIES sandwiched between Ghana and Benin in West Africa. The 1993–1994 elections were the first since its independence in 1960.

GEOGRAPHY
Central forested region bounded by savanna lands to the north and south. Mountain range stretches southwest to northeast.

CLIMATE
Coast hot and humid; drier inland. Rainy season March–July, with heaviest falls in the west.

PEOPLE AND SOCIETY
Harsh resentment between Ewe in the south and Kabye in the north. Kabye control military, but are far less developed than people of the south. Extended family is important. Tribalism and nepotism are key factors in everyday life. Some ethnic groups, such as the Mina, have matriarchal societies.

◆ INSIGHT: The "Nana Benz," the market-women of Lomé market, control Togo's retail trade

THE ECONOMY
Most people are farmers. Self-sufficient in basic foodstuffs. Main export crops are coffee, cocoa, and cotton. Half of all export revenues come from phosphate deposits with the world's highest mineral content.

500m/1640ft
200m/656ft
Sea Level

0   50 km
0   50 miles

FACT FILE
OFFICIAL NAME: Togolese Republic
DATE OF FORMATION: 1960
CAPITAL: Lomé
POPULATION: 3.9 million
TOTAL AREA: 21,927 sq miles
(56,790 sq km)
DENSITY: 177 people per sq mile

LANGUAGES: French*, Ewe, Kabye, Gurma, other
RELIGIONS: Traditional beliefs 70%, Christian 20%, Muslim 10%
ETHNIC MIX: Ewe 43%, Kabye 26%, Gurma 16%, other 15%
GOVERNMENT: Multiparty republic
CURRENCY: CFA franc = 100 centimes

BENIN

STRETCHES NORTH from the West African coast. In 1990, it became one of the pioneers of African democratization, ending years of military rule.

GEOGRAPHY
Long, sandy coastal region. Numerous lagoons lie just behind the shoreline. Forested plateaus inland. Mountains in the northwest.

CLIMATE
Hot and humid in the south. Two rainy seasons. Hot, dusty *harmattan* winds blow during December–February dry season.

PEOPLE AND SOCIETY
Around 50 ethnic groups. Fon people in the south dominate politics. Other major groups are Adja and Yoruba. In the far north, Fulani follow a nomadic lifestyle. Tension between north and south, partly reflecting Muslim–Christian divide, and partly because south is more developed. Women hold positions of power in retail trade. Substantial differences in wealth reflect strongly hierarchical society.

THE ECONOMY
Mostly subsistence farming. Cash crops include cotton, cocoa beans, and coffee. Some oil and limestone are produced. France is the main aid donor.

◆ INSIGHT: Benin trains many doctors, but more of them work in France than in Benin

500m/1640ft
200m/656ft
Sea Level

0   100 km
0   100 miles

FACT FILE
OFFICIAL NAME: Republic of Benin
DATE OF FORMATION: 1960
CAPITAL: Porto-Novo
POPULATION: 5.1 million
TOTAL AREA: 43,480 sq miles
(112,620 sq km)
DENSITY: 117 people per sq mile

LANGUAGES: French*, Fon, Bariba, Yoruba, Adja, Houeda, Fulani
RELIGIONS: Traditional beliefs 70%, Muslim 15%, Christian 15%
ETHNIC MIX: Fon 39%, Yoruba 12%, Adja 10%, other 39%
GOVERNMENT: Multiparty republic
CURRENCY: CFA franc = 100 centimes

NIGERIA

FOUR TIMES the size of the United Kingdom, from which it gained independence in 1960, Nigeria in West Africa is a federation of 30 states.

GEOGRAPHY
Coastal area of beaches, swamps, and lagoons gives way to rain forest, and then to savanna on high plateaus. Semidesert in north.

CLIMATE
South is hot, rainy, and humid for most of the year. Arid north has one very humid wet season. Jos plateau and highlands are cooler.

PEOPLE AND SOCIETY
Some 250 ethnic groups: the largest are Hausa, Yoruba, Ibo, and Fulani. Tensions between groups constantly threaten national unity, although they have largely been contained in recent years. Members of one group tend to blame those of another for their problems, rather than the political system. Except in the Islamic north, women are allowed economic independence.

THE ECONOMY
Oil has been the economic mainstay since 1970s, accounting for 90% of export earnings.

◆ INSIGHT: Nigeria is Africa's most populous state – one in every six Africans is Nigerian

FACT FILE
OFFICIAL NAME: Federal Republic of Nigeria
DATE OF FORMATION: 1960
CAPITAL: Abuja
POPULATION: 119 million
TOTAL AREA: 356,668 sq miles (923,770 sq km)

DENSITY: 333 people per sq mile
LANGUAGES: English*, Hausa, Yoruba
RELIGIONS: Muslim 50%, Christian 40%, traditional beliefs 10%
ETHNIC MIX: Hausa 21%, Yoruba 20%, Ibo 17%, Fulani 9%, other 33%
GOVERNMENT: Military regime
CURRENCY: Naira = 100 kobo

CAMEROON

SITUATED ON the central West African coast, Cameroon was in effect a one-party state for 30 years. Multiparty elections were held in 1992.

GEOGRAPHY
Over half the land is forested: equatorial rain forest in north, evergreen forest and wooded savanna in south. Mountains in the west.

CLIMATE
South is equatorial, with plentiful rainfall, declining inland. Far north is beset by drought.

PEOPLE AND SOCIETY
Around 230 ethnic groups; no single group is dominant. Bamileke is the largest, but it has never held political power. Some tension between more affluent south and poorer north, albeit diminished by the ethnic diversity. Also rivalry between majority French-speakers and minority English-speakers.

◆ INSIGHT: *Cameroon's name derives from the Portuguese* camarões – *after the shrimp fished by the early explorers*

THE ECONOMY
Moderate oil reserves. Very diversified agricultural economy – timber, cocoa, coffee, rubber. Self-sufficient in food. Growing national debt owing to failure to adjust to falling oil revenues.

FACT FILE

OFFICIAL NAME: Republic of Cameroon
DATE OF FORMATION: 1961
CAPITAL: Yaoundé
POPULATION: 12.5 million
TOTAL AREA: 183,570 miles
475,440 sq km)
DENSITY: 26 people per sq mile

LANGUAGES: English*, French*, Fang, Bulu, Yaunde, Duala, Mbum
RELIGIONS: Traditional beliefs 51%, Christian 33%, Muslim 16%
ETHNIC MIX: Bamileke and Manum 20%, Fang 19%, other 61%
GOVERNMENT: Multiparty republic
CURRENCY: CFA franc = 100 centimes

EQUATORIAL GUINEA

COMPRISES THE mainland territory of Rio Muni and five islands on the west coast of central Africa. In 1993, the first free elections were held.

GEOGRAPHY

Islands are mountainous and volcanic. Mainland is lower, with mangrove swamps along coast.

CLIMATE
Bioko is extremely wet and humid. The mainland is only marginally drier and cooler.

PEOPLE AND SOCIETY

The mainland is sparsely populated. Most people are Fang, who dominate politics. Ruling Mongomo clan have most of the wealth. Bioko populated mostly by Bubi and minority of Creoles known as *Fernandinos*. Extended family ties have remained strong despite disruptive social pressure during the years of dictatorship.

◆ INSIGHT: *Some 100,000 Equatorial Guineans now live outside the country, having fled its dictatorial regimes*

THE ECONOMY
Bioko generates the most income. Main exports are tropical timber and cocoa. Oil and gas reserves yet to be fully exploited.

2000m/6562ft
1000m/3281ft
500m/1640ft
200m/656ft
Sea Level

MALABO

3°30' N

Bioko

Bight of Biafra

ATLANTIC OCEAN

CAMEROON

Mikomeseng

Gulf of Guinea

Bata   Niefang

Mbini

Mongomo

Mbini

R i o   M u n i

Cabo San Juan

Etembue

Kogo

Nsok

Isla de Corisco

GABON

FACT FILE

OFFICIAL NAME: Republic of Equatorial Guinea
DATE OF FORMATION: 1968
CAPITAL: Malabo
POPULATION: 400,000
TOTAL AREA: 10,830 sq miles (28,050 sq km)

DENSITY: 36 people per sq mile
LANGUAGES: Spanish*, Fang, other
RELIGIONS: Christian (mainly Roman Catholic) 89%, other 11%
ETHNIC MIX: Fang 72%, Bubi 14%, Duala 3%, Ibibio 2%, other 9%
GOVERNMENT: Multiparty republic
CURRENCY: CFA franc = 100 centimes

SAO TOME & PRINCIPE

A FORMER Portuguese colony off Africa's west coast, comprising two main islands and smaller islets. 1991 elections ended 15 years of Marxism.

GEOGRAPHY
Islands are scattered across equator. São Tomé and Príncipe are heavily forested and mountainous.

CLIMATE
Hot and humid, slightly cooled by Benguela Current. Plentiful rainfall, but dry July–August.

PEOPLE AND SOCIETY
Population is mostly black, although Portuguese culture predominates. Blacks run the political parties. Society is well integrated and free of racial prejudice. Wealth disparities are not great, although there is a growing business class. Extended family offers main form of social security. Príncipe assumed autonomous status in April 1995.

◆ INSIGHT: The population is entirely of immigrant descent: the islands were uninhabited when colonized in 1470

THE ECONOMY
Cocoa provides 90% of export earnings. Palm oil, pepper, and coffee are farmed. One of Africa's highest aid-to-population ratios.

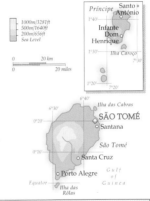

1000m/3281ft
500m/1640ft
200m/656ft
Sea Level

0   20 km
0   20 miles

Príncipe

Santo Antônio

Infante Dom Henrique

Ilha Caroço

Ilha das Cabras

SÃO TOMÉ
Santana

São Tomé

Santa Cruz

Porto Alegre

Gulf of Guinea

Equator   Ilha das Rôlas

FACT FILE
OFFICIAL NAME: Democratic Republic of Sao Tome and Principe
DATE OF FORMATION: 1975
CAPITAL: São Tomé
POPULATION: 121,000
TOTAL AREA: 372 sq miles (964 sq km)
DENSITY: 352 people per sq mile

LANGUAGES: Portuguese*, Portuguese Creole, other
RELIGIONS: Roman Catholic 90%, other Christian 10%
ETHNIC MIX: Black 90%, Portuguese and Creole 10%
GOVERNMENT: Multiparty republic
CURRENCY: Dobra = 100 centimos

GABON

A FORMER French colony straddling the equator on Africa's west coast. It returned to multiparty politics in 1990, after 22 years of one-party rule.

GEOGRAPHY
Low plateaus and mountains lie beyond the coastal strip. Two-thirds of the land is rain forest.

CLIMATE
Hot and tropical, with little distinction between seasons. Cold Benguela Current cools the coast.

PEOPLE AND SOCIETY
Some 40 different languages are spoken. The Fang, who live mainly in the north, are the largest ethnic group, but have yet to gain control of the government. Oil wealth has led to growth of an affluent middle class. Menial jobs are done by immigrant workers. Education follows the French system. With almost half its population living in towns, Gabon is one of Africa's most urbanized countries. The government is encouraging population growth.

THE ECONOMY
Oil is the main source of revenue. Tropical hardwoods are being exploited. Cocoa beans, coffee, and rice grown for export.

◆ INSIGHT: *Libreville was founded as a settlement for freed French slaves in 1849*

FACT FILE

OFFICIAL NAME: The Gabonese Republic
DATE OF FORMATION: 1960
CAPITAL: Libreville
POPULATION: 1.3 million
TOTAL AREA: 103,347 sq miles (267,670 sq km)

DENSITY: 13 people per sq mile
LANGUAGES: French*, Fang, other
RELIGIONS: Catholic, other Christian 96%, Muslim 2%, other 2%
ETHNIC MIX: Fang 36%, Mpongwe 15%, Mbete 14%, other 35%
GOVERNMENT: Multiparty republic
CURRENCY: CFA franc = 100 centimes

CONGO

ASTRIDE THE equator in west central Africa, this former French colony emerged from 20 years of Marxist-Leninist rule in 1990.

GEOGRAPHY
Mostly forest- or savanna-covered plateaus, drained by Ubangui and Zaire River systems. Narrow coastal plain is lined with sand dunes and lagoons.

CLIMATE
Hot, tropical. Temperatures rarely fall below 86°F (30°C). Two wet and two dry seasons. Rainfall is heaviest south of the equator.

PEOPLE AND SOCIETY
One of the most tribally conscious nations in Africa. Four main ethnic groups: Bakongo, Sangha, Teke, and Mboshi. Main tensions between Bakongo in the north and Mboshi in the south. Middle class is sustained by oil wealth. Schools are run according to the French system and are still subject to inspection from Paris. Multiparty elections held in 1992.

THE ECONOMY
Oil is main source of revenue. Cash crops include sugar, coffee, cocoa, and palm oil. Substantial industrial base. Large foreign debt.

◆ *INSIGHT: In 1970, Congo became Africa's first declared communist state*

FACT FILE
OFFICIAL NAME: The Republic of the Congo
DATE OF FORMATION: 1960
CAPITAL: Brazzaville
POPULATION: 2.4 million
TOTAL AREA: 132,040 sq miles (342,000 sq km)

DENSITY: 18 people per sq mile
LANGUAGES: French*, Kongo, other
RELIGIONS: Catholic 50%, traditional beliefs 48%, other (inc. Muslim) 2%
ETHNIC MIX: Bakongo 48%, Teke 17%, Mboshi 17%, Sangha 5%, other 13%
GOVERNMENT: Multiparty republic
CURRENCY: CFA franc = 100 centimes

ANGOLA

LOCATED IN southwest Africa, Angola was in an almost continuous state of civil war from 1975–1994, following independence from Portugal.

GEOGRAPHY
Most of the land is hilly and grass-covered. Desert in the south. Mountains in the center and north.

CLIMATE
Varies from temperate to tropical. Rainfall decreases north to south. Coast is cooler and dry.

PEOPLE AND SOCIETY
Civil war was fought by two groups. UNITA cast itself as sole representative of the Ovimbundu, in order to attack ruling Kimbundu-dominated MPLA. In 1991–92, MPLA abandoned Marxist rule and held free elections. UNITA lost, and resumed civil war. Up to 500,000 people died as a result. In 1995, UN troops were deployed to begin a phased demilitarization operation.

◆ INSIGHT: *Angola has some of the world's richest alluvial diamond deposits*

THE ECONOMY
Potentially one of Africa's richest countries, but civil war has hampered economic development. Oil and diamonds are exported.

FACT FILE
OFFICIAL NAME: Republic of Angola
DATE OF FORMATION: 1975
CAPITAL: Luanda
POPULATION: 10.3 million
TOTAL AREA: 481,551 sq miles (1,246,700 sq km)
DENSITY: 21 people per sq mile

LANGUAGES: Portuguese*, other
RELIGIONS: Catholic/Protestant 64%, traditional beliefs 34%, other 2%
ETHNIC MIX: Ovimbundu 37%, Kimbundu 25%, Bakongo 13%, mixed 1%, other 24%
GOVERNMENT: Multiparty republic
CURRENCY: Kwanza = 100 lwei

ZAMBIA

ZAMBIA LIES landlocked at the heart of southern Africa. In 1991, it made a peaceful transition from single-party rule to multiparty democracy.

GEOGRAPHY
A high savanna plateau, broken by mountains in northeast. Vegetation mainly trees and scrub.

CLIMATE
Tropical, with three seasons: cool and dry, hot and dry, and wet. Southwest is prone to drought.

PEOPLE AND SOCIETY
One of the continent's most urbanized countries. More than 70 different ethnic groups, but it has been less affected by ethnic tensions than many African states. Largest group is Bemba in northeast. Other major groups are Tonga in the south, and Lozi in the west. Urban life has done little to change the traditionally subordinate role of women in the family and politics. Rural population live by subsistence farming.

THE ECONOMY
Copper mining is the main industry – exports bring in 80% of foreign income. However, domestic reserves are declining rapidly.

◆ *INSIGHT: Zambia's Victoria Falls is known to Africans as* Musi-o-Tunyi *(The Smoke That Thunders)*

FACT FILE

OFFICIAL NAME: Republic of Zambia

DATE OF FORMATION: 1964

CAPITAL: Lusaka

POPULATION: 8.9 million

TOTAL AREA: 290,563 sq miles (752,610 sq km)

DENSITY: 12 people per sq mile

LANGUAGES: English*, Bemba, Tonga, Nyanja, Lozi, Lunda

RELIGIONS: Christian 63%, traditional beliefs 35%, other 2%

ETHNIC MIX: Bemba 36%, Maravi 18%, Tonga 15%, other 31%

GOVERNMENT: Multiparty republic

CURRENCY: Kwacha = 100 ngwee

TANZANIA

THE EAST African state of Tanzania was formed in 1964 by the union of Tanganyika and Zanzibar. A third of its area is game reserve or national park.

GEOGRAPHY
Mainland is mostly a high plateau lying to the east of the Great Rift Valley. Forested coastal plain. Highlands in the north and south.

CLIMATE
Tropical on the coast and Zanzibar. Semiarid on central plateau, semitemperate in the highlands. March–May rains.

PEOPLE AND SOCIETY
99% of people belong to one of 120 small ethnic Bantu groups. Arabs, Asians, and Europeans make up remaining population. Use of Swahili as *lingua franca* has eliminated ethnic rivalries. Politics is moving towards democracy.

THE ECONOMY
Reliant on agriculture, including forestry and livestock. Cotton, coffee, tea, and cloves are cash crops. Diamonds are mined.

◆ *INSIGHT: At 19,340 ft (5,895 m), Kilimanjaro in northeast Tanzania is Africa's highest mountain*

FACT FILE

OFFICIAL NAME: United Republic of Tanzania
DATE OF FORMATION: 1964
CAPITAL: Dodoma
POPULATION: 28.8 million
TOTAL AREA: 364,900 sq miles (945,090 sq km)

DENSITY: 79 people per sq mile
LANGUAGES: English*, Swahili*
RELIGIONS: Traditional beliefs 42%, Muslim 31%, Christian 27%
ETHNIC MIX: 120 ethnic Bantu groups 99%, other 1%
GOVERNMENT: Single-party republic
CURRENCY: Shilling = 100 cents

MALAWI

A FORMER British colony, Malawi lies landlocked in southeast Africa. Its name means "the land where the sun is reflected in the water like fire."

 GEOGRAPHY
Lake Malawi takes up one fifth of the country. Highlands lie west of the lake. Much of the land is covered by forests and savanna.

CLIMATE
Mainly subtropical. South is hot and humid. Highlands are cooler. May–October dry season.

 PEOPLE AND SOCIETY
Few ethnic tensions as most people share common Bantu origin. However, tensions between north and south have arisen in recent years. Northerners are increasingly disaffected by their lack of political representation. Many Asians are involved in the retail trade. Multi-party politics introduced in 1993.

◆ INSIGHT: Lake Malawi is 353 miles (568 km) in length and contains at least 500 species of fish

THE ECONOMY
Tobacco accounts for 76% of export earnings. Tea and sugar production. Coal, bauxite reserves.

2000m/6562ft
1000m/3281ft
500m/1640ft
200m/656ft
Sea Level

0   100 km
0   100 miles

FACT FILE

OFFICIAL NAME: Republic of Malawi
DATE OF FORMATION: 1964
CAPITAL: Lilongwe
POPULATION: 10.7 million
TOTAL AREA: 45,745 sq miles
(118,480 sq km)
DENSITY: 234 people per sq mile

LANGUAGES: English*, Chewa*, other
RELIGIONS: Protestant/Catholic 66%,
traditional beliefs 18%, other 16%
ETHNIC MIX: Maravi 55%, Lomwe
17%, Yao 13%, Ngoni 7%, other
(including Asian) 8%
GOVERNMENT: Multiparty republic
CURRENCY: Kwacha = 100 tambala

ZIMBABWE

THE FORMER British colony of Southern Rhodesia became fully independent as Zimbabwe in 1980, after 15 years of troubled white minority rule.

 GEOGRAPHY
High plateaus in center bordered by Zambezi River in the north and Limpopo in the south. Rivers crisscross central area.

 CLIMATE
Tropical, though moderated by the altitude. Wet season November–March. Drought is common in eastern highlands.

 PEOPLE AND SOCIETY
Two main ethnic groups, Ndebele in the north, and Shona in the south. Shona outnumber Ndebele by four to one. Whites make up just 1% of the population. Because of past colonial rule, whites are generally far more affluent than blacks. This imbalance has been somewhat redressed by government policies to increase black education and employment. Families are large and 45% of people are under 15.

 THE ECONOMY
Most broadly based African economy after South Africa. Virtually self-sufficient in food and energy. Tobacco is main cash crop.

◆ *INSIGHT: The city of Great Zimbabwe, after which the country is named, was built in the 8th century. Its ruins are found near Masvingo*

FACT FILE

OFFICIAL NAME: Republic of Zimbabwe
DATE OF FORMATION: 1980
CAPITAL: Harare
POPULATION: 10.9 million
TOTAL AREA: 150,800 sq miles
(390,580 sq km)
DENSITY: 70 people per sq mile

LANGUAGES: English*, Shona, Ndebele
RELIGIONS: Syncretic (Christian and traditional beliefs) 50%, Christian 26%, traditional beliefs 24%
ETHNIC MIX: Shona 71%, Ndebele 16%, other 11%, White, Asian 2%
GOVERNMENT: Multiparty republic
CURRENCY: Zimbabwe $ = 100 cents

MOZAMBIQUE

MOZAMBIQUE LIES on the southeast African coast. It was torn by a civil war between the Marxist government and a rebel group from 1977 to 1992.

GEOGRAPHY
Largely a savanna-covered plateau. Coast is fringed by coral reefs and lagoons. Zambezi River bisects country from east to west.

CLIMATE
Tropical. Hottest along the coast. Wet season usually March–October, but rains frequently fail.

PEOPLE AND SOCIETY
Racially diverse, but tensions in society are between northerners and southerners, rather than ethnic groups. Life is based around the extended family, which in some regions is matriarchal. Polygamy is fairly common. Government has faced huge task of resettling the one million war refugees. 90% of the population live in poverty.

◆ INSIGHT: *Maputo, the capital, has Africa's second largest harbor*

THE ECONOMY
Almost entirely dependent on foreign aid. 85% of the population is engaged in agriculture.

	2000m/6562ft
	1000m/3281ft
	500m/1640ft
	200m/656ft
	Sea Level

0   200 km
0   200 miles

FACT FILE

OFFICIAL NAME: Republic of Mozambique
DATE OF FORMATION: 1975
CAPITAL: Maputo
POPULATION: 15.3 million
TOTAL AREA: 309,493 sq miles (801,590 sq km)

DENSITY: 49 people per sq mile
LANGUAGES: Portuguese* other
RELIGIONS: Traditional beliefs 60%, Christian 30%, Muslim 10%
ETHNIC MIX: Makua-Lomwe 47%, Tsonga 23%, Malawi 12%, other 18%
GOVERNMENT: Multiparty republic
CURRENCY: Metical = 100 centavos

NAMIBIA

LOCATED IN southwestern Africa, Namibia became free of South African control in 1990, after years of uncertainty and guerrilla activity.

GEOGRAPHY
Namib Desert stretches along coastal strip. Inland, a ridge of mountains rises to 8,200 ft (2,500 m). Kalahari Desert lies in the east.

CLIMATE
Almost rainless. Coast usually shrouded in thick fog, unless hot dry *berg* wind blows.

PEOPLE AND SOCIETY
Largest ethnic group, the Ovambo, live mainly in the north. Whites, including a large German community, are centred around Windhoek. Ethnic strife predicted at time of independence has not materialized. High illiteracy among blacks due to legacy of apartheid. Whites still control the economy.

THE ECONOMY
Third wealthiest country in sub-Saharan Africa. Varied mineral resources, including uranium and diamonds. Rich offshore fishing grounds. Lack of skilled labor.

◆ INSIGHT: *The Namib is the Earth's oldest, and one of its driest deserts*

FACT FILE	
OFFICIAL NAME: Republic of Namibia	LANGUAGES: English*, Afrikaans, Ovambo, Kavango, German, other
DATE OF FORMATION: 1990	RELIGIONS: Christian 90%, other 10%
CAPITAL: Windhoek	ETHNIC MIX: Ovambo 50%, Kavango 9%, Herero 7%, Damara 7%, White 6%, other 21%
POPULATION: 1.6 million	
TOTAL AREA: 318,260 sq miles (824,290 sq km)	GOVERNMENT: Multiparty republic
DENSITY: 5 people per sq mile	CURRENCY: Rand = 100 cents

BOTSWANA

ONCE THE British protectorate of Bechuanaland, Botswana lies landlocked in southern Africa. Diamonds provide it with a prosperous economy.

GEOGRAPHY
Lies on vast plateau, high above sealevel. Hills in the east. Kalahari Desert in center and southwest. Swamps and saltpans elsewhere and in Okavango Basin.

CLIMATE
Dry and prone to drought. Summer wet season, April–October. Winters are warm, with cold nights.

PEOPLE AND SOCIETY
Tswana make up 75% of the population. San, or Kalahari Bushmen, the first inhabitants, have been marginalized. 72% of people live in rural areas. Traditional forms of authority such as the village *kgotla*, or parliament, remain important.

◆ INSIGHT: *Water, Botswana's most precious resource, is honored in the name of the currency – pula*

THE ECONOMY
Diamonds are the leading export. Also deposits of copper, nickel, coal, salt, soda ash. Beef is exported to Europe. Tourism aimed at wealthy wildlife enthusiasts.

Map labels
ZAMBIA · Kwando · Kasane · Okavango Delta · Maun · NAMIBIA · ZIMBABWE · Makgadikgadi · Ghanzi · Francistown · Selebi Phikwe · Serowe · Mahalapye · Kalahari Desert · Limpopo · GABORONE · Mochudi · Kanye · Lobatse · SOUTH AFRICA

200m/656ft Sea Level

0 200 km
0 200 miles

FACT FILE

OFFICIAL NAME: Republic of Botswana

DATE OF FORMATION: 1966

CAPITAL: Gaborone

POPULATION: 1.4 million

TOTAL AREA: 224,600 sq miles (581,730 sq km)

DENSITY: 6.2 people per sq mile

LANGUAGES: English*, Tswana, Shona, San, Khoikhoi, Ndebele

RELIGIONS: Traditional beliefs 50%, Christian (mostly Anglican) 50%

ETHNIC MIX: Tswana 75%, Shona 12%, San 3%, White 1%, other 9%

GOVERNMENT: Multiparty republic

CURRENCY: Pula = 100 thebe

LESOTHO

THE KINGDOM of Lesotho is entirely surrounded by South Africa, which provides all its land transportation links with the outside world.

GEOGRAPHY
High mountainous plateau, cut by valleys and ravines. Maluti range in center. Drakensberg range in the east. Lowlands in the west.

CLIMATE
Temperate. Summers are hot and wet. Snow is frequent in the mountains in winter.

PEOPLE AND SOCIETY
Almost everyone is Basotho, although there are some South Asians, Europeans, and Taiwanese. Strong sense of national identity has tended to minimize ethnic tensions. Many men work as migrant laborers in South Africa, leaving 72% of households, and most of the farms, run by women.

◆ INSIGHT: Lesotho has one of the highest literacy rates in Africa, and the highest female literacy rate – 84%

THE ECONOMY
Few natural resources. Heavy reliance on incomes of its migrant workers. Subsistence farming is the main activity. Exports include livestock, wool, mohair.

3000m/9843ft
2000m/6562ft
1000m/328ft

0   50 km
0   50 miles

FACT FILE
OFFICIAL NAME: Kingdom of Lesotho
DATE OF FORMATION: 1966
CAPITAL: Maseru
POPULATION: 1.9 million
TOTAL AREA: 11,718 sq miles (30,350 sq km)

DENSITY: 162 people per sq mile
LANGUAGES: English*, Sesotho*, Zulu
RELIGIONS: Roman Catholic and other Christian 93%, other 7%
ETHNIC MIX: Basotho 99%, other 1%
GOVERNMENT: Constitutional monarchy
CURRENCY: Loti = 100 lisente

SWAZILAND

THE SOUTHERN African kingdom of Swaziland gained independence from Britain in 1968. It is economically dependent on South Africa.

GEOGRAPHY
Mainly high plateaus and mountains. Rolling grasslands and low scrub plains to the east. Pine forests on western border.

CLIMATE
Temperatures rise and rainfall declines as land descends eastward, from high to low *veld*.

PEOPLE AND SOCIETY
One of Africa's most homogenous states. Also among its most conservative, although it is now coming under pressure from urban-based modernizers. Political system promotes Swazi tradition and is dominated by a powerful monarchy. Society is patriarchal and focused around clans and chiefs.

◆ *INSIGHT: Polygamy is practised in Swaziland. When King Sobhuza died in 1982, he left 100 wives and 600 children*

THE ECONOMY
Sugarcane is the main cash crop. Others are pineapples, cotton, rice, and tobacco. Asbestos, coal, and wood pulp are also exported.

FACT FILE

OFFICIAL NAME: Kingdom of Swaziland
DATE OF FORMATION: 1968
CAPITAL: Mbabane
POPULATION: 800,000
TOTAL AREA: 6,703 sq miles (17,360 sq km)

DENSITY: 120 people per sq mile
LANGUAGES: Siswati*, English*, Zulu
RELIGIONS: Protestant and other Christian 60%, traditional beliefs 40%
ETHNIC MIX: Swazi 95%, other 5%
GOVERNMENT: Executive monarchy
CURRENCY: Lilangeni = 100 cents

SOUTH AFRICA

Namibia Botswana
SOUTH — Swaziland
AFRICA — Lesotho

SOUTH AFRICA is the southernmost nation on the African continent. After 80 years of white minority rule, and racial segregation under apartheid from 1948, the country's first multiracial, multiparty elections were held in 1994.

GEOGRAPHY

Much of the country is grassland plateaus, drained in the west by the Orange River system and in the east by the Limpopo and its tributaries. Mountain ridges stretch across south. Drakensberg range overshadows eastern coastal lowlands.

CLIMATE

Warm, temperate, and dry. Interior of country gets most of its rain in summer. Coast around Cape Town has Mediterranean climate, with winter rains.

◆ *INSIGHT: South Africa dominates the world market in gold and diamonds. Over the past century, it has produced almost half of the world's gold*

PEOPLE AND SOCIETY

Since dismantling of apartheid in early 1990s, racial segregation has ended, but tensions remain. Some Zulus and whites have made demands for independent homelands. Government aims to redress social and economic imbalance between blacks and whites, focusing on education, housing, land reform.

THE ECONOMY

Africa's largest economy; highly diversified, with modern infrastructure. Growing manufacturing sector. Varied agriculture. Diamonds, gold, platinum, coal, silver, uranium, copper, and asbestos mined.

2000m/6562ft
1000m/3281ft
500m/1640ft
Sea Level

◉ Judicial capital
◎ Legislative capital

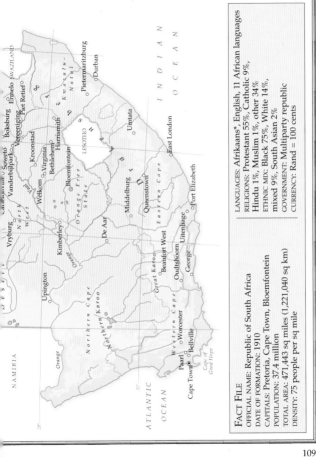

NAMIBIA

ATLANTIC
OCEAN

INDIAN OCEAN

SWAZILAND

LESOTHO

Pretoria
Johannesburg
Soweto
Vanderbijlpark
Vereeniging
Boksburg
Ermelo
Piet Retief
Pietermaritzburg
Durban
Kroonstad
Harrismith
Virginia
Bethlehem
Welkom
Vryburg
Umtata
Bloemfontein
Kimberley
De Aar
East London
Middelburg
Queenstown
Beaufort West
Port Elizabeth
Uitenhage
Oudtshoorn
George
Worcester
Paarl
Bellville
Cape Town
Upington

Orange

Great Karoo
Northern Cape
Western Cape
Eastern Cape
Orange Free State
North West
KwaZulu-Natal

Cape of Good Hope

Kalahari Desert

Drakensberg

FACT FILE

OFFICIAL NAME: Republic of South Africa
DATE OF FORMATION: 1910
CAPITALS: Pretoria, Cape Town, Bloemfontein
POPULATION: 37.4 million
TOTAL AREA: 471,443 sq miles (1,221,040 sq km)
DENSITY: 75 people per sq mile

LANGUAGES: Afrikaans*, English, 11 African languages
RELIGIONS: Protestant 55%, Catholic 9%,
Hindu 1%, Muslim 1%, other 34%
ETHNIC MIX: Black 75%, White 14%,
mixed 9%, South Asian 2%
GOVERNMENT: Multiparty republic
CURRENCY: Rand = 100 cents

SEYCHELLES

A FORMER British colony, comprising 115 islands in the Indian Ocean. Under one-party rule for 16 years, it became a multiparty democracy in 1993.

GEOGRAPHY
Mostly low-lying coral atolls, but 40 islands, including the largest, Mahé, are mountainous and are the only granitic islands in the world.

CLIMATE
Tropical oceanic climate. Hot and humid all year round. Rainy season December–May.

PEOPLE AND SOCIETY
The islands were uninhabited when French settlers arrived in the 18th century. Today, the population is homogeneous – a result of inter-marriage between ethnic groups. Almost 90% of people live on Mahé. Living standards are among Africa's highest. Poverty is rare and the welfare system serves all.

◆ INSIGHT: Host to unique flora and fauna – it is the only country to have two natural World Heritage sites

THE ECONOMY
Tourism is main source of income, based on appeal of beaches and exotic plants and animals. Tuna fished and canned for export. Virtually no mineral resources. All domestic requirements imported.

FACT FILE

OFFICIAL NAME: Republic of the Seychelles
DATE OF FORMATION: 1976
CAPITAL: Victoria
POPULATION: 69,000
TOTAL AREA: 108 sq miles (280 sq km)

DENSITY: 638 people per sq mile
LANGUAGES: Creole*, French, English
RELIGIONS: Catholic 90%, other 10%
ETHNIC MIX: Seychellois (mixed African, South Asian and European) 95%, Chinese and South Asian 5%
GOVERNMENT: Multiparty republic
CURRENCY: Rupee = 100 cents

COMOROS

IN THE Indian Ocean between Mozambique and Madagascar lie the Comoros, comprising three main islands and a number of smaller islets.

GEOGRAPHY
Main islands are of volcanic origin and are heavily forested. The remainder are coral atolls.

CLIMATE
Hot and humid all year round. November–May is hottest and wettest period.

PEOPLE AND SOCIETY
Country has absorbed a diversity of people over the years: African, Arab, Polynesian, and Persian. Also Portuguese, Dutch, French, and Indian immigrants. Ethnic tension is rare. Wealth concentrated among political and business elite. Schools equipped to teach only basic literacy, hygiene, and agricultural skills. Politically unstable – frequent coup attempts have been made during 1990s.

THE ECONOMY
One of the world's poorest countries. 80% of people are farmers Vanilla and cloves are main cash crops. Lack of basic infrastructure.

◆ INSIGHT: *The Comoros is the world's largest producer of ylang-ylang – an extract from trees used in manufacturing perfumes*

Grande Comore (Njazidja)

Koimbani
✦ MORONI
Foumbouni
Dembéni

INDIAN OCEAN

12°30'
12°

Mozambique Channel

Mohéli (Mwali)
43°30'
Fomboni

Ouani
Mutsamudu
Moya
Anjouan (Nzwani)

44°
44°30'

1000m/3281ft
500m/1640ft
200m/656ft
Sea Level

0   20 km
0   20 miles

FACT FILE

OFFICIAL NAME: Federal Islamic Republic of the Comoros
DATE OF FORMATION: 1975
CAPITAL: Moroni
POPULATION: 600,000
TOTAL AREA: 8,865 sq miles (22,960 sq km)

DENSITY: 700 people per sq mile
LANGUAGES: Arabic*, French*, other
RELIGIONS: Muslim 86%, Roman Catholic 14%
ETHNIC MIX: Comorian 96%, Makua 2%, other (inc. French) 2%
GOVERNMENT: Islamic republic
CURRENCY: Franc = 100 centimes

MADAGASCAR

LYING IN the Indian Ocean, Madagascar is the world's fourth largest island. Free elections in 1993 ended 18 years of socialist government.

GEOGRAPHY
More than two thirds of country is a savanna-covered plateau, which drops sharply to narrow coastal belt in the east.

CLIMATE
Tropical, and often hit by cyclones. Monsoons affect the east coast. Southwest is much drier.

PEOPLE AND SOCIETY
People are Malay-Indonesian in origin, intermixed with later migrants from African mainland. Main ethnic division is between Merina of the central plateau and the poorer *côtier* (coastal) peoples. Merina were the country's historic rulers. They remain the social elite, and largely run the government.

◆ INSIGHT: *80% of Madagascar's plants, and many of its animal species, such as the lemur, are found nowhere else*

THE ECONOMY
Over 80% of people are farmers. Coffee is the most important cash crop. World's largest producer of vanilla. Shrimp are a valuable export commodity.

Antsirānana
Analalava
Sambava
Mahajanga
Marovoay
Toamasina
ANTANANARIVO
Antsirabe
Fandriana
Morondava
Ambositra
Fianarantsoa
Mozambique Channel
INDIAN OCEAN
Toliara
Farafangana
Amboasary

2000m/6562ft
1000m/3281ft
500m/1640ft
200m/656ft
Sea Level

0   200 km
0   200 miles

FACT FILE

OFFICIAL NAME: Democratic Republic of Madagascar
DATE OF FORMATION: 1960
CAPITAL: Antananarivo
POPULATION: 13.3 million
TOTAL AREA: 226,660 sq miles (587,040 sq km)

DENSITY: 57 people per sq mile
LANGUAGES: Malagasy*, French*
RELIGIONS: Traditional beliefs 52%, Catholic/Protestant 41%, Muslim 7%
ETHNIC MIX: Merina 26%, Betsimisaraka 15%, Betsileo 12%, other 47%
GOVERNMENT: Multiparty republic
CURRENCY: Franc = 100 centimes

MAURITIUS

LOCATED TO the east of Madagascar in the Indian Ocean. Independent in 1968, as part of the Commonwealth, it became a republic in 1993.

GEOGRAPHY
Main island, of volcanic origin, is ringed by coral reefs. Rises from coast to fertile central plateau. Outer islands lie some 311 miles (500 km) to the north.

CLIMATE
Warm and humid. March–December are hottest and wettest months, with tropical storms.

PEOPLE AND SOCIETY
Most people are descendants of laborers brought over from India in the 19th century. Small minority of French descent are the wealthiest group. Literacy rate for under-30s is 95%. Crime rates on the main island are fairly low; outer islands are virtually crime-free.

◆ INSIGHT: The islands lie on what was once a land bridge between Asia and Africa – the Mascarene Archipelago

THE ECONOMY
Sugar, tourism, and clothing manufacture are main sources of income. Sugar accounts for 30% of exports. Potential as offshore financial center is being developed.

FACT FILE

OFFICIAL NAME: Mauritius
DATE OF FORMATION: 1968
CAPITAL: Port Louis
POPULATION: 1.1 million
TOTAL AREA: 718 sq miles (1,860 sq km)
DENSITY: 1,532 people per sq mile

LANGUAGES: English*, French Creole, Hindi, Bhojpuri, Chinese
RELIGIONS: Hindu 52%, Catholic 26%, Muslim 17%, other 5%
ETHNIC MIX: Creole 55%, South Asian 40%, Chinese 3%, other 2%
GOVERNMENT: Multiparty republic
CURRENCY: Rupee = 100 cents

113

EUROPE

EUROPE IS the smallest continent after Australia, yet it has a wide range of climates, land forms, and types of vegetation. The tundra of the far north gives way to a cool, wet, heavily forested region. The North European Plain is well-drained, fertile, and rich in natural resources. The shores of the Mediterranean are generally warm, dry, and hilly. A great curve of mountain ranges, including the Pyrenees, Alps, and Carpathians, roughly divide the continent from north to south. To the east lie the rolling plains of European Russia and the Ukraine.

3000m/9843ft
2000m/6562ft
1000m/3281ft
200m/656ft
Sea Level
Below Sea Level

0   500 km
0   500 miles

Asiatic Russia

Novaya Zemlya

CEAN

Barents Sea

orth Cape

Kola Peninsula

apland

FINLAND

Lake Onega

Lake Ladoga

Ural Mountains

RUSSIAN FEDERATION

Irtysh

Lake Balkhash

ESTONIA

Baltic Sea

LATVIA

LITHUANIA

USS. FED.

aliningrad)

orth European Plain

BELARUS

European Russia

Volga

KAZAKHSTAN

Aral Sea

UZBEKISTAN

OLAND

Dnieper

UKRAINE

Don

• Volga Delta
-92ft

Caspian Sea

TURKMENISTAN

SLOVAKIA

MOLDAVA

Carpathian Mts.

Crimea

Caucasus

El'brus
18,510ft

GEOR.

AZ.

HUNGARY

SLVNA·

ROATIA

BOS.

HERZ.

ROMANIA

Danube

Black Sea

ARM.

IRAN

YUGO.

BULGARIA

TURKEY

MAC.

ALBANIA

GREECE

Ionian Sea

Aegean Sea

tna
11,054ft

MALTA

Crete

Mediterranean Sea

LIBYA

CONTINENTAL FACTS

HIGHEST POINT:
El'Brus, Caucasus Mts.,
European Russia
18,510 ft (5,642 m)

LOWEST POINT: Volga
Delta, Caspian Sea,
European Russia 92 ft
(28 m) below sea level

LARGEST LAKE:
Ladoga, European
Russia 7,100 sq miles
(18,390 sq km)

LONGEST RIVER:
Volga, European
Russia 2,290 miles
(3,699 km)

115

ICELAND

EUROPE'S WESTERNMOST country, Iceland lies in the north Atlantic, straddling the mid-Atlantic ridge. Its spectacular landscape is largely uninhabited.

GEOGRAPHY
Grassy coastal lowlands, with fjords in the north. Central plateau of cold lava desert, glaciers, and geothermal springs. Around 200 volcanoes.

CLIMATE
Location in middle of Gulf Stream moderates climate. Mild winters and brief, cool summers.

PEOPLE AND SOCIETY
Prosperous and homogeneous society includes only 4,000 foreign residents. High social mobility, free health care and heating (using geothermal power). Longevity rates are among the highest in the world. Equivocal attitude toward Europe accompanies increasing US influence. Strong emphasis on education and reading. Low crime rate, but concerns of alcohol abuse.

THE ECONOMY
Fish or fish products make up 80% of exports. Developing light industry produces knitwear, textiles, paint. Ecotourism potential.

◆ INSIGHT: Iceland has the world's oldest parliament, founded in 930 A.D.

1000m/3281ft
500m/1640ft
200m/656ft
Sea Level
Ice Cap

Denmark Strait
Arctic Circle
Norwegian Sea
Akureyri
Húsavík
Keflavík
Akranes
REYKJAVÍK
Hafnarfjördhur
Kópavogur
Selfoss
Egilsstadhir
Vestmannaeyjar
Vatnajökull
ATLANTIC OCEAN

0   50 km
0   50 miles

FACT FILE

OFFICIAL NAME: Republic of Iceland
DATE OF FORMATION: 1944
CAPITAL: Reykjavik
POPULATION: 300,000
TOTAL AREA: 39,770 sq miles (103,000 sq km)

DENSITY: 8 people per sq mile
LANGUAGES: Icelandic*, English, other
RELIGIONS: Evangelical Lutheran 96%, other Christian 3%, other 1%
ETHNIC MIX: Icelandic (Norwegian-Celtic descent) 98%, other 2%
GOVERNMENT: Constitutional republic
CURRENCY: Krona = 100 aurar

NORWAY

NORWAY
Sweden
Finland
Russian Federation

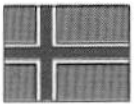

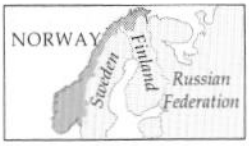

THE KINGDOM of Norway traces the rugged western coast of Scandinavia. Settlements are largely restricted to southern and coastal areas.

GEOGRAPHY

Highly indented coast with fjords and tens of thousands of islands. Mountains and plateaus cover most of the country.

CLIMATE

Mild coastal climate. Inland east is more extreme, with warm summers, and cold, snowy winters.

PEOPLE AND SOCIETY

Homogeneous, with some recent refugees from Bosnian conflict. Strong family tradition despite high divorce rate. Fair-minded consensus promotes female equality, boosted by generous childcare provision. Wealth more evenly distributed than in most developed countries.

◆ INSIGHT: *At a point near Narvik, mainland Norway is only 4 miles (7 km wide)*

THE ECONOMY

Europe's largest producer and exporter of oil and gas. Engineering, chemical, and metal industries.

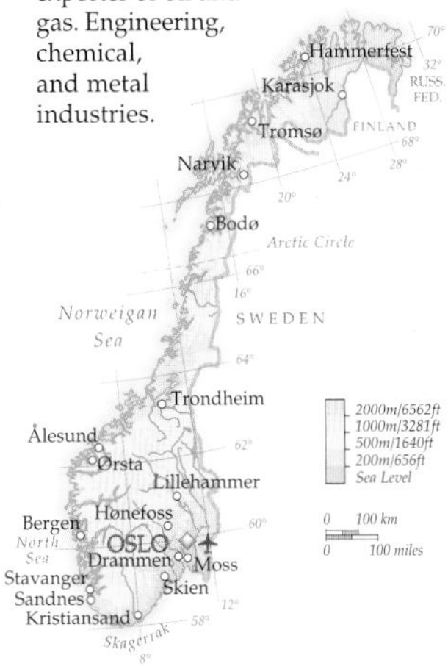
Hammerfest
Karasjok
RUSS. FED.
Tromsø
FINLAND
Narvik
Bodø
Arctic Circle
Norweigan Sea
SWEDEN
Trondheim
Ålesund
Ørsta
Lillehammer
Hønefoss
Bergen
North Sea
OSLO
Drammen
Moss
Stavanger
Sandnes
Skien
Kristiansand
Skagerrak
70°
32°
68°
28°
24°
20°
66°
16°
64°
62°
60°
12°
58°
8°
2000m/6562ft
1000m/3281ft
500m/1640ft
200m/656ft
Sea Level
0 100 km
0 100 miles

FACT FILE

OFFICIAL NAME: Kingdom of Norway
DATE OF FORMATION: 1905
CAPITAL: Oslo
POPULATION: 4.3 million
TOTAL AREA: 125,060 sq miles (323,900 sq km)
DENSITY: 34 people per sq mile

LANGUAGES: Norwegian* (*Bokmal* and *Nynorsk*), Lappish, Finnish
RELIGIONS: Evangelical Lutheran 88%, other Christian 12%
ETHNIC MIX: Norwegian 95%, Lapp 1%, other 4%
GOVERNMENT: Constitutional monarchy
CURRENCY: Krone = 100 øre

see also Overseas Territories pp 230–236

DENMARK

OCCUPIES THE Jutland peninsula and over 400 islands in Scandinavia. Greenland and the Faeroe islands are self-governing associated territories.

GEOGRAPHY
Fertile farmland covers two thirds of the terrain, which is among the flattest in the world. About 100 islands are inhabited.

CLIMATE
Damp, temperate climate with mild summers and cold, wet winters. Rainfall is moderate.

PEOPLE AND SOCIETY
Prosperous population maintains traditions of tolerance and welfare provision. High rates of divorce and cohabitation mean that almost 40% of children are brought up by unmarried couples or single parents. Over 75% of women work, due to generous state-funded childcare.

◆ INSIGHT: Denmark is Europe's oldest kingdom – the monarchy dates back to the 10th century

THE ECONOMY
Few natural resources but a diverse manufacturing base. Skilled work force a key to high-tech industrial success. Bacon, ham, and dairy products are exported.

FACT FILE
OFFICIAL NAME: Kingdom of Denmark
DATE OF FORMATION: 960 A.D.
CAPITAL: Copenhagen
POPULATION: 5.2 million
TOTAL AREA: 16,629 sq miles
(43,069 sq km)
DENSITY: 312 people per sq mile

LANGUAGES: Danish*, other
RELIGIONS: Evangelical Lutheran 91% other Protestant and Catholic 9%
ETHNIC MIX: Danish 96%, Faeroese and Inuit 1%, other 3%
GOVERNMENT: Constitutional monarchy
CURRENCY: Krone = 100 øre

see also Overseas Territories pp 230–236

SWEDEN

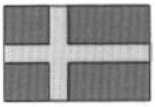

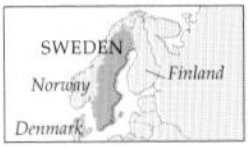

THE LARGEST Scandinavian country in both population and area, Sweden's strong industrial base helps to fund its extensive welfare system.

GEOGRAPHY
Heavily forested, with many lakes. Northern plateau extends beyond the Arctic Circle. Southern lowlands are widely cultivated.

CLIMATE
Southern coasts warmed by Gulf Stream. Northern areas have more extreme continental climate.

PEOPLE AND SOCIETY
Traditions of hard work and economic success are balanced by permissiveness and egalitarianism. High taxes pay for extensive child-care provision, medical protection, and state education. Most industries and the bulk of the population are based in and around the southern cities. A 15,000-strong minority of Sami (Lapps) live in the north.

◆ INSIGHT: *Sweden has maintained a position of armed neutrality since 1815*

THE ECONOMY
Companies of global importance, including Volvo, Saab, SKF, Ericsson. Highly developed infrastructure. Up-to-date technology Skilled labor force.

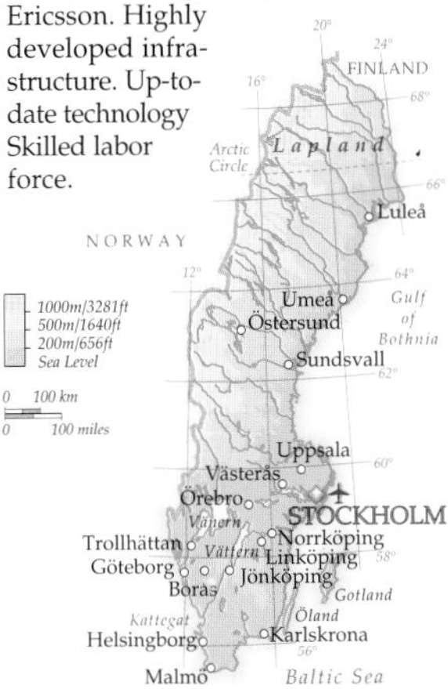

Map labels: FINLAND, Lapland, Arctic Circle, NORWAY, Luleå, Umeå, Östersund, Sundsvall, Gulf of Bothnia, Uppsala, Västerås, STOCKHOLM, Örebro, Norrköping, Trollhättan, Linköping, Göteborg, Jönköping, Borås, Gotland, Öland, Kattegat, Helsingborg, Karlskrona, Malmö, Baltic Sea, Vänern, Vättern

1000m/3281ft, 500m/1640ft, 200m/656ft, Sea Level, 0 100 km, 0 100 miles

FACT FILE
OFFICIAL NAME: Kingdom of Sweden
DATE OF FORMATION: 1905
CAPITAL: Stockholm
POPULATION: 8.7 million
TOTAL AREA: 173,730 sq miles (449,960 sq km)
DENSITY: 50 people per sq mile

LANGUAGES: Swedish*, Finnish, Lappish, other
RELIGIONS: Evangelical Lutheran 94%, Catholic 2%, other 4%
ETHNIC MIX: Swedish 87%, Finnish and Lapp 1%, other European 12%
GOVERNMENT: Constitutional monarchy
CURRENCY: Krona = 100 öre

FINLAND

FINLAND'S DISTINCTIVE language and national identity have been influenced by both its Scandinavian and its Russian neighbors.

 GEOGRAPHY
South and center are flat, with low hills and many lakes. Uplands and low mountains in the north. 60% of the land area is forested.

 CLIMATE
Long, harsh winters with frequent snowfalls. Short, warmer summers. Rainfall is low, and decreases northward.

PEOPLE AND SOCIETY
More than half the population live in the five districts around Helsinki. The Swedish minority live mainly in the Åland Islands in the southwest. The Sami (Lapps) lead a seminomadic existence in the north. Over 50% of women go out to work, continuing a tradition of equality between the sexes.

◆ *INSIGHT: Finland has Europe's largest inland waterway system*

THE ECONOMY
Wood-based industries account for 40% of exports. Strong engineering and electronics sectors.

FACT FILE

OFFICIAL NAME: Republic of Finland
DATE OF FORMATION: 1917
CAPITAL: Helsinki
POPULATION: 5 million
TOTAL AREA: 130,552 sq miles (338,130 sq km)
DENSITY: 38 people per sq mile

LANGUAGES: Finnish*, Swedish, Lappish
RELIGIONS: Evangelical Lutheran 89%, Greek Orthodox 1%, other 10%
ETHNIC MIX: Finnish 93%, Swedish 6%, other (inc. Sami) 1%
GOVERNMENT: Multiparty republic
CURRENCY: Markka = 100 pennia

ESTONIA

ESTONIA IS the smallest and most developed of the three Baltic states and has the highest standard of living of any former Soviet republic.

GEOGRAPHY
Flat, boggy, and partly forested, with over 1,500 islands. Lake Peipus forms much of the eastern border with Russia.

CLIMATE
Maritime, with some continental extremes. Harsh winters, cool summers, and damp springs.

PEOPLE AND SOCIETY
The Estonians are related linguistically and ethnically to the Finns. Friction between ethnic Estonians and the large Russian minority has led to reassertion of Estonian culture and language, as well as job discrimination. Some post-independence political upheaval reflects disenchantment with free-market economics. Families are small; divorce rates are high.

THE ECONOMY
Agricultural machinery, electric motors, and ships are the leading manufactures. Strong timber industry. Increased trade links with Finland and Germany.

◆ INSIGHT: *Estonia is still pressing for the return of territories ceded to Russia during the Soviet period*

FACT FILE

OFFICIAL NAME: Republic of Estonia
DATE OF FORMATION: 1991
CAPITAL: Tallinn
POPULATION: 1.6 million
TOTAL AREA: 17,423 sq miles (45,125 sq km)

DENSITY: 91 people per sq mile
LANGUAGES: Estonian*, Russian
RELIGIONS: Evangelical Lutheran 98%, Eastern Orthodox, Baptist 2%
ETHNIC MIX: Estonian 62%, Russian 30%, Ukrainian 3%, other 5%
GOVERNMENT: Multiparty republic
CURRENCY: Kroon = 100 cents

LATVIA

SITUATED ON the east coast of the Baltic Sea. Like its Baltic neighbors, it became independent in 1991. It retains a large Russian population.

GEOGRAPHY
Flat coastal plain deeply indented by the Gulf of Riga. Poor drainage creates many bogs and swamps in the forested interior.

CLIMATE
Temperate: warm summers and cold winters. Steady rainfall throughout the year.

PEOPLE AND SOCIETY
Latvia is the most urbanized of the three Baltic states, with more than 70% of the population living in cities and towns. Delicate relations with Russia are dictated by a large Russian minority, and energy and infrastructure investment dating from the Soviet period. The status of women is on a par with that in Western Europe. The divorce rate is high.

THE ECONOMY
Transportation and defense equipment lead strong industrial sector. Developed papermaking industry. Good ports. Russia remains main trading partner.

◆ INSIGHT: Latvia's flag is said to represent a sheet stained with the blood of a 13th-century Latvian hero

FACT FILE

OFFICIAL NAME: Republic of Latvia
DATE OF FORMATION: 1991
CAPITAL: Riga
POPULATION: 2.7 million
TOTAL AREA: 24,938 sq miles
(64,589 sq km)
DENSITY: 109 people per sq mile

LANGUAGES: Latvian*, Russian
RELIGIONS: Evangelical Lutheran 85%, other Christian 15%
ETHNIC MIX: Latvian 52%, Russian 34%, Belorussian 5%, Ukrainian 4%, Polish 3%, other 2%
GOVERNMENT: Multiparty republic
CURRENCY: Lats = 100 santimi

LITHUANIA

THE LARGEST and most powerful of the Baltic states, Lithuania was the first Soviet republic to declare independence from Moscow, in 1991.

GEOGRAPHY
Mostly flat with moors, bogs, and an intensively farmed central lowland. Numerous lakes and forested sandy ridges in the east.

CLIMATE
Coastal location moderates continental extremes. Cold winters, cool summers and steady rainfall.

PEOPLE AND SOCIETY
Homogeneous population, with Lithuanians forming a large majority. Strong Roman Catholic tradition and historical links with Poland. Better relations among ethnic groups than in other Baltic states and interethnic marriages are fairly common. However, some ethnic Russians and Poles see a threat of "Lithuanianization." Russian army presence until 1993, when all troops were withdrawn.

THE ECONOMY
Wide range of high-tech and heavy industries, includes textiles, engineering, shipbuilding, and food processing. Agricultural surpluses.

◆ INSIGHT: *The Baltic states produce two thirds of the world's amber – the fossilized sap of ancient trees. Most is found along Lithuania's "amber coast"*

FACT FILE

OFFICIAL NAME: Republic of Lithuania
DATE OF FORMATION: 1991
CAPITAL: Vilnius
POPULATION: 3.8 million
TOTAL AREA: 25,174 sq miles (65,200 sq km)

DENSITY: 151 people per sq mile
LANGUAGES: Lithuanian*, Russian
RELIGIONS: Roman Catholic 87%, Russian Orthodox 10%, other 3%
ETHNIC MIX: Lithuanian 80%, Russian 9%, Polish 8%, other 3%
GOVERNMENT: Multiparty republic
CURRENCY: Litas = 100 centas

POLAND

WITH ITS seven international borders and strategic location, Poland has always played an important role in European affairs.

 GEOGRAPHY
Lowlands, part of the North European plain, cover most of the country. Carpathian Mountains run along the southern borders.

CLIMATE
Peak rainfall during hot summers. Cold winters with snow, especially in mountains.

 PEOPLE AND SOCIETY
Ethnic homogeneity masks a number of tensions. Secular liberals criticize semiofficial status of Catholic Church; emerging wealth disparities resented by those unaffected by free-market reforms. German minority presses for action on Green issues. Many women hold policy-making posts.

◆ INSIGHT: Poland's eastern forests are home to Europe's largest remaining herds of European bison

THE ECONOMY
High growth, with foreign investment linked to government privatization program. Heavy industries still dominate, but service sector is quickly emerging.

```
1000m/3281ft
500m/1640ft
200m/656ft
Sea Level

0        100 km
0        100 miles
```

FACT FILE

OFFICIAL NAME: Republic of Poland
DATE OF FORMATION: 1945
CAPITAL: Warsaw
POPULATION: 38.5 million
TOTAL AREA: 120,720 sq miles (312,680 sq km)

DENSITY: 318 people per sq mile
LANGUAGES: Polish*, German, other
RELIGIONS: Roman Catholic 95%, other (inc. Protestant and Eastern Orthodox) 5%
ETHNIC MIX: Polish 98%, other 2%
GOVERNMENT: Multiparty republic
CURRENCY: Zloty = 100 groszy

GERMANY

EUROPE'S STRONGEST economic power, Germany's democratic west and communist east were re-unified in 1990, after the fall of the east's regime.

GEOGRAPHY
Coastal plains in the north, rising to rolling hills of central region. Alpine region in the south.

CLIMATE
Damp, temperate in northern and central regions. Continental extremes in mountainous south.

PEOPLE AND SOCIETY
Social and economic differences reflect former divisions. Some prosperous Western Germans resent added taxes since re-unification. Far-right political groups have emerged. Immigrant "guest workers" – mainly Turks – face citizenship problems and occasional racial attacks. Strong feminist and Green movements.

◆ INSIGHT: *Germany's rivers and canals carry as much freight as its roads*

THE ECONOMY
Massive exports of cars, heavy engineering, electronics, and chemicals. Postwar "miracle" powered by efficiency and good labor relations.

FACT FILE

OFFICIAL NAME: Federal Republic of Germany
DATE OF FORMATION: 1990
CAPITAL: Berlin
POPULATION: 80.6 million
TOTAL AREA: 356,910 sq km (137,800 sq miles)

DENSITY: 585 people per sq mile
LANGUAGES: German*, Sorbian, other
RELIGIONS: Protestant 45%, Roman Catholic 37%, other 18%
ETHNIC MIX: German 92%, other 8%
GOVERNMENT: Multiparty republic
CURRENCY: Deutsche Mark = 100 pfennigs

NETHERLANDS

ASTRIDE THE delta of five major rivers in north-west Europe, the Netherlands has a long trading tradition. Rotterdam is the world's largest port.

GEOGRAPHY
Mainly flat, with 27% of the land below sea level and protected by dunes, dikes, and canals. Low hills in the south and east.

CLIMATE
Mild, rainy winters and cool summers. Gales from the North Sea are common in autumn and winter.

PEOPLE AND SOCIETY
The Dutch see their country as the most tolerant in Europe. This reflects a long history of welcoming refugees and immigrants. Large urban concentration (89%) accounts for high population density. Laws concerning issues such as sexuality, euthanasia, and drug taking are among the world's most liberal.

THE ECONOMY
Diverse industrial sector exports metals, machinery, chemicals, and electronics. Many high-profile multinationals.

◆ INSIGHT: *A century ago there were 10,000 windmills in the Netherlands, compared with only 1,000 today*

FACT FILE

OFFICIAL NAME: Kingdom of the Netherlands
DATE OF FORMATION: 1815
CAPITALS: Amsterdam, The Hague
POPULATION: 15.3 million
TOTAL AREA: 14,410 sq miles (37,330 sq km)

DENSITY: 1,061 people per sq mile
LANGUAGES: Dutch*, Frisian, other
RELIGIONS: Catholic 36%, Protestant 27%, other (inc. unaffiliated) 37%
ETHNIC MIX: Dutch 96%, other 4%
GOVERNMENT: Constitutional monarchy
CURRENCY: Guilder = 100 cents

---

see also Overseas Territories pp 230–236

BELGIUM

BELGIUM LIES in northwestern Europe. Its history has been marked by the division between its Flemish- and French-speaking communities.

GEOGRAPHY
Low-lying coastal plain covers two thirds of the country. Land becomes hilly and forested in the southeast (Ardennes) region.

CLIMATE
Maritime climate with Gulf stream influences. Temperatures are mild, with heavy cloud cover and rain. More rainfall and weather fluctuations on coast.

PEOPLE AND SOCIETY
Since 1970, Flemish-speaking regions have become more prosperous than those of the minority French-speakers (Walloons), overturning the traditional roles and increasing friction. In order to contain tensions, Belgium began to move toward federalism in 1980. Both groups now have their own governments and control most of their own affairs.

THE ECONOMY
Variety of industrial exports, including steel, glassware, cut diamonds, and textiles. Many foreign multinationals.

◆ *INSIGHT: The motorway network is extensive and so well lit that, along with the Great Wall of China, it is the most visible sight from space*

FACT FILE

OFFICIAL NAME: Kingdom of Belgium
DATE OF FORMATION: 1830
CAPITAL: Brussels
POPULATION: 10 million
TOTAL AREA: 12,780 sq miles (33,100 sq km)

DENSITY: 782 people per sq mile
LANGUAGES: French*, Dutch*, German*
RELIGIONS: Catholic 75%, other 25%
ETHNIC MIX: Flemish 58%, Walloon 32%, other European 6%, other 4%
GOVERNMENT: Constitutional monarchy
CURRENCY: Franc = 100 centimes

IRELAND

THE REPUBLIC of Ireland occupies 85% of the island of Ireland, with the remainder (Northern Ireland) being part of the United Kingdom.

GEOGRAPHY
Low mountain ranges along an irregular coastline surround an inland plain punctuated by lakes, undulating hills and peat bogs.

CLIMATE
The Gulf Stream accounts for the mild and wet climate. Snow is rare, except in the mountains.

PEOPLE AND SOCIETY
Although homogeneous in ethnicity and Catholic religion, the population show signs of change. Younger Irish question Vatican teachings on birth control, divorce, abortion. Many people still emigrate to find jobs. 1994 terrorist ceasefire in Northern Ireland tempered the traditional aim of reunification.

◆ INSIGHT: About 20,000 people, in areas collectively known as the Gaeltacht, use Irish Gaelic as an everyday language

THE ECONOMY
High unemployment tarnishes high-tech export successes and trade surplus. Highly educated work force. Efficient agriculture and food-processing industries.

FACT FILE

OFFICIAL NAME: Republic of Ireland
DATE OF FORMATION: 1921
CAPITAL: Dublin
POPULATION: 3.5 million
TOTAL AREA: 27,155 sq miles (70,280 sq km)

DENSITY: 128 people per sq mile
LANGUAGES: English*, Irish Gaelic*
RELIGIONS: Catholic 93%, Protestant (mainly Anglican) 5%, other 2%
ETHNIC MIX: Irish 95%, other (mainly British) 5%
GOVERNMENT: Multiparty republic
CURRENCY: Irish £ = 100 pence

UNITED KINGDOM

SEPARATED FROM continental Europe by the North Sea and the English Channel, the UK comprises England, Wales, Scotland, and Northern Ireland.

GEOGRAPHY
Mountainous in the north and west, undulating hills and lowlands in the south and east.

CLIMATE
Generally mild and temperate. Rainfall is heaviest in the west. Winter snow in mountainous areas.

PEOPLE AND SOCIETY
Although of mixed stock themselves, the British have an insular and ambivalent attitude toward Europe. The Welsh and Scottish are ethnically and culturally distinct. Asian and West Indian minorities in most cities. Class, the traditional source of division, is fading in the face of popular culture.

◆ INSIGHT: *The UK has produced 90 nobel laureates – more than any other nation in the world, except from the US*

THE ECONOMY
World leader in financial services, pharmaceuticals, and defense industries. Exports of steel, vehicles, aircraft, high-tech goods.

FACT FILE

OFFICIAL NAME: United Kingdom of Great Britain and Northern Ireland
DATE OF FORMATION: 1921
CAPITAL: London
POPULATION: 57.8 million
TOTAL AREA: 94,550 sq miles (244,880 sq km)

DENSITY: 611 people per sq mile
LANGUAGES: English*, other
RELIGIONS: Protestant 52%, Catholic 9%, Muslim 3%, other 36%
ETHNIC MIX: English 81%, Scottish 10%, Welsh 2%, other 7%
GOVERNMENT: Constitutional monarchy
CURRENCY: £ sterling = 100 pence

---

see also Overseas Territories pp 230–236

FRANCE

STRADDLING WESTERN Europe from the English Channel to the Mediterranean Sea, France is one of the world's leading industrial powers.

GEOGRAPHY
Broad plain covers northern half of the country. Tall mountain ranges in the east and southwest. Mountainous plateau in the center.

CLIMATE
Three main climates: temperate and damp northwest; continental east; and Mediterranean south.

PEOPLE AND SOCIETY
Strong French national identity coexists with pronounced regional differences, including local languages. Long tradition of absorbing immigrants (European Jews, North African Muslims, economic migrants from Southern Europe). Catholic Church is no longer central to daily life.

◆ INSIGHT: The French wine industry dates back to around 600 B.C.

THE ECONOMY
Steel, chemicals, electronics, heavy engineering, wine, and aircraft typify a strong and diversified export sector.

3000m/9843ft	
2000m/6562ft	
1000m/3281ft	
500m/1640ft	
200m/656ft	
Sea Level	

0   100 km
0   100 miles

FACT FILE
OFFICIAL NAME: The French Republic
DATE OF FORMATION: 1685
CAPITAL: Paris
POPULATION: 57.4 million
TOTAL AREA: 551,500 sq km (212,930 sq miles)
DENSITY: 270 people per sq mile

LANGUAGES: French*, Provençal, German, Breton, Catalan, Basque
RELIGIONS: Catholic 90%, Protestant 2%, Jewish 1%, Muslim 1%, other 6%
ETHNIC MIX: French 92%, North African 3%, German 2%, other 3%
GOVERNMENT: Multiparty republic
CURRENCY: Franc = 100 centimes

see also Overseas Territories pp 230–236

LUXEMBOURG

MAKING UP part of the plateau of the Ardennes in Western Europe, Luxembourg is Europe's last independent duchy and one of its richest states.

GEOGRAPHY
Dense Ardennes forests in the north, low, open southern plateau. Undulating terrain throughout.

CLIMATE
Moist climate with warm summers and mild winters. Snow is common only in the Ardennes.

PEOPLE AND SOCIETY
Society is peaceable, despite large proportion of foreigners (half the work force and one third of the residents). Integration has been straightforward; most are fellow Western Europeans and Catholics, mainly from Italy and Portugal. High salaries and very low unemployment promote stability.

◆ INSIGHT: *Luxembourg's capital, Luxembourg, is home to over 980 investment funds and 192 banks – more than any other city in the world*

THE ECONOMY
Traditional industries such as steel-making have given way in recent years to a thriving banking and service sector. Tax-haven status attracts foreign companies.

	500m/1640ft
	200m/656ft
	Sea Level

0   10 km
0   10 miles

Clervaux

GERMANY

Ettelbruck

Echternach

Mersch

BELGIUM

LUXEMBOURG

Pétange

Differdange
Esch-sur-Alzette
Dudelange

FRANCE

FACT FILE

OFFICIAL NAME: Grand Duchy of Luxembourg
DATE OF FORMATION: 1867
CAPITAL: Luxembourg
POPULATION: 400,000
TOTAL AREA: 998 sq miles (2,586 sq km)

DENSITY: 400 people per sq mile
LANGUAGES: Letzeburgish*, French*, German*, Italian, Portuguese, other
RELIGIONS: Catholic 97%, other 3%
ETHNIC MIX: Luxemburger 72%, Portuguese 9%, Italian 5%, other 14%
GOVERNMENT: Constitutional monarchy
CURRENCY: Franc = 100 centimes

MONACO

A JET-SET image and a thriving service sector define the modern identity of this tiny enclave on the Côte d'Azur in southeastern France.

GEOGRAPHY
A rocky promontory overlooking a narrow coastal strip that has been enlarged through land reclamation.

CLIMATE
Mediterranean. Summers are hot and dry; days with 12 hours of sunshine are not uncommon. Winters are mild and sunny.

PEOPLE AND SOCIETY
Less than 20% of residents are Monégasques. The rest are Europeans – mainly French – attracted by the tax-haven, upscale lifestyle. Nationals enjoy considerable privileges, including housing benefits to protect them from high housing prices, and the right of first refusal before foreigners can take a job. Women have equal status but only acquired the vote in 1962.

THE ECONOMY
Tourism and gambling are the mainstays. Banking secrecy laws and tax-haven conditions attract foreign investment. Almost totally dependent on imports due to lack of natural resources.

◆ INSIGHT: The Grimaldi princes (Rainier since 1949) have been Monaco's hereditary rulers for 700 years

Lycée l'Annonciade
FRANCE
43°45'
Musée Nation
Larvotto
Centre de la
Culture et
d'Expositions
Monte-Carlo
Sporting
Club d'Été
Hospitalier
Grace
La Condamine
Grand Prix
Circuit
Casino
Centre de Congrès
Monte-Carlo
Railway
Station
Palais du Prince
Port de Monaco
Ministère d'État
Côte d'Azur
Stade Louis II
Fontvieille
Cathédrale
Musée Océanographique
Mediterranean Sea
7°25'

0   1000 m
0   1500 yds

FACT FILE

OFFICIAL NAME: Principality of Monaco

DATE OF FORMATION: 1861

CAPITAL: Monaco

POPULATION: 28,000

TOTAL AREA: 1.95 sq km (0.75 sq miles)

DENSITY: 37,333 people per sq mile

LANGUAGES: French*, Italian, other

RELIGIONS: Catholic 95%, other 5%

ETHNIC MIX: French 47%, Monégasque 17%, Italian 16%, other 20%

GOVERNMENT: Constitutional monarchy

CURRENCY: French franc = 100 centimes

ANDORRA

A TINY landlocked principality, Andorra lies high in the eastern Pyrenees between France and Spain. It held its first full elections in 1993.

GEOGRAPHY
High mountains, and six deep, glaciated valleys that drain into the River Valira as it flows into Spain.

CLIMATE
Cool, wet springs followed by dry, warm summers. Mountain snows linger until March.

PEOPLE AND SOCIETY
Immigration is strictly monitored and restricted by quota to French and Spanish nationals seeking employment. A referendum in 1993 ended 715 years of semifeudal status but society remains conservative. Divorce is illegal.

◆ INSIGHT: *Andorra is a co-principality whose status dates back to the 13th century, the "princes" being the President of France and the Bishop of Urgel in Spain*

THE ECONOMY
Tourism and duty-free sales dominate the economy. Banking secrecy laws and low consumer taxes promote investment and commerce. Dependence on imported food and raw materials.

FRANCE

Pyrenees

Arinsal   Soldeu
Ordino   Canillo
           Encamp   Port
Escaldes   d'Envalira

ANDORRA LA VELLA
Sant Julià de Lòria

SPAIN

2000m/6562ft
1000m/3281ft
500m/1640ft

0   5 km
0   5 miles

FACT FILE

OFFICIAL NAME: Principality of Andorra
DATE OF FORMATION: 1278
CAPITAL: Andorra la Vella
POPULATION: 58,000
TOTAL AREA: 181 sq miles (468 sq km)

DENSITY: 320 people per sq mile
LANGUAGES: Catalan*, Spanish, other
RELIGIONS: Catholic 86%, other 14%
ETHNIC MIX: Catalan 61%, Spanish Castilian 30%, other 9%
GOVERNMENT: Parliamentary democracy
CURRENCY: French franc, Spanish peseta

PORTUGAL

FACING THE Atlantic on the western side of the Iberian peninsula, Portugal is the most westerly country on the European mainland.

GEOGRAPHY
The River Tagus bisects the country roughly east to west, dividing mountainous north from lower and more undulating south.

CLIMATE
North is cool and moist. South is warmer with dry, mild winters.

PEOPLE AND SOCIETY
Homogeneous and stable society, losing some of its conservative traditions. Small, well-assimilated immigrant population, mainly from former colonies. Urban areas and south are more socially progressive. North is more responsive to traditional Catholic values. Family ties remain all-important.

◆ INSIGHT: Portugal is the world's leading producer of cork, which comes from the bark of the cork oak

THE ECONOMY
Agricultural exports include grain, vegetables, fruits, and wine, but farming methods are outdated. Strong banking and tourism sectors.

1000m/3281ft
500m/1640ft
200m/656ft
Sea Level

0 — 100 km
0 — 100 miles

Viana do Castelo
Braga
Póvoa de Varzim
Porto
Vila Real
Vila Nova de Gaia
ATLANTIC OCEAN
Coimbra
Santarém
SPAIN
Amadora
Estoril
Barreiro
LISBON
Évora
Setúbal
Beja
Algarve
Portimão
Faro

Madeira
Madeira Is.
0 — 50 km
0 — 50 miles

São Miguel
Azores
0 — 200 km
0 — 200 miles

FACT FILE
OFFICIAL NAME: Republic of Portugal
DATE OF FORMATION: 1640
CAPITAL: Lisbon
POPULATION: 9.9 million
TOTAL AREA: 35,670 sq miles (92,390 sq km)

DENSITY: 277 people per sq mile
LANGUAGES: Portuguese*
RELIGIONS: Catholic 97%, Protestant 1%, other 2%
ETHNIC MIX: Portuguese 98%, African 1%, other 1%
GOVERNMENT: Multiparty republic
CURRENCY: Escudo = 100 centavos

see also Overseas Territories pp 230–236

SPAIN

LODGED BETWEEN Europe, and Africa, the Atlantic, and the Mediterranean, Spain has occupied a pivotal position since it was united in 1492.

GEOGRAPHY
Mountain ranges in north, center, and south. Huge central plateau. Verdant valleys in northwest, Mediterranean lowlands.

CLIMATE
Maritime in north. Hotter and drier in south. Central plateau has an extreme climate.

PEOPLE AND SOCIETY
Ethnic regionalism, suppressed under General Franco's regime (1936–1975), is increasing. 17 regions are now autonomous. People remain church-going, although Catholic teachings on social issues are often flouted. Status of women rising quickly, with strong political representation.

THE ECONOMY
Outdated labor practices and low investment hinder growth. Heavy industry, textiles, and food-processing lead exports. Tourism and agriculture are important.

◆ INSIGHT: *Over 3,000 festivals and feasts take place each year in Spain*

2000m/6562ft	
1000m/3281ft	
500m/1640ft	
200m/656ft	
Sea Level	

FACT FILE
OFFICIAL NAME: Kingdom of Spain
DATE OF FORMATION: 1492
CAPITAL: Madrid
POPULATION: 39.2 million
TOTAL AREA: 194,900 sq miles
(504,780 sq km)
DENSITY: 201 people per sq mile

LANGUAGES: Castilian Spanish*, Catalan*, Galician*, Basque*, other
RELIGIONS: Catholic 99%, other 1%
ETHNIC MIX: Castilian Spanish 72%, Catalan 16%, Galician 7%, Basque 2%, Gypsy 1%, other 2%
GOVERNMENT: Constitutional monarchy
CURRENCY: Peseta = 100 céntimos

ITALY

PROJECTING INTO the Mediterranean Sea in Southern Europe, Italy is an ancient land but also one of the continent's newest unified states.

GEOGRAPHY
Appennino form the backbone of a rugged peninsula, extending from the Alps into the Mediterranean Sea. Alluvial plain in the north.

CLIMATE
Mediterranean in the south. Seasonal extremes in mountains and on northern plain.

PEOPLE AND SOCIETY
Ethnically homogeneous, but gulf between prosperous, industrial north and poorer, agricultural south. Strong regional identities, especially on islands of Sicily and Sardinia. State institutions viewed as inefficient and corrupt. Allegiance to the family survives lessened influence of the Church.

◆ INSIGHT: Italy was a collection of city states, dukedoms, and monarchies before it became a unified nation in 1871

THE ECONOMY
World leader in industrial and product design and textiles. Strong tourism and agriculture sectors. Weak currency. Large public-sector debt.

3000m/9843ft	
2000m/6562ft	
1000m/3281ft	
500m/1640ft	
200m/656ft	
Sea Level	

FACT FILE

OFFICIAL NAME: Italian Republic
DATE OF FORMATION: 1871
CAPITAL: Rome
POPULATION: 57.8 million
TOTAL AREA: 116,320 sq miles (301,270 sq km)
DENSITY: 497 people per sq mile

LANGUAGES: Italian*, German, French, Rhaeto-Romanic, Sardinian
RELIGIONS: Catholic 99%, other 1%
ETHNIC MIX: Italian 98%, other (inc. German, French, Greek, Slovenian, Albanian) 2%
GOVERNMENT: Multiparty republic
CURRENCY: Lira = 100 centesimi

MALTA

THE MALTESE archipelago lies off southern Sicily, midway between Europe and Africa. The only inhabited islands are Malta, Gozo, and Kemmuna.

GEOGRAPHY
The main island of Malta has low hills and a ragged coastline with numerous harbors, bays, sandy beaches, and rocky coves. Gozo is more densely vegetated.

CLIMATE
Mediterranean climate. Many hours of sunshine throughout the year but very low rainfall.

PEOPLE AND SOCIETY
Over the centuries, the Maltese have been subject to Arab, Sicilian, Spanish, French, and English influences. Today, the population is socially conservative and devoutly Roman Catholic. Divorce is illegal. Many young Maltese go abroad to find work – notably to the United States and Australia – as opportunities for them on the islands are few.

THE ECONOMY
Tourism is the chief source of income. Offshore banking potential. Schemes to attract foreign high-tech industry. Almost all requirements have to be imported.

◆ INSIGHT: *The Maltese language has Phoenician origins but features Arabic etymology and intonation*

FACT FILE

OFFICIAL NAME: Republic of Malta
DATE OF FORMATION: 1964
CAPITAL: Valletta
POPULATION: 400,000
TOTAL AREA: 124 sq miles (320 sq km)
DENSITY: 3,225 people per sq mile

LANGUAGES: Maltese*, English
RELIGIONS: Catholic 98%, other (mostly Anglican) 2%
ETHNIC MIX: Maltese (mixed Arab, Sicilian, Norman, Spanish, Italian, English) 98%, other 2%
GOVERNMENT: Multiparty republic
CURRENCY: Lira = 100 cents

VATICAN CITY

THE VATICAN City, the seat of the Roman Catholic Church, is a walled enclave in the city of Rome. It is the world's smallest fully independent state.

GEOGRAPHY
Territory includes ten other buildings in Rome, plus the papal residence. The Vatican Gardens cover half the City's area.

CLIMATE
Mild winters with regular rainfall. Hot, dry summers with occasional thunderstorms.

PEOPLE AND SOCIETY
The Vatican has about 1,000 permanent inhabitants, including several hundred lay persons, and employs a further 3,400 lay staff. Citizenship can be acquired through stable residence and holding an office or job within the City. Reigning Pope has supreme legislative and judicial powers, and holds office for life. State maintains a neutral stance in world affairs and has observer status in many international organizations.

THE ECONOMY
Investments and voluntary contributions by Catholics world-wide (known as Peter's Pence), backed up by tourist revenue and issue of Vatican stamps and coins.

◆ INSIGHT: The Vatican City is the only state to have Latin as an official language

FACT FILE

OFFICIAL NAME: State of the Vatican City

DATE OF FORMATION: 1929

CAPITAL: Not applicable

POPULATION: 1,000

TOTAL AREA: 0.17 sq miles (0.44 sq km)

DENSITY: 5,882 people per sq mile

LANGUAGES: Italian*, Latin*, other

RELIGIONS: Catholic 100%

ETHNIC MIX: Italian 90%, Swiss 10% (including the Swiss Guard, which is responsible for papal security)

GOVERNMENT: Papal Commission

CURRENCY: Italian lira = 100 centesimi

SAN MARINO

PERCHED ON the slopes of Monte Titano in the Italian Appennino, San Marino has maintained its independence since the 4th century A.D.

GEOGRAPHY
Distinctive limestone outcrop of Monte Titano dominates wooded hills and pastures near Italy's Adriatic coast.

CLIMATE
Altitude and sea breezes moderate Mediterranean climate. Hot summers and cool, wet winters.

PEOPLE AND SOCIETY
Territory is divided into nine "castles," or districts. Tightly knit society, with 16 centuries of tradition. Strict immigration rules require 30-year residence before applying for citizenship. Catholic Church remains a more powerful influence than in neighboring Italy. Living standards are similar to those of northern Italy.

THE ECONOMY
Tourism provides 60% of government income. Light industries – led by mechanical engineering and high-quality clothing – generate export revenue. Italian infrastructure is a boon.

◆ INSIGHT: *Sales of postage stamps contribute 10% of the national income*

FACT FILE	
OFFICIAL NAME: Republic of San Marino	DENSITY: 958 people per sq mile
	LANGUAGES: Italian*, other
DATE OF FORMATION: 301 A.D.	RELIGIONS: Catholic 96%, Protestant 2%, other 2%
CAPITAL: San Marino	ETHNIC MIX: Sammarinese 95%, Italian 4%, other 1%
POPULATION: 23,000	GOVERNMENT: Multiparty republic
TOTAL AREA: 24 sq miles (61 sq km)	CURRENCY: Italian lira = 100 centesimi

SWITZERLAND

ONE OF the world's most prosperous countries, with a long tradition of neutrality in foreign affairs, it lies at the center of Western Europe.

GEOGRAPHY
Mostly mountainous, with river valleys. Alps cover 60% of its area; Jura in west cover 10%. Lowlands lie along east–west axis.

CLIMATE
Most rain falls in the warm summer months. Snowy winters, but milder and foggy away from the mountains.

PEOPLE AND SOCIETY
Composed of distinct Swiss-German, Swiss-French, and Swiss-Italian linguistic groups, but national identity is strong. Country divided into 26 autonomous cantons (states), each with control over housing and economic policy. Tensions over membership of EU, drug abuse, and role of guest workers in economy. Some young see society as regimented and conformist.

THE ECONOMY
Diversified economy relies on services – with strong tourism and banking sectors – and specialized industries (engineering, watches).

◆ INSIGHT: Genève is the headquarters of many UN agencies, although Switzerland itself is not a UN member

3000m/9843ft	
2000m/6562ft	
1000m/3281ft	
500m/1640ft	
200m/656ft	

0   50 km

0   50 miles

FACT FILE

OFFICIAL NAME: Swiss Confederation
DATE OF FORMATION: 1815
CAPITAL: Bern
POPULATION: 6.9 million
TOTAL AREA: 15,940 sq miles
(41,290 sq km)
DENSITY: 432 people per sq mile

LANGUAGES: German*, French*, Italian*, Romansch*, other
RELIGIONS: Catholic 48%, Protestant 44%, other 8%
ETHNIC MIX: German 65%, French 18%, Italian 10%, other 7%
GOVERNMENT: Federal republic
CURRENCY: Franc = 100 centimes

LIECHTENSTEIN

TUCKED IN the Alps between Switzerland and Austria, Liechtenstein became an independent principality of the Holy Roman Empire in 1719.

GEOGRAPHY
Upper Rhine valley covers western third. Mountains and narrow valleys of the eastern Alps make up the remainder.

CLIMATE
Warm, dry summers. Cold winters, with heavy snow in mountains December–March.

PEOPLE AND SOCIETY
Country's role as a financial center accounts for its many foreign residents (over 35% of the population), of whom half are Swiss and the rest mostly German. High standard of living results in few social tensions. Sovereignty cherished, despite close alliance with Switzerland, which handles its foreign relations and defense.

THE ECONOMY
Banking secrecy and low taxes attract foreign investment. Well-diversified exports include dental products, furniture, and chemicals.

◆ INSIGHT: *Women in Liechtenstein only received the vote in 1984*

FACT FILE

OFFICIAL NAME: Principality of Liechtenstein

DATE OF FORMATION: 1719

CAPITAL: Vaduz

POPULATION: 29,000

TOTAL AREA: 62 sq miles (160 sq km)

DENSITY: 468 people per sq mile

LANGUAGES: German*, Alemannish

RELIGIONS: Catholic 87%, Protestant 8%, other 5%

ETHNIC MIX: Liechtensteiner 63%, Swiss 15%, German 9%, other 13%

GOVERNMENT: Constitutional monarchy

CURRENCY: Swiss franc = 100 centimes

141

AUSTRIA

BORDERING EIGHT countries in the heart of Europe, Austria was created in 1920 after the collapse of the Austro-Hungarian Empire the previous year.

GEOGRAPHY
Mainly mountainous. Alps and foothills cover the west and south. Lowlands in the east are part of the Danube River basin.

CLIMATE
Temperate continental climate. Western Alpine regions have colder winters and more rainfall.

PEOPLE AND SOCIETY
Although all are German-speaking, Austrians consider themselves ethnically distinct from Germans. Minorities are few; there are a small number of Hungarians, Slovenes, and Croats, plus refugees from conflict in former Yugoslavia. Some Austrians are beginning to challenge patriarchal and class-conscious social values. Legislation reflects strong environmental concerns.

THE ECONOMY
Large manufacturing base, despite lack of energy resources. Skilled labor force the key to high-tech exports. Strong tourism sector.

◆ INSIGHT: *Many of the world's great composers were Austrian, including Mozart, Haydn, Schubert, and Strauss*

3000m/9843ft	
2000m/6562ft	
1000m/3281ft	
500m/1640ft	
200m/656ft	
Sea Level	

FACT FILE
OFFICIAL NAME: Republic of Austria
DATE OF FORMATION: 1920
CAPITAL: Vienna
POPULATION: 7.8 million
TOTAL AREA: 32,375 sq miles (83,850 sq km)
DENSITY: 241 people per sq mile

LANGUAGES: German*, Croatian, Slovene, Hungarian (Magyar)
RELIGIONS: Catholic 85%, Protestant 6%, other 9%
ETHNIC MIX: German 99%, other (inc. Hungarian, Slovene, Croat) 1%
GOVERNMENT: Multiparty republic
CURRENCY: Schilling = 100 groschen

HUNGARY

HUNGARY IS bordered by seven states in Central Europe. It has changed its economic and political policies to develop closer ties with the EU.

GEOGRAPHY
Fertile plains in east and northwest; west and north are hilly. River Danube bisects the country from north to south.

CLIMATE
Continental. Wet springs; late, but very hot summers, and cold, cloudy winters.

PEOPLE AND SOCIETY
Ethnically homogenous and stable society, showing signs of stress since change to market economy. Most homes are overcrowded, due to a severe housing shortage. Since 1989, a middle class has emerged, but life for the unemployed and unskilled is harder than under communism. Concern over treatment of Hungarian nationals in neighboring states.

THE ECONOMY
Weak banking sector and unemployment hamper moves to open economy. Heavy industries and agriculture remain strong. Growing tourism and services.

◆ INSIGHT: *The Hungarian language is Asian in origin and has features not found in any other Western language*

FACT FILE
OFFICIAL NAME: Republic of Hungary
DATE OF FORMATION: 1918
CAPITAL: Budapest
POPULATION: 10.5 million
TOTAL AREA: 35,919 sq miles (93,030 sq km)
DENSITY: 292 people per sq mile

LANGUAGES: Hungarian (Magyar)*, German, Slovak, other
RELIGIONS: Catholic 68%, Protestant 25%, other 7%
ETHNIC MIX: Hungarian (Magyar) 90%, German 2%, other 8%
GOVERNMENT: Multiparty republic
CURRENCY: Forint = 100 filler

CZECH REPUBLIC

ONCE PART of Czechoslovakia in Central Europe, it became independent in 1993, after peacefully dissolving its federal union with Slovakia.

GEOGRAPHY

Western territory of Bohemia is a plateau surrounded by mountains. Moravia, in the east, has hills and lowlands.

CLIMATE

Cool, sometimes cold winters, and warm summer months, which bring most of the annual rainfall.

PEOPLE AND SOCIETY

Secular and urban society, with high divorce rates. Czechs make up the vast majority of the population. The 300,000 Slovaks left after partition now form largest ethnic minority. Ethnic tensions are few, but there is some hostility towards the Gypsy community. A new commercial elite is emerging alongside ex-communist entrepreneurs.

THE ECONOMY

Traditional heavy industries (machinery, iron, car-making) have been successfully privatized. Large tourism revenues. Skilled labor force. Rising unemployment.

◆ INSIGHT: The Czech Republic is the most polluted country in Europe. Acid rain has devastated many of its forests

FACT FILE

OFFICIAL NAME: Czech Republic
DATE OF FORMATION: 1993
CAPITAL: Prague
POPULATION: 10.4 million
TOTAL AREA: 30,260 sq miles
(78,370 sq km)
DENSITY: 343 people per sq mile

LANGUAGES: Czech*, Slovak, Romany, other
RELIGIONS: Catholic 44%, Protestant 6%, other Christian 12%, other 38%
ETHNIC MIX: Czech 85%, Moravian 13%, other (inc. Slovak, Gypsy) 2%
GOVERNMENT: Multiparty republic
CURRENCY: Koruna = 100 halura

SLOVAKIA

LANDLOCKED IN Central Europe, Slovakia has been independent since 1993. It is the less-developed half of the former Czechoslovakia.

GEOGRAPHY
Carpathian Mountains stretch along northern border with Poland. Southern lowlands include the fertile Danube plain.

CLIMATE
Continental. Moderately warm summers and steady rainfall. Cold winters with heavy snowfalls.

PEOPLE AND SOCIETY
Slovaks are largest and most dominant group. Tension between them and the Hungarian minority has increased, particularly over directive that Hungarians should adopt Slovak name endings. Before partition, many skilled Slovaks took jobs in Prague, but few have returned to help structure the new Slovakia. Catholic Church remains influential.

THE ECONOMY
Narrow emphasis on heavy industry, with poor record on innovation and capital investment. High inflation and unemployment. Growing tourism sector.

◆ INSIGHT: *Separation from the Czech Republic gave Slovakia full independence for the first time in over 1,000 years*

2000m/6562ft	
1000m/3281ft	
500m/1640ft	
200m/656ft	
Sea Level	

0   50 km
0   50 miles

FACT FILE

OFFICIAL NAME: Slovak Republic
DATE OF FORMATION: 1993
CAPITAL: Bratislava
POPULATION: 5.3 million
TOTAL AREA: 19,100 sq miles (49,500 sq km)
DENSITY: 277 people per sq mile

LANGUAGES: Slovak*, Hungarian (Magyar), Romany, Czech, other
RELIGIONS: Catholic 80%, Protestant 12%, other 8%
ETHNIC MIX: Slovak 85%, Hungarian 9%, Czech 1%, other (inc. Gypsy) 5%
GOVERNMENT: Multiparty republic
CURRENCY: Koruna = 100 halura

SLOVENIA

NORTHERNMOST of the former Yugoslav republics, it has the closest links with Western Europe. In 1991, it gained independence with little violence.

GEOGRAPHY
Alpine terrain with hills and mountains. Forests cover almost half the country's area. Short Adriatic coastline.

CLIMATE
Mediterranean climate on small coastal strip. Alpine interior has continental extremes.

PEOPLE AND SOCIETY
Homogeneous population accounts for relatively peaceful transition to independence. Traditional links with Austria and Italy, each with Slovene populations, account for the "Alpine" rather than "Balkan" outlook. Wages are the highest in central Europe, but unemployment is rising. Institutional change is proceeding slowly.

THE ECONOMY
Competitive manufacturing industry. Prospects for growth in electronics industry. Well-developed tourist sector.

◆ INSIGHT: *Slovenia is a major producer of mercury, used in thermo-meters, barometers, and batteries*

AUSTRIA

HUNGA

Murska Sobota

Jesenice

Maribor

Kranj

Celje

Ptuj

LJUBLJANA ✈

Nova Gorica

Krško

Postojna

Brežice

CROATIA

Adriatic Sea

| 1000m/3281ft |
| 500m/1640ft |
| 200m/656ft |
| Sea Level |

0   25 km
0   25 miles

FACT FILE

OFFICIAL NAME: Republic of Slovenia
DATE OF FORMATION: 1991
CAPITAL: Ljubljana
POPULATION: 2 million
TOTAL AREA: 7,820 sq miles (20,250 sq km)

DENSITY: 255 people per sq mile
LANGUAGES: Slovene*, Serbo-Croatian
RELIGIONS: Roman Catholic 96%, Muslim 1%, other 3%
ETHNIC MIX: Slovene 92%, Croat 3%, Serb 1%, other 4%
GOVERNMENT: Multiparty republic
CURRENCY: Tolar = 100 stotins

CROATIA

A FORMER Yugoslav republic. Postindependence fighting thwarted its plans to capitalize on its prime location along the east Adriatic coast.

GEOGRAPHY
Rocky, mountainous Adriatic coastline is dotted with islands. Interior is a mixture of wooded mountains and broad valleys.

CLIMATE
The interior has a temperate continental climate. Mediterranean climate along the Adriatic coast.

PEOPLE AND SOCIETY
Turbulence was triggered by long-held ethnic hostilities. Open warfare between Croats and Serbs began in 1990. Some areas with local Serb majorities achieved de facto autonomy after fierce fighting in 1992. Destruction was widespread; thousands of people were made homeless.

◆ INSIGHT: The Croatian language uses the Roman alphabet, while Serbian employs Cyrillic (Russian) script

THE ECONOMY
Economy was severely strained by fighting and influx of refugees. Potential for renewed success in manufacturing, tourism. Exports to the West have grown, despite conflict.

FACT FILE

OFFICIAL NAME: Republic of Croatia
DATE OF FORMATION: 1991
CAPITAL: Zagreb
POPULATION: 4.9 million
TOTAL AREA: 21,830 sq miles (56,540 sq km)
DENSITY: 211 people per sq mile

LANGUAGES: Croatian*, Serbian
RELIGIONS: Roman Catholic 77%, Orthodox Catholic 11%, Protestant 1%, Muslim 1%, other 10%
ETHNIC MIX: Croat 80%, Serb 12%, Hungarian, Slovenian, other 8%
GOVERNMENT: Multiparty republic
CURRENCY: Kuna = 100 para

BOSNIA & HERZEGOVINA

DOMINATING THE western Balkans, Bosnia and Herzegovina was the focus of the bitter conflict surrounding the breakup of former Yugoslavia.

GEOGRAPHY
Hills and mountains, with narrow river valleys. Lowlands in the north. Mainly deciduous forest covers about half of the total area.

CLIMATE
Continental. Hot summers and cold, often snowy winters.

PEOPLE AND SOCIETY
Civil war between rival ethnic groups. Ethnic Bosnians (mainly Muslim) form the largest group, with large minorities of Serbs and Croats. Communities have been destroyed or uprooted ("ethnic cleansing") as Serbs and Croats established separate ethnic areas. The UN and Nato have been involved as peacekeepers.

◆ INSIGHT: *By 1995, over two million people had been made homeless and a further million had fled the country*

THE ECONOMY
Before 1991, Bosnia was home to five of former Yugoslavia's largest companies. It has the potential to become a thriving market economy with a strong manufacturing base.

FACT FILE
OFFICIAL NAME: The Republic of Bosnia and Herzegovina
DATE OF FORMATION: 1992
CAPITAL: Sarajevo
POPULATION: 4.5 million
TOTAL AREA: 19,741 sq miles (51,130 sq km)

DENSITY: 227 people per sq mile
LANGUAGES: Serbo-Croatian*, other
RELIGIONS: Muslim 40%, Orthodox Catholic 31%, other 29%
ETHNIC MIX: Bosnian 44%, Serb 31%, Croat 17%, other 8%
GOVERNMENT: Multiparty republic
CURRENCY: Dinar = 100 para

YUGOSLAVIA (SERBIA & MONTENEGRO)

THE FEDERAL Republic of Yugoslavia, comprising Serbia and Montenegro, lays claim to being the successor state to the former Yugoslavia.

GEOGRAPHY
Fertile Danube plain in north, rolling uplands in center. Mountains in south, and behind narrow Adriatic coastal plain.

CLIMATE
Mediterranean along coast, continental inland. Hot summers and cold winters, with heavy snow.

PEOPLE AND SOCIETY
Social order has disintegrated since dissolution of the former Yugoslavia. Serbia was vilified in the international community for its role in the conflict in the region. Serbian concerns over Bosnia and Croatia have masked domestic tensions, particularly unrest among the Albanian population in the southern province of Kosovo.

◆ INSIGHT: *Belgrade means "White City." Its site has been settled for 7,000 years*

THE ECONOMY
Bosnian war and UN trade sanctions crippled the economy. Fuel and food shortages. Hyper-inflation created a barter economy.

FACT FILE

OFFICIAL NAME: Federal Republic of Yugoslavia
DATE OF FORMATION: 1992
CAPITAL: Belgrade
POPULATION: 10.6 million
TOTAL AREA: 9,929 sq miles (25,715 sq km)

DENSITY: 1,067 people per sq mile
LANGUAGES: Serbo-Croatian*, other
RELIGIONS: Orthodox Catholic 65%, Muslim 19%, other 16%
ETHNIC MIX: Serb 63%, Albanian 14%, Montenegrin 6%, other 17%
GOVERNMENT: Multiparty republic
CURRENCY: Dinar = 100 para

ALBANIA

LYING AT the southeastern end of the Adriatic Sea, Albania held its first multiparty elections in 1991, after nearly five decades of communism.

GEOGRAPHY
Narrow coastal plain. Interior is mostly hills and mountains. Forest and scrub cover over 40% of the land. Large lakes in the east.

CLIMATE
Mediterranean coastal climate, with warm summers and cool winters. Mountains receive heavy rains or snows in winter.

PEOPLE AND SOCIETY
Last eastern European country to move toward Western economic liberalism – pace of change remains a sensitive issue. Mosques and churches have reopened in what was once the world's only officially atheist state. Greek minority in the south suffers much discrimination.

◆ INSIGHT: *The Albanians' name for their nation,* Shqipërisë, *means "Land of the Eagle"*

THE ECONOMY
Oil and gas reserves plus high growth rate have potential to offset rudimentary infrastructure and lack of foreign investment.

2000m/6562ft	
1000m/3281ft	
500m/1640ft	
200m/656ft	
Sea Level	

0   50 km
0   50 miles

FACT FILE
OFFICIAL NAME: Republic of Albania
DATE OF FORMATION: 1913
CAPITAL: Tirana
POPULATION: 3.3 million
TOTAL AREA: 11,100 sq miles (28,750 sq km)

DENSITY: 297 people per sq mile
LANGUAGES: Albanian*, Greek
RELIGIONS: Muslim 70%, Greek Orthodox 20%, Roman Catholic 10%
ETHNIC MIX: Albanian 96%, Greek 2%, other (inc. Macedonian) 2%
GOVERNMENT: Multiparty republic
CURRENCY: Lek = 100 qindars

MACEDONIA

LANDLOCKED in the southern Balkans, Macedonia is affected by sanctions imposed on its northern trading partners and by Greek antagonism.

GEOGRAPHY
Mainly mountainous or hilly, with deep river basins in center. Plains in northeast and southwest.

CLIMATE
Continental climate with wet springs and dry autumns. Heavy snowfalls in northern mountains.

PEOPLE AND SOCIETY
Slav Macedonians comprise two thirds of the population. Officially 20% are Albanian, although Albanians claim they account for 40%. Tensions between the two groups have so far been restrained. Greek government is hostile toward the state because it suspects it may try to absorb northern Greece – also called Macedonia – in a "Greater Macedonia." Social structures remain essentially socialist.

THE ECONOMY
Serbian sanctions paralyze exports, but foreign aid and grants boost foreign exchange reserves. Growing private sector. Thriving black market in the capital.

◆ INSIGHT: *Lake Ohrid is the deepest lake in Europe at 964 ft (294 m)*

FACT FILE

OFFICIAL NAME: Former Yugoslav Republic of Macedonia

DATE OF FORMATION: 1991

CAPITAL: Skopje

POPULATION: 1.9 million

TOTAL AREA: 9,929 sq miles (25,715 sq km)

DENSITY: 192 people per sq mile

LANGUAGES: Macedonian, Serbo-Croatian (no official language)

RELIGIONS: Christian 80%, Muslim 20%

ETHNIC MIX: Macedonian 67%, Albanian 20%, Turkish 4%, other 9%

GOVERNMENT: Multiparty republic

CURRENCY: Denar = 100 deni

BULGARIA

LOCATED IN southeastern Europe, Bulgaria has made slow progress toward democracy since the fall of its communist regime in 1990.

 GEOGRAPHY
Mountains run east–west across center and along southern border. Danube plain in north, Thracian plain in southeast.

CLIMATE
Warm summers and snowy winters, especially in mountains. East winds bring seasonal extremes.

 PEOPLE AND SOCIETY
Government has sought to assimilate separate ethnic groups, thereby suppressing cultural identities. Large exodus of Bulgarian Turks in 1989. Recent privatization program has left many Turks landless and prompted further emigration. Gypsies suffer much discrimination. Female equality exists only in theory. Ruling party, mainly ex-communists, have resisted change.

THE ECONOMY
Political and technical delays hinder privatization program. Good agricultural production – including grapes for the well-developed wine industry – and tobacco.

◆ *INSIGHT: Shaking one's head implies "yes" in Bulgaria while a nod means "no"*

FACT FILE

OFFICIAL NAME: Republic of Bulgaria
DATE OF FORMATION: 1908
CAPITAL: Sofia
POPULATION: 8.9 million
TOTAL AREA: 42,822 sq miles (110,910 sq km)
DENSITY: 211 people per sq mile

LANGUAGES: Bulgarian*, Turkish, Macedonian, Romany, Armenian
RELIGIONS: Christian 85%, Muslim 13%, Jewish 1%, other 1%
ETHNIC MIX: Bulgarian 85%, Turkish 9%, Macedonian 3%, Gypsy 3%
GOVERNMENT: Multiparty republic
CURRENCY: Lev = 100 stotinki

GREECE

GREECE IS the southernmost Balkan nation. Surrounded by the Mediterranean, Aegean, and Ionian seas, it has a strong seafaring tradition.

GEOGRAPHY
Mountainous peninsula with over 2,000 islands. Large central plain along the Aegean coast.

CLIMATE
Mainly Mediterranean with dry, hot summers. Alpine climate in northern mountain areas.

PEOPLE AND SOCIETY
Postwar industrial development altered the dominance of agriculture and seafaring. Rural exodus to industrial cities has been stemmed but over half the population now live in the two largest cities. Age-old culture and Greek Orthodox Church balance social mobility.

THE ECONOMY
High inflation and poor investment work against strong economic sectors: tourism, shipping, agriculture. Thriving black market.

◆ INSIGHT: *The Parthenon in Athens has suffered more erosion in the last 20 years than in the previous 2,000*

FACT FILE

OFFICIAL NAME: Hellenic Republic
DATE OF FORMATION: 1913
CAPITAL: Athens
POPULATION: 10.2 million
TOTAL AREA: 50,961 sq miles (131,990 sq km)
DENSITY: 203 people per sq mile

LANGUAGES: Greek*, Turkish, Albanian, Macedonian
RELIGIONS: Greek Orthodox 98%, Muslim 1%, other (mainly Roman Catholic and Jewish) 1%
ETHNIC MIX: Greek 98%, other 2%
GOVERNMENT: Multiparty republic
CURRENCY: Drachma = 100 lepta

ROMANIA

ROMANIA LIES on the Black Sea coast. Since the overthrow of its communist regime in 1989, it has been slowly converting to a free-market economy.

GEOGRAPHY
Carpathian Mountains encircle Transylvanian plateau. Wide plains to the south and east. River Danube on southern border.

CLIMATE
Continental. Hot, humid summers and cold, snowy winters. Very heavy spring rains.

PEOPLE AND SOCIETY
Since 1989, there has been a rise in Romanian nationalism, aggravated by the hardships brought by economic reform. Incidence of ethnic violence has also risen, particularly toward Hungarians and Gypsies. Decrease in population in recent years due to emigration and falling birth rate.

THE ECONOMY
Outdated, polluting heavy industries and unmechanized agricultural sector. Wages have fallen since demise of communism. High number of small-scale foreign joint ventures. Tourism potential.

2000m/6562ft	
1000m/3281ft	
500m/1640ft	
200m/656ft	
Sea Level	

0   50 km
0   50 miles

◆ INSIGHT: *Romania is the only nation with a Romance language that does not have a Roman Catholic background*

FACT FILE
OFFICIAL NAME: Romania
DATE OF FORMATION: 1947
CAPITAL: Bucharest
POPULATION: 23.4 million
TOTAL AREA: 91,700 sq miles (237,500 sq km)
DENSITY: 255 people per sq mile

LANGUAGES: Romanian*, Hungarian
RELIGIONS: Romanian Orthodox 70%, Roman Catholic 6%, Protestant 6%, Greek Catholic 3%, other 15%
ETHNIC MIX: Romanian 89%, Hungarian 8%, other (inc. Gypsy) 3%
GOVERNMENT: Multiparty republic
CURRENCY: Leu = 100 bani

MOLDOVA

SMALLEST AND most densely populated of the ex-Soviet republics, Moldova has strong linguistic and cultural links with Romania to the west.

GEOGRAPHY
Steppes and hilly plains, drained by Dniester and Prut rivers.

CLIMATE
Warm summers and relatively mild winters. Moderate rainfall, evenly spread throughout the year.

PEOPLE AND SOCIETY
Shared heritage with Romania defines national identity, although in 1994 Moldovans voted against possible unification with Romania. Most of the population is engaged in intensive agriculture. The 1994 constitution granted special autonomous status to the Gagauz people in the south (Orthodox Christian Turks), and to the Slav peoples on the east bank of the River Dniester.

◆ INSIGHT: Moldova's vast underground wine vaults contain entire "streets" of bottles built into rock quarries

THE ECONOMY
Well-developed agricultural sector: wine, tobacco, cotton, food processing. Light manufacturing. Progress in establishing markets for exports. High unemployment.

FACT FILE	
OFFICIAL NAME: Republic of Moldova	LANGUAGES: Moldovan*, Russian
DATE OF FORMATION: 1991	RELIGIONS: Romanian Orthodox 98%, Jewish 1%, other 1%
CAPITAL: Chişinău	ETHNIC MIX: Moldovan (Romanian) 65%, Ukrainian 14%, Russian 13%, Gagauz 4%, other 4%
POPULATION: 4.4 million	
TOTAL AREA: 13,000 sq miles (33,700 sq km)	GOVERNMENT: Multiparty republic
DENSITY: 338 people per sq mile	CURRENCY: Leu = 100 bani

BELARUS

FORMERLY KNOWN as White Russia, Belarus lies landlocked in Eastern Europe. It reluctantly became independent of the USSR in 1991.

GEOGRAPHY
Mainly plains and low hills. Dnieper and Dvina rivers drain eastern lowlands. Vast Pripet Marshes in the southwest.

CLIMATE
Extreme continental climate. Long, subfreezing, but mainly dry winters, and hot summers.

PEOPLE AND SOCIETY
Only 2% of people are non-Slav; ethnic tension is minimal. Entire population have right to citizenship, although only 11% are fluent in Belarussian. Slowest of the ex-Soviet states to implement political reform, a post-Soviet constitution was not adopted until 1994. Wealth is held by a small ex-communist elite. Fallout from 1986 Chornobil' nuclear disaster in Ukraine seriously affected Belarussians' health and environment.

THE ECONOMY
Food processing and heavy industries stagnate while politicians argue over market reforms. Low unemployment but high inflation.

◆ INSIGHT: *The number of cancer and leukemia cases is 10,000 above the pre-Chornobil' annual average*

FACT FILE

OFFICIAL NAME: Republic of Belarus
DATE OF FORMATION: 1991
CAPITAL: Minsk
POPULATION: 10.3 million
TOTAL AREA: 80,154 sq miles
(207,600 sq km)
DENSITY: 127 people per sq mile

LANGUAGES: Belarussian*, Russian
RELIGIONS: Russian Orthodox 60%, Catholic 8%, other (inc. Uniate, Protestant, Muslim, Jewish) 32%
ETHNIC MIX: Belarussian 78%, Russian 13%, Polish 4%, other 5%
GOVERNMENT: Multiparty republic
CURRENCY: Rouble = 100 kopeks

UKRAINE

THE FORMER "breadbasket of the Soviet Union," Ukraine balances assertive nationalism with concerns over its relations with Russia.

GEOGRAPHY
Mainly fertile steppes and forests. Carpathian Mountains in southwest, Crimean chain in south. Pripet Marshes in northwest.

CLIMATE
Mainly continental climate, with distinct seasons. Southern Crimea has Mediterranean climate.

PEOPLE AND SOCIETY
Over 90% of the population in western Ukraine is Ukrainian. However, in several cities in the east and south, Russians form a majority. In the Crimea, the Tartars comprise around 10% of the population. At independence in 1991, most Russians accepted Ukrainian sovereignty. However, tensions are now rising as both groups adopt more extremist nationalist policies.

THE ECONOMY
Hyperinflation, corruption, and hostility from economic elite stifle any reforms. Heavy industries and agriculture largely unchanged since independence.

◆ INSIGHT: *The name Ukraine means "frontier," a reference to the country's position along the Russian border*

	2000m/6562ft
	1000m/3281ft
	500m/1640ft
	200m/656ft
	Sea Level

FACT FILE

OFFICIAL NAME: Ukraine
DATE OF FORMATION: 1991
CAPITAL: Kiev
POPULATION: 52.2 million
TOTAL AREA: 223,090 sq miles (603,700 sq km)
DENSITY: 233 people per sq mile

LANGUAGES: Ukrainian*, Russian, Tartar
RELIGIONS: Mostly Ukrainian Orthodox, with Roman Catholic, Protestant and Jewish minorities
ETHNIC MIX: Ukrainian 73%, Russian 22%, other (inc. Tartar) 5%
GOVERNMENT: Multiparty republic
CURRENCY: Karbovanets (coupons)

RUSSIAN FEDERATION

STILL THE world's largest state, despite the break-up of the USSR in 1991, the Russian Federation is struggling to capitalize on its diversity.

GEOGRAPHY
Ural Mountains divide European steppes and forests from tundra and forests of Siberia. South-central deserts and mountains.

CLIMATE
Continental in European Russia. Elsewhere from subarctic to Mediterranean and hot desert.

PEOPLE AND SOCIETY
Ethnic Russians now make up 80% of the population, but there are many minority groups. 57 nationalities have territorial status, a further 95 lack their own territory. 1994 war with Chechnya indicated potential for ethnic crisis. Wealth disparities, rising crime, and black market activities have accompanied reforms. Extremist politicians have exploited standard-of-living and ethnic concerns. Strong resurgence of religious practice since late 1980s.

◆ INSIGHT: The Trans-Siberian railroad, which runs 5,800 miles (9,335 km) from Moscow to Vladivostok, is the world's longest. It crosses seven time zones

FACT FILE

OFFICIAL NAME: Russian Federation
DATE OF FORMATION: 1991
CAPITAL: Moscow
POPULATION: 149.2 million
TOTAL AREA: 6,592,800 sq miles (17,075,400 sq km)

DENSITY: 5 people per sq mile
LANGUAGES: Russian*, other
RELIGIONS: Russian Orthodox 80%, other (inc. Jewish, Muslim) 20%
ETHNIC MIX: Russian 80%, Tatar 4%, Ukrainian 3%, other 13%
GOVERNMENT: Multiparty republic
CURRENCY: Rouble = 100 kopeks

ARCTIC OCEAN

Zemlya
ntsa-Iosifa

Novaya Zemlya

Severnaya
Zemlya

Novosibirskiye
Ostrova

Chukchi
Sea

Ostrov
Vrangel'ya

Bering
Sea

Karskoye
More

More
Laptevykh

Vostochno-
Sibirskoye
More

Poluostrov
Taymyr

Kolyma

Khrebet Kolyma

Noril'sk

Central
Siberian Plateau

Verkhoyanskiy Khrebet

Kamchatka

Magadan

Nizhnyaya Tunguska

Yakutsk

Petropavlovsck-
Kamchatskiy

Western
Siberian Plateau

Yenisey

S i b e r i a

Lena

Sea
of
Okhotsk

us-Siberian railway

Angara

Stanovoy Khrebet

Sakhalin

Tomsk

Krasnoyarsk

Bratsk

Komsomol'sk-
na-Amure

Kurile
Islands

ovosibirsk

Ozero
Baykal

Amur

Khabarovsk

Yuzhno-
Sakhalinsk

Barnaul

Novokuznetsk
Abakan

Irkutsk
Ulan-Ude

Chita

Argun

Blagoveshchensk

Sea
of
Japan

ubtsovsk

Ob

MONGOLIA

CHINA

Vladivostok

3000m/9843ft	
2000m/6562ft	
1000m/3281ft	
500m/1640ft	
200m/656ft	
Sea Level	
Below Sea Level	

0   500 km
0   500 miles

$ THE ECONOMY
Lingering inefficiencies since transition to market economy sap Russia's obvious strengths: huge natural resources, in particular oil and gas, precious metals, timber, and hydrocarbons. Enormous engineering and scientific base. Privatization, which is proceeding fast, and foreign investment could transform industry and agriculture. Many of the skills developed under communism are not relevant in a competitive economy.

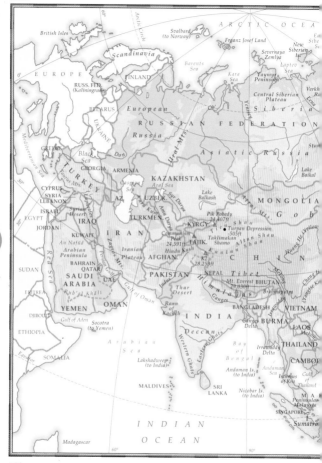

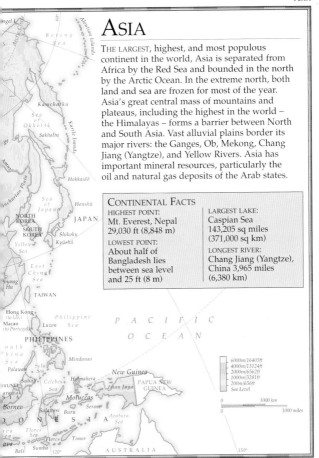

ASIA

THE LARGEST, highest, and most populous
continent in the world, Asia is separated from
Africa by the Red Sea and bounded in the north
by the Arctic Ocean. In the extreme north, both
land and sea are frozen for most of the year.
Asia's great central mass of mountains and
plateaus, including the highest in the world –
the Himalayas – forms a barrier between North
and South Asia. Vast alluvial plains border its
major rivers: the Ganges, Ob, Mekong, Chang
Jiang (Yangtze), and Yellow Rivers. Asia has
important mineral resources, particularly the
oil and natural gas deposits of the Arab states.

CONTINENTAL FACTS

HIGHEST POINT:
Mt. Everest, Nepal
29,030 ft (8,848 m)

LOWEST POINT:
About half of
Bangladesh lies
between sea level
and 25 ft (8 m)

LARGEST LAKE:
Caspian Sea
143,205 sq miles
(371,000 sq km)

LONGEST RIVER:
Chang Jiang (Yangtze),
China 3,965 miles
(6,380 km)

	6000m/16405ft
	4000m/13124ft
	2000m/6562ft
	1000m/3281ft
	200m/656ft
	Sea Level

0   1000 km

0   1000 miles

AZERBAIJAN

SITUATED ON the western coast of the Caspian Sea, Azerbaijan was the first Soviet republic to declare independence from Moscow in 1991.

GEOGRAPHY
Caucasus Mountains in west, including Naxçivan enclave in south of Armenia. Flat, low-lying terrain on the coast of the Caspian Sea.

CLIMATE
Continental with pronounced seasonal extremes. Low rainfall, with peak months during summer.

PEOPLE AND SOCIETY
Azerbaijanis now form a large majority. Thousands of Armenians, Russians, and Jews have left as a result of rising nationalism among Azerbaijanis. Racial hostility against those who remain is increasing. Influx of half a million Azerbaijani refugees fleeing war with Armenia over the disputed enclave of Nagorno Karabakh. Once-effective social security system has collapsed.

THE ECONOMY
Oil and gas have considerable potential. War is a major drain on state resources. Market reforms attract foreign interest.

◆ INSIGHT: The fire-worshipping Zoroastrian faith originated in Azerbaijan in the 6th century B.C.

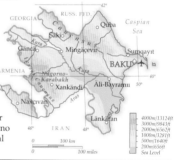

	4000m/13124ft
	3000m/9843ft
	2000m/6562ft
	1000m/3281ft
	500m/1640ft
	200m/656ft
	Sea Level

FACT FILE

OFFICIAL NAME: Republic of Azerbaijan
DATE OF FORMATION: 1991
CAPITAL: Baku
POPULATION: 7.3 million
TOTAL AREA: 33,436 sq miles (86,600 sq km)
DENSITY: 218 people per sq mile

LANGUAGES: Azerbaijani*, Russian, Armenian, other
RELIGIONS: Muslim 83%, Armenian Apostolic , Russian Orthodox 17%
ETHNIC MIX: Azerbaijani 83%, Russian 6%, Armenian 6%, other 5%
GOVERNMENT: Multiparty republic
CURRENCY: Manat = 100 gopik

ARMENIA

SMALLEST OF the former USSR's republics, Armenia lies in the Lesser Caucasus Mountains. Since 1988, it has been at war with Azerbaijan.

GEOGRAPHY
Rugged and mountainous, with expanses of semidesert and a large lake in the east, Sevana Lich.

CLIMATE
Continental climate, little rainfall in the lowlands. Winters are often bitterly cold.

PEOPLE AND SOCIETY
Strong commitment to Christianity, and to Armenian culture. Minority groups are well integrated. War with Azerbaijan over the enclave of Nagorno Karabakh has meant 100,000 Armenians living in Azerbaijan forced to return home to live in poverty. In 1988, 25,000 people died in an earthquake in the west.

◆ INSIGHT: *In the 4th century, Armenia became the first country to adopt Christianity as its state religion*

THE ECONOMY
Few natural resources, though lead, copper, and zinc are mined. Main agricultural products are wine, tobacco, olives, and rice. Well-developed machine-building and manufacturing – includes textiles and bottling of mineral water.

3000m/9843ft
2000m/6562ft
1000m/3281ft
500m/1640ft

0   50 km
0   50 miles

FACT FILE

OFFICIAL NAME: Republic of Armenia
DATE OF FORMATION: 1991
CAPITAL: Yerevan
POPULATION: 3.6 million
TOTAL AREA: 11,505 sq miles
(29,000 sq km)
DENSITY: 312 people per sq mile

LANGUAGES: Armenian*, Azerbaijani, Russian, Kurdish
RELIGIONS: Armenian Apostolic 90%, other Christian and Muslim 10%
ETHNIC MIX: Armenian 93%, Azerbaijani 3%, Russian, Kurdish 4%
GOVERNMENT: Multiparty republic
CURRENCY: Dram = 100 louma

TURKEY

LYING PARTLY in Europe, but mostly in Asia, Turkey's position gives it significant influence in the Mediterranean, Black Sea and Middle East.

GEOGRAPHY
Asian Turkey (Anatolia) is dominated by two mountain ranges, separated by a high, semidesert plateau. Coastal regions are fertile.

CLIMATE
Coast has a Mediterranean climate. Interior has cold, snowy winters and hot, dry summers.

PEOPLE AND SOCIETY
The Turks are racially diverse. Many are refugees or descendants of refugees, often from the Balkans or other territories once under Russian rule. However, the sense of national identity is strong. Since 1984, southeastern region has been the scene of a civil war waged by the Kurdish minority, demanding their rights within the country.

THE ECONOMY
Since the early 1980s, textiles, manufacturing, and construction sectors all booming. Tourism is also a major foreign currency earner.

◆ INSIGHT: Turkey had two of the seven wonders of the ancient world: the tomb of King Mausolus at Halicarnassus (now Bodrum), and the temple of Artemis at Ephesus

3000m/9843ft	
2000m/6562ft	
1000m/3281ft	
500m/1640ft	
200m/656ft	
Sea Level	

FACT FILE

OFFICIAL NAME: Republic of Turkey

DATE OF FORMATION: 1923

CAPITAL: Ankara

POPULATION: 59.6 million

TOTAL AREA: 300,950 sq miles (779,450 sq km)

DENSITY: 198 people per sq mile

LANGUAGES: Turkish*, Kurdish, Arabic, Circassian, Armenian

RELIGIONS: Muslim 99%, other 1%

ETHNIC MIX: Turkish 80%, Kurdish 17%, other 3%

GOVERNMENT: Multiparty republic

CURRENCY: Turkish lira = 100 krural

GEORGIA

LOCATED ON the eastern shore of the Black Sea, Georgia has been torn by civil war since achieving independence from the USSR in 1991.

GEOGRAPHY
Kura valley lies between Caucasus Mountains in the north and Lesser Caucasus range in south. Lowlands along the Black Sea coast.

CLIMATE
Subtropical along the coast, changing to continental extremes at high altitudes. Rainfall is moderate.

PEOPLE AND SOCIETY
Paternalistic society, with strong family, cultural, and literary traditions. Georgians are the majority group. An uneasy truce has followed 1990–1993 civil war, and the political scene remains volatile. In 1994, another civil war was fought, as ethnic Abkhazians attempted to secede from Georgia. Around one in five Georgians live in poverty, but a small, wealthy elite is found in the capital.

THE ECONOMY
Food processing and wine production are the main industries. Economy has broken down due to war and severance of links with other former Soviet republics.

◆ INSIGHT: *Western Georgia was the land of the legendary Golden Fleece of Greek mythology*

FACT FILE

OFFICIAL NAME: Republic of Georgia
DATE OF FORMATION: 1991
CAPITAL: Tbilisi
POPULATION: 5.5 million
TOTAL AREA: 26,911 sq miles
(69,700 sq km)
DENSITY: 205 people per sq mile

LANGUAGES: Georgian*, Russian, other
RELIGIONS: Georgian Orthodox 70%, Russian Orthodox 10%, other 20%
ETHNIC MIX: Georgian 69%, Armenian 9%, Russian 6%, Azerbaijani 5%, other 11%
GOVERNMENT: Republic
CURRENCY: Coupons

LEBANON

LEBANON IS dwarfed by its two powerful neighbors, Syria and Israel. The country is rebuilding after 14 years of civil war.

 GEOGRAPHY
Behind a narrow coastal plain, two parallel mountain ranges run the length of the country, separated by the fertile El Beqaa valley.

CLIMATE
Hot summers, with high humidity on the coast. Mild winters.

PEOPLE AND SOCIETY
Population is split between Christians and Muslims. Although in the minority, Christians have been the traditional rulers. In 1975, civil war broke out between the two groups. A settlement, which gave the Muslims more power, was reached in 1989. Elections in 1992 brought hope of greater stability. A huge gulf exists between the poor and a small, immensely rich elite.

◆ INSIGHT: The Cedar of Lebanon has been the nation's symbol for 2,000 years

THE ECONOMY
Infrastructure wrecked by civil war. Postwar opportunity to regain position as Arab center for banking and services. Potentially a major producer of wine and fruit.

FACT FILE

OFFICIAL NAME: Republic of Lebanon
DATE OF FORMATION: 1944
CAPITAL: Beirut
POPULATION: 2.9 million
TOTAL AREA: 4,015 sq miles (10,400 sq km)
DENSITY: 722 people per sq mile

LANGUAGES: Arabic*, French, Armenian, Assyrian
RELIGIONS: Muslim (mainly Sunni) 57%, Christian (mainly Maronite) 43%
ETHNIC MIX: Arab 93% (Lebanese 83%, Palestinian 10%), other 7%
GOVERNMENT: Multiparty republic
CURRENCY: Pound = 100 piastres

SYRIA

STRETCHING FROM the eastern Mediterranean to the River Tigris, Syria's borders were created on its independence from France in 1946.

GEOGRAPHY
Northern coastal plain is backed by a low range of hills. The River Euphrates cuts through a vast interior desert plateau.

CLIMATE
Mediterranean coastal climate. Inland areas are arid. In winter, snow is common on the mountains.

PEOPLE AND SOCIETY
Most Syrians live near the coast, where the biggest cities are sited. 90% are Muslim, including the politically dominant Alawis. In the north and west are groups of Kurds, Armenians, and Turkish-speaking peoples. Some 300,000 Palestinian refugees have also settled in Syria. They, together with the urban unemployed, make up the poorest groups in a growing gulf between rich and poor.

THE ECONOMY
High defense spending is major drain on economy. Exporter of crude oil. Agriculture is thriving: crops include cotton, wheat, olives.

◆ INSIGHT: *Aramaic, the language of the Bible, is still spoken in two villages in Syria*

FACT FILE

OFFICIAL NAME: Syrian Arab Republic
DATE OF FORMATION: 1946
CAPITAL: Damascus
POPULATION: 13.8 million
TOTAL AREA: 71,500 sq miles (185,180 sq km)

DENSITY: 193 people per sq mile
LANGUAGES: Arabic*, French, Kurdish, Armenian, Circassian, Aramaic
RELIGIONS: Sunni Muslim 74%, other Muslim 16%, Christian 10%
ETHNIC MIX: Arab 90%, other 10%
GOVERNMENT: Single-party republic
CURRENCY: Pound = 100 piastres

CYPRUS

CYPRUS LIES in the eastern Mediterranean. Since 1974, it has been partitioned between the Turkish-occupied north and the Greek south.

GEOGRAPHY
Mountains in the center-west give way to a fertile plain in the east, flanked by hills to the northeast.

CLIMATE
Mediterranean. Summers are hot and dry. Winters are mild, with snow in the mountains.

PEOPLE AND SOCIETY
Majority of the population is Greek Christian. Since the 16th century, a minority community of Turkish Muslims has lived in the north of the island. In 1974 Turkish troops occupied the north, which was proclaimed the Turkish Republic of Northern Cyprus, but is recognized only by Turkey. The north remains poor, while the south, where the tourist industry is booming, is richer.

THE ECONOMY
In the south, tourism is the key industry. Shipping and light manufacturing also important. In the north, the main exports are citrus fruits and live animals.

◆ INSIGHT: The buffer zone that divides Cyprus is manned by UN forces, at an estimated cost of $100m a year

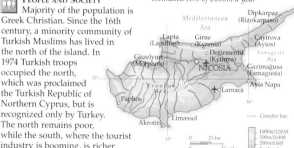

FACT FILE

OFFICIAL NAME: Republic of Cyprus
DATE OF FORMATION: 1974
CAPITAL: Nicosia
POPULATION: 700,000
TOTAL AREA: 3,572 sq miles (9,251 sq km)

DENSITY: 198 people per sq mile
LANGUAGES: Greek*, Turkish, other
RELIGIONS: Greek Orthodox 77%, Muslim 18%, other 5%
ETHNIC MIX: Greek 77%, Turkish 18%, other (mostly British) 5%
GOVERNMENT: Multiparty republic
CURRENCY: Cypriot £/Turkish lira

ISRAEL

CREATED AS a new state in 1948, on the east coast of the Mediterranean. Following wars with its Arab neighbors, it has extended its boundaries.

GEOGRAPHY
Coastal plain. Desert in the south. In the east lie the Great Rift valley and the Dead Sea – the lowest point on the Earth's surface.

CLIMATE
Summers are hot and dry. Wet season, March–November, is mild.

PEOPLE AND SOCIETY
Large numbers of Jews settled in Palestine before Israel was founded. After World War II there was a huge increase in immigration. Sephardi Jews from the Middle East and Mediterranean are now in the majority, but Ashkenazi Jews from Central Europe still dominate politics and business. Palestinians in Gaza and Jericho gained limited autonomy in 1994.

◆ INSIGHT: *All Jews worldwide have the right of Israeli citizenship*

THE ECONOMY
Huge potential of industrial, agricultural, and manufacturing products. Major exporter of mineral salts. Important banking sector.

The West Bank, Gaza Strip and Golan Heights have been occupied by Israel since the Six Day War in 1967

Palestinians gained limited home rule of the Gaza Strip and Jericho in 1994

1000m/3281ft
500m/1640ft
200m/656ft
Sea Level
Below Sea Level

FACT FILE
OFFICIAL NAME: State of Israel
DATE OF FORMATION: 1948
CAPITAL: Jerusalem
POPULATION: 5.4 million
TOTAL AREA: 7,992 sq miles (20,700 sq km)
DENSITY: 675 people per sq mile

LANGUAGES: Hebrew*, Arabic, Yiddish, German, Russian, Polish, Romanian, Persian, English
RELIGIONS: Jewish 83%, Muslim 13%, Christian 2%, other 2%
ETHNIC MIX: Jewish 83%, Arab 17%
GOVERNMENT: Multiparty republic
CURRENCY: New shekel = 100 agorat

JORDAN

THE KINGDOM of Jordan lies east of Israel. In 1993, King Hussein responded to calls for greater democracy by agreeing to multiparty elections.

GEOGRAPHY
Mostly desert plateaus, with occasional saltpans. Lowest parts lie along eastern shore of Dead Sea and East Bank of the River Jordan.

CLIMATE
Hot, dry summers. Cool, wet winters. Areas below sea level very hot in summer, and warm in winter.

PEOPLE AND SOCIETY
A predominantly Muslim country with a strong national identity, Jordan's population has Bedouin roots. There is a Christian minority and a large Palestinian population who have moved to Jordan from Israeli-occupied territory. Jordan gave up its claim to the West Bank to the PLO in 1988. The monarchy's power base lies among the rural tribes, which also provide the backbone of the military.

THE ECONOMY
Phosphates, chemicals, and fertilizers are principal exports. Skilled, educated work force.

◆ INSIGHT: King Hussein, who succeeded to the throne in 1952, is the longest-reigning Arab ruler

FACT FILE

OFFICIAL NAME: Hashemite Kingdom of Jordan

DATE OF FORMATION: 1949

CAPITAL: Amman

POPULATION: 4.4 million

TOTAL AREA: 34,440 sq miles (89,210 sq km)

DENSITY: 125 people per sq mile

LANGUAGES: Arabic*, other

RELIGIONS: Muslim 95%, Christian 5%

ETHNIC MIX: Arab 98% (Palestinian 49%), Armenian 1%, Circassian 1%

GOVERNMENT: Constitutional monarchy

CURRENCY: Dinar = 1,000 fils

SAUDI ARABIA

OCCUPYING MOST of the Arabian peninsula, the oil- and gas-rich kingdom of Saudi Arabia covers an area the size of Western Europe.

GEOGRAPHY
Mostly desert or semidesert plateau. Mountain ranges in the west run parallel to the Red Sea and drop steeply to a coastal plain.

CLIMATE
In summer, temperatures often soar above 118°F (48°C), but in winter they may fall below freezing. Rainfall is rare.

PEOPLE AND SOCIETY
Most Saudis are Sunni Muslims who follow the strictly orthodox *wahabi* interpretation of Islam and embrace *sharia* (Islamic law) in their daily lives. Women are obliged to wear the veil, cannot hold driver's licenses, and have no role in public life. The Al-Saud family have been absolutist rulers since 1932. With the support of the religious establishment, they control all political life.

THE ECONOMY
Vast oil and gas reserves. Other minerals include coal, iron, and gold. Most food is imported.

◆ *INSIGHT: Over two million Muslims a year make the* haj – *the pilgrimage to the holy city of Mecca*

FACT FILE

OFFICIAL NAME: Kingdom of Saudi Arabia

DATE OF FORMATION: 1932

CAPITAL: Riyadh

POPULATION: 16.5 million

TOTAL AREA: 829,995 sq miles (2,149,690 sq km)

DENSITY: 18 people per sq mile

LANGUAGES: Arabic*, other

RELIGIONS: Sunni Muslim 85%, Shi'a Muslim 14%, Christian 1%

ETHNIC MIX: Arab 90%, Yemeni 8%, other Arab 1%, other 1%

GOVERNMENT: Absolute monarchy

CURRENCY: Riyal = 100 malalah

YEMEN

LOCATED IN southern Arabia, Yemen was formerly two countries: a socialist regime in the south, and a republic in the north, which united in 1990.

 GEOGRAPHY
Mountainous north with fertile strip along the Red Sea. Arid desert and mountains in south and east.

 CLIMATE
Desert climate, modified by altitude, which affects temperatures by as much as 54°F (12°C).

 PEOPLE AND SOCIETY
Yemenis are almost entirely of Arab and Bedouin descent. The majority are Sunni Muslims, of the Shafi sect. In rural areas and in the north, Islamic orthodoxy is strong and most women wear the veil. Tension continues to exist between the south, led by the cosmopolitan city of 'Adan, and the more conservative north. Clashes between their former armies escalated into a brief civil war in 1994.

THE ECONOMY
Poor economic development due to political instability. Large oil and gas reserves discovered in 1984. Agriculture is the largest employer.

◆ *INSIGHT: Al Mukha (Mokha) on the Red Sea gave its name to the first coffee beans to be exported to Europe in the 17th and 18th centuries*

FACT FILE

OFFICIAL NAME: Republic of Yemen
DATE OF FORMATION: 1990
CAPITAL: Sana
POPULATION: 13 million
TOTAL AREA: 203,849 sq miles (527,970 sq km)
DENSITY: 62 people per sq mile

LANGUAGES: Arabic*, other
RELIGIONS: Sunni Muslim 55%, Shi'a Muslim 42%, other 3%
ETHNIC MIX: Arab 95%, Afro-Arab 3%, South Asian, African, European 2%
GOVERNMENT: Multiparty republic
CURRENCY: Rial (North), Dinar (South) – both are legal currency

OMAN

SITUATED ON the eastern coast of the Arabian peninsula, Oman is the least developed of the Gulf states, despite modest oil exports.

GEOGRAPHY
Mostly gravel desert, with mountains in the north and south. Some narrow fertile coastal strips.

CLIMATE
Blistering heat in the north. Summer temperatures often climb above 110°F (44°C). Southern uplands receive rains June–September.

PEOPLE AND SOCIETY
Most Omanis still live on the land, especially in the south. The majority are Ibadi Muslims who follow an appointed leader, the Imam. Ibadism is not opposed to freedom for women, and a few women hold positions of authority. Baluchis from Pakistan are the largest group of foreign workers.

◆ INSIGHT: Until the late 1980s, Oman was closed to all but business or official visitors

THE ECONOMY
Oil accounts for most export revenue. Gas is set to eventually supplant oil. Other exports include fish, dates, limes, and coconuts.

FACT FILE

OFFICIAL NAME: Sultanate of Oman
DATE OF FORMATION: 1650
CAPITAL: Muscat
POPULATION: 1.7 million
TOTAL AREA: 82,030 sq miles
(212,460 sq km)
DENSITY: 21 people per sq mile

LANGUAGES: Arabic*, Baluchi, other
RELIGIONS: Ibadi Muslim 75%, other Muslim 11%, Hindu 14%
ETHNIC MIX: Arab 75%, Baluchi 15%, other (mainly South Asian) 10%
GOVERNMENT: Monarchy with Consultative Council
CURRENCY: Rial = 1,000 baizas

UNITED ARAB EMIRATES

BORDERING THE Persian Gulf on the northern coast of the Arabian peninsula is the United Arab Emirates, a federation of seven states.

 GEOGRAPHY
Mostly flat, semiarid desert with sand dunes, saltpans, and occasional oases. Cities are watered by extensive irrigation systems.

 CLIMATE
Summers are humid, despite minimal rainfall. Sand-laden *shamal* winds blow in winter and spring.

PEOPLE AND SOCIETY
People are mostly Sunni Muslims of Bedouin descent, and largely city-dwellers. In theory, women enjoy equal rights with men. Poverty is rare. Emirians make up only one fifth of the population. They are out-numbered by immigrants who arrived during 1970s oil boom. Western expatriates are permitted a virtually unrestricted lifestyle. Islamic fundamentalism, however, is a growing force among the young.

THE ECONOMY
Major exporter of oil and natural gas. Fish and shellfish are caught in the Persian Gulf, as well as oysters for their pearls. Most food and raw materials are imported.

◆ *INSIGHT: At present levels of production, the country's crude oil reserves should last for over 100 years*

FACT FILE

OFFICIAL NAME: United Arab Emirates
DATE OF FORMATION: 1971
CAPITAL: Abu Dhabi
POPULATION: 1.7 million
TOTAL AREA: 32,278 sq miles (83,600 sq km)
DENSITY: 52 people per sq mile

LANGUAGES: Arabic*, Farsi (Persian), Urdu, Hindi, English
RELIGIONS: Sunni Muslim 77%, Shi'a Muslim 19% other 4%
ETHNIC MIX: South Asian 50%, Emirian 19%, other Arab 23%, other 8%
GOVERNMENT: Federation of monarchs
CURRENCY: Dirham = 100 fils

QATAR

PROJECTING NORTH from the Arabian peninsula into the Persian Gulf, Qatar's reserves of oil and gas make it one of the region's wealthiest states.

GEOGRAPHY
Flat, semiarid desert with sand dunes and saltpans. Vegetation limited to small patches of scrub.

CLIMATE
Hot and humid. Summer temperatures soar to over 104°F (40°C). Rainfall is rare.

PEOPLE AND SOCIETY
Only one in five Qataris is native-born. Most of the population are guest workers from the Indian subcontinent, Iran, and North Africa. Qataris were once nomadic Bedouins, but since advent of oil wealth, have become city-dwellers. As a result, the north is dotted with abandoned villages. Political and religious life is dominated by the ruling Al-Thani family.

◆ INSIGHT: *There are over 700 mosques in the capital, Doha*

THE ECONOMY
Steady supply of crude oil and huge gas reserves, plus related industries. Economy is heavily dependent on foreign work force. All raw materials and most foods, except vegetables, are imported.

FACT FILE
OFFICIAL NAME: State of Qatar
DATE OF FORMATION: 1971
CAPITAL: Doha
POPULATION: 500,000
TOTAL AREA: 4,247 sq miles (11,000 sq km)
DENSITY: 117 people per sq mile

LANGUAGES: Arabic*, Farsi (Persian), Urdu, Hindi, English
RELIGIONS: Sunni Muslim 86%, Hindu 10%, Christian 4%
ETHNIC MIX: Arab 40%, South Asian 35%, Persian 12%, other 13%
GOVERNMENT: Absolute monarchy
CURRENCY: Riyal = 100 dirhams

BAHRAIN

BAHRAIN IS an archipelago of 33 islands between the Qatar peninsula and the Saudi Arabian mainland. Only three islands are inhabited.

GEOGRAPHY
All islands are low-lying. The largest, Bahrain Island, is mainly sandy plains and salt marshes.

CLIMATE
Summers are hot and humid. Winters are mild. Low rainfall.

PEOPLE AND SOCIETY
Largely Muslim population is divided between Shi'a majority and Sunni minority. Tensions between the two groups. Ruling Sunni class hold the best jobs in bureaucracy and business. Shi'ites tend to do menial work. Al-Khalifa family has ruled since 1783. Regime is autocratic and political dissent is not tolerated. Bahrain is the most liberal of the Gulf States. Women have access to education and jobs.

◆ INSIGHT: Bahrain was the first Gulf emirate to export oil, in the 1930s

THE ECONOMY
Main exports are refined petroleum and aluminum products. As oil reserves run out, gas is of increasing importance. Bahrain is also the Arab world's major offshore banking center.

FACT FILE

OFFICIAL NAME: State of Bahrain

DATE OF FORMATION: 1971

CAPITAL: Manama

POPULATION: 500,000

TOTAL AREA: 263 sq miles (680 sq km)

DENSITY: 1,911 people per sq mile

LANGUAGES: Arabic*, English, Urdu

RELIGIONS: Muslim (Shi'a majority) 85%, Christian 7%, other 8%

ETHNIC MIX: Arab 73%, South Asian 14%, Persian 8%, other 5%

GOVERNMENT: Absolute monarchy (emirate)

CURRENCY: Dinar = 1,000 fils

KUWAIT

KUWAIT LIES on the north of the Persian Gulf. The state was a British protectorate from 1914 until 1961, when full independence was granted.

 GEOGRAPHY
Low-lying desert. Lowest land in the north. Cultivation is only possible along the coast.

CLIMATE
Summers are very hot and dry. Winters are cooler, with some rain and occasional frost.

PEOPLE AND SOCIETY
Oil-rich monarchy, ruled by the Al-Sabah family. Oil wealth has attracted workers from India, Pakistan, and other Arab states. In 1990, Iraq invaded Kuwait, claiming it as a province. A US-led alliance, backed by the UN, ousted Iraqi forces following a short war in 1991. Many foreign workers expelled after the war, in attempt to ensure Kuwaiti majority.

THE ECONOMY
Oil and gas production has been restored to pre-invasion levels. Skilled labor, raw materials, and food have to be imported. Vulnerability to Iraqi attack deters Western industrial investment.

◆ INSIGHT: *During the Gulf War, 800 of Kuwait's 950 oil wells were damaged*

FACT FILE

OFFICIAL NAME: State of Kuwait

DATE OF FORMATION: 1961

CAPITAL: Kuwait City

POPULATION: 1.8 million

TOTAL AREA: 6,880 sq miles (17,820 sq km)

DENSITY: 291 people per sq mile

LANGUAGES: Arabic*, English, other

RELIGIONS: Muslim 92%, Christian 6%, other 2%

ETHNIC MIX: Arab 85%, South Asian 9%, Persian 4%, other 2%

GOVERNMENT: Constitutional monarchy

CURRENCY: Dinar = 1,000 fils

IRAQ

IRAQ IS situated in the central Middle East. Since the removal of the monarchy in 1958, it has experienced considerable political turmoil.

GEOGRAPHY
Mainly desert. Rivers Tigris and Euphrates water fertile regions and create southern marshland. Mountains along northeast border.

CLIMATE
South has hot, dry summers and mild winters. North has dry summers, but winters can be harsh in the mountains. Rainfall is low.

PEOPLE AND SOCIETY
Population mainly Arab and Kurdish. Small minorities of Turks and Persians. After coming to power in 1979, President Saddam Hussein led the country into an inconclusive war with Iran (1980–1988). In 1990, invasion of Kuwait precipitated the Gulf War against UN forces. In recent years, drainage schemes in the southern marshlands have threatened the ancient and unique lifestyle of the Marsh Arabs.

THE ECONOMY
Gulf War and resulting UN sanctions had a devastating effect. Iraq is unable to sell its oil on the international market.

◆ INSIGHT: As Mesopotamia, Iraq was the site where the Sumerians established the world's first civilization c. 4,000 B.C.

FACT FILE

OFFICIAL NAME: Republic of Iraq
DATE OF FORMATION: 1932
CAPITAL: Baghdad
POPULATION: 19.9 million
TOTAL AREA: 169,235 sq miles
(438,320 sq km)
DENSITY: 114 people per sq mile

LANGUAGES: Arabic*, Kurdish, Turkish, Farsi (Persian)
RELIGIONS: Shi'a Muslim 63%, Sunni Muslim 34%, other 3%
ETHNIC MIX: Arab 79%, Kurdish 16%, Persian 3%, Turkish 2%
GOVERNMENT: Single-party republic
CURRENCY: Dinar = 1,000 fils

IRAN

Since the 1979 revolution led by Ayatollah Khomeini, the Middle Eastern country of Iran has become the world's largest theocracy.

GEOGRAPHY
High desert plateau with large saltpans in the east. West and north are mountainous. Fertile coastal land borders Caspian Sea.

CLIMATE
Mostly desert climate. Hot summers, and bitterly cold winters. Area around the Caspian Sea is more temperate.

PEOPLE AND SOCIETY
Many ethnic groups, including Persians, Azerbaijanis, and Kurds. Large number of refugees, mainly from Afghanistan. Since 1979 Islamic revolution, political life has been dominated by militant Islamic idealism. Mullahs' belief that adherence to religious values is more important than economic welfare has resulted in declining living standards. The role of women in public life is restricted.

THE ECONOMY
One of the world's biggest oil producers. Government restricts contact with the West, blocking acquisition of vital technology. High unemployment and inflation.

◆ INSIGHT: *In Iran, a total of 109 offenses carry the death penalty*

FACT FILE

OFFICIAL NAME: Islamic Republic of Iran
DATE OF FORMATION: 1906
CAPITAL: Tehran
POPULATION: 63.2 million
TOTAL AREA: 636,293 sq miles (1,648,000 sq km)

DENSITY: 99 people per sq mile
LANGUAGES: Farsi (Persian)*, other
RELIGIONS: Shi'a Muslim 95%, Sunni Muslim 4%, other 1%
ETHNIC MIX: Persian 52%, Azerbaijani 24%, Kurdish 9%, other 15%
GOVERNMENT: Islamic republic
CURRENCY: Rial = 100 dinars

TURKMENISTAN

STRETCHING FROM the Caspian Sea into the deserts of Central Asia, the ex-Soviet state of Turkmenistan has adjusted better than most to independence.

GEOGRAPHY
Low Karakumy desert covers 80% of the country. Mountains on southern border with Iran. Fertile Amu Darya valley in north.

CLIMATE
Arid desert climate with extreme summer heat, but sub-freezing winter temperatures.

PEOPLE AND SOCIETY
Before Czarist Russia annexed the country in 1884, the Turkmen were a largely nomadic tribal people. Today, the tribal unit remains strong, with most of the population clustered around desert oases. Generally peaceful relations between Turkmen and Uzbek and Russian minorities. Resurgence of Islam fosters ties with its Muslim neighbors to the south.

THE ECONOMY
Abundant reserves of natural gas. Least industrialized of the ex-Soviet states. Large cotton crop, but most food has to be imported.

◆ INSIGHT: *Ashgabat is a breeding center for the Akhal-Teke, a prized race horse able to maintain its speed in the desert*

FACT FILE	
OFFICIAL NAME: Republic of Turkmenistan	DENSITY: 21 people per sq mile
DATE OF FORMATION: 1991	LANGUAGES: Turkmen*, Uzbek, other
CAPITAL: Ashgabat	RELIGIONS: Muslim 85%, Eastern Orthodox 10%, other 5%
POPULATION: 4 million	ETHNIC MIX: Turkmen 72%, Russian 9%, Uzbek 9%, other 10%
TOTAL AREA: 188,455 sq miles (488,100 sq km)	GOVERNMENT: Single-party republic
	CURRENCY: Manat = 100 tenge

UZBEKISTAN

SHARING THE Aral Sea coastline with its northern neighbor, Kazakhstan, Uzbekistan lies on the ancient Silk Road between Asia and Europe.

GEOGRAPHY
Arid and semi-arid plains in much of the west. Fertile, irrigated eastern farmland below peaks of the western Pamirs.

CLIMATE
Harsh continental climate. Summers can be extremely hot and dry, winters are cold.

PEOPLE AND SOCIETY
Complex ethnic make-up, with potential for racial and regional conflict. Ex-communists are in firm control, but traditional social patterns based on family, religion, clan, and region have reemerged. Population is concentrated in the fertile east. High birth rates, continued low status of women. Constitutional measures aim to control influence of Islam.

THE ECONOMY
Strong agricultural sector, led by cotton production. Large unexploited deposits of oil and natural gas, gold, and uranium. Very limited economic reform.

◆ INSIGHT: *The Aral Sea has shrunk to half of the area it covered in 1960, due to diversion of rivers for irrigation*

FACT FILE

OFFICIAL NAME: Republic of Uzbekistan
DATE OF FORMATION: 1991
CAPITAL: Tashkent
POPULATION: 21.9 million
TOTAL AREA: 439,733 sq miles (1,138,910 sq km)

DENSITY: 122 people per sq mile
LANGUAGES: Uzbek*, Russian, other
RELIGIONS: Muslim 88%, other (mostly Eastern Orthodox) 12%
ETHNIC MIX: Uzbek 71%, Russian 8%, Tajik 5%, Kazakh 4%, other 12%
GOVERNMENT: Single-party republic
CURRENCY: Sum = 100 teen

KAZAKHSTAN

LARGEST OF the former Soviet republics, mineral-rich Kazakhstan has the potential to become the major Central Asian economic power.

GEOGRAPHY
Mainly steppe. Volga delta and Caspian Sea in the west. Central plateau. Mountains in the east. Semidesert in the south.

CLIMATE
Dry continental. Hottest summers in desert south, coldest winters in northern steppes.

PEOPLE AND SOCIETY
Kazakhs only just outnumber Russians in a multiethnic society. Stable relations with Russia, plus increased international profile, preserve relative harmony. Few Kazakhs maintain a nomadic lifestyle, but Islam and loyalty to the three Hordes (clan federations) remain strong. Wealth is concentrated among former communists in the capital.

THE ECONOMY
Vast mineral resources, notably gas, oil, coal, uranium, and gold. Increasing foreign investment, but living standards have fallen with market reforms to date.

◆ INSIGHT: Russia's space program was based at Baykonur, in the south

FACT FILE
OFFICIAL NAME: Republic of Kazakhstan
DATE OF FORMATION: 1991
CAPITAL: Alma-Ata
POPULATION: 17.2 million
TOTAL AREA: 1,049,150 sq miles (2,717,300 sq km)

DENSITY: 16 people per sq mile
LANGUAGES: Kazakh*, Russian, other
RELIGIONS: Muslim 47%, other 53% (mostly Russian Orthodox, Lutheran)
ETHNIC MIX: Kazakh 40%, Russian 38%, Ukrainian 6%, other 16%
GOVERNMENT: Multiparty republic
CURRENCY: Tenge = 100 tein

MONGOLIA

LYING BETWEEN Russia and China, Mongolia is a vast and isolated country with a tiny population. It is the world's largest landlocked nation.

GEOGRAPHY
High steppe plateau, with mountains in the north. Lakes in the north and west. Desert region of the Gobi dominates the south.

CLIMATE
Continental. Mild summers, and long, dry, very cold winters, with heavy snowfall. Temperatures can drop to −30°C (−22°F).

PEOPLE AND SOCIETY
Mongolia was unified by Genghis Khan in 1206 and was later absorbed into Manchu China. It became a communist People's Republic in 1924, and after 66 years of Soviet-style communist rule, introduced democracy in 1990. Most Mongolians still follow a traditional nomadic way of life, living in circular felt tents called *gers*. Others live on state-run farms.

THE ECONOMY
Rich in oil, coal, copper, and other minerals, which were barely exploited under communism. In 1990s, some shift in agriculture away from traditional herding and toward a market economy.

◆ *INSIGHT: Horse-racing, wrestling, and archery are the national sports. During the* Nadam *festival each July, competitions are held all over Mongolia*

FACT FILE

OFFICIAL NAME: Mongolia
DATE OF FORMATION: 1921
CAPITAL: Ulan Bator
POPULATION: 2.4 million
TOTAL AREA: 604,247 sq miles
(1,565,000 sq km)
DENSITY: 3.6 people per sq mile

LANGUAGES: Khalkha Mongol*, Turkic, Russian, Chinese
RELIGIONS: Predominantly Tibetan Buddhist, with a Muslim minority
ETHNIC MIX: Khalkha Mongol 90%, Kazakh 4%, Chinese 2%, other 4%
GOVERNMENT: Multiparty republic
CURRENCY: Tughrik = 100 möngös

KYRGYZSTAN

A MOUNTAINOUS, landlocked state in Central Asia. The most rural of the ex-Soviet republics, it only gradually developed its own cultural nationalism.

GEOGRAPHY
Mountainous spurs of Tien Shan range have glaciers, alpine meadows, forests, and narrow valleys. Semi-desert in the west.

CLIMATE
Varies from permanent snow and cold deserts at altitude to hot deserts in low regions.

PEOPLE AND SOCIETY
Ethnic Kyrgyz majority status dates only from the late 1980s, and is due to their higher birth rate. Considerable tension between Kyrgyz and other groups, particularly Uzbeks. Large Russian community no longer wields power, but is seen as necessary for transfer of skills. Concerns over rising crime rate and opium poppy cultivation accompany political reforms.

THE ECONOMY
Still dominated by the state and tradition of collective farming. Small quantities of commercially exploitable coal, oil, and gas. Great hydroelectric power potential.

◆ INSIGHT: Kyrgyz folklore is based around the 1,000-year-old epic poem, Manas, which takes a week to recite

4000m/13124ft	
3000m/9843ft	
2000m/6562ft	
1000m/3281ft	
500m/1640ft	

0   100 km
0   100 miles

FACT FILE

OFFICIAL NAME: Kyrgyz Republic
DATE OF FORMATION: 1991
CAPITAL: Bishkek
POPULATION: 4.6 million
TOTAL AREA: 76,640 sq miles
(198,500 sq km)
DENSITY: 60 people per sq mile

LANGUAGES: Kyrgyz*, Russian, Uzbek
RELIGIONS: Muslim 65%, other
(mostly Russian Orthodox) 35%
ETHNIC MIX: Kyrgyz 52%, Russian
21%, Uzbek 13%, other (mostly
Kazakh and Tajik) 14%
GOVERNMENT: Mutiparty republic
CURRENCY: Som = 100 teen

TAJIKISTAN

LIES LANDLOCKED on the western slopes of the Pamirs in Central Asia. The Tajiks' language and traditions are similiar to those of Iran.

GEOGRAPHY
Mainly mountainous: bare slopes of Pamir ranges cover most of the country. Small but fertile Fergana Valley in northwest.

CLIMATE
Continental extremes in valleys. Bitterly cold winters in mountains. Low rainfall.

PEOPLE AND SOCIETY
Conflict between Tajiks, a Persian people, and minority Uzbeks (of Turkic origin), coupled with civil war between supporters of the government and Tajik Islamic rebels. Despite a ceasefire in late 1994, clashes continued in 1995. Already low living standards have been worsened by the conflict. Many Russians have left to escape discrimination.

THE ECONOMY
Formal economy crippled by conflict. All sectors in decline; barter economy is widespread. Uranium potential and hydro-electric schemes depend on peace.

◆ INSIGHT: *Carpet-making, an ancient tradition learned from Persia, was a major source of revenue before the war*

FACT FILE	
OFFICIAL NAME: Republic of Tajikistan	DENSITY: 101 people per sq mile
DATE OF FORMATION: 1991	LANGUAGES: Tajik*, Uzbek, Russian
CAPITAL: Dushanbe	RELIGIONS: Sunni Muslim 85%, Shi'a Muslim 5%, other 10%
POPULATION: 5.7 million	ETHNIC MIX: Tajik 62%, Uzbek 24%, Russian 4%, Tartar 2%, other 8%
TOTAL AREA: 55,251 sq miles (143,100 sq km)	GOVERNMENT: Single-party republic
	CURRENCY: Tajik rouble = 100 kopeks

AFGHANISTAN

LANDLOCKED IN southwestern Asia, about three-quarters of Afghanistan is inaccessible. Civil war means the country effectively has no government.

GEOGRAPHY
Predominantly mountainous. Highest range is the Hindu Kush. Mountains are bordered by fertile plains. Desert plateau in the south.

CLIMATE
Harsh continental. Hot, dry summers. Cold winters with heavy snow, especially in Hindu Kush.

PEOPLE AND SOCIETY
In 1979, Soviet forces invaded to support communist government against Islamic guerrillas. Last Soviet troops pulled out in 1989. Civil war continues between Pashtuns, the country's traditional rulers, and minority groups of Tajiks, Hazaras, and Uzbeks. Health and education systems have collapsed. Many Afghans are nomadic sheep farmers and most live in extreme poverty.

THE ECONOMY
Economy has collapsed. The largest sector, agriculture, has been damaged. Illicit opium trade is the main currency earner.

◆ INSIGHT: *The UN estimates that it will take 100 years to remove the ten million landmines laid in the country*

FACT FILE

OFFICIAL NAME: Islamic State of Afghanistan
DATE OF FORMATION: 1919
CAPITAL: Kābul
POPULATION: 20.5 million
TOTAL AREA: 251,770 sq miles (652,090 sq km)

DENSITY: 75 people per sq mile
LANGUAGES: Persian*, Pashtu*, other
RELIGIONS: Sunni Muslim 84%, Shi'a Muslim 15%, other 1%
ETHNIC MIX: Pashtun 38%, Tajik 25%, Hazara 19%, Uzbek 6%, other 12%
GOVERNMENT: *Mujahideen* coalition
CURRENCY: Afghani = 100 puls

PAKISTAN

ONCE A part of British India, Pakistan was created in 1947 as an independent Muslim state. Today, it is divided into four provinces.

GEOGRAPHY
East and south is great flood plain drained by River Indus. Hindu Kush range in north. West is semi-desert plateau and mountains.

CLIMATE
Temperatures can soar to 122°F (50°C) in south and west, and fall to −4°F (−20°C) in the Hindu Kush.

PEOPLE AND SOCIETY
Majority Punjabis control bureaucracy and the army. Many tensions with minority groups. Vast gap between rich and poor. Bonded laborers, often recent converts to Islam, or Christians, form the underclass. Strong family ties, reflected in dynastic and nepotistic political system.

◆ INSIGHT: In 1988, Pakistan elected the first female prime minister in the Muslim world

THE ECONOMY
Leading producer of cotton and rice, but unpredictable weather conditions often affect the crop. Oil, gas reserves. Inefficient, haphazard government economic policies.

5000m/16405ft	
4000m/13124ft	
3000m/9843ft	
2000m/6562ft	
1000m/3281ft	
500m/1640ft	
200m/656ft	
Sea Level	

FACT FILE

OFFICIAL NAME: Islamic Republic of Pakistan
DATE OF FORMATION: 1947
CAPITAL: Islāmābād
POPULATION: 128.1 million
TOTAL AREA: 307,374 sq miles (796,100 sq km)

DENSITY: 421 people per sq mile
LANGUAGES: Urdu*, Punjabi, other
RELIGIONS: Sunni Muslim 77%, Shi'a Muslim 20%, Hindu 2%, Christian 1%
ETHNIC MIX: Punjabi 56%, Sindhi 13%, Pashtun 8%, other 23%
GOVERNMENT: Multiparty republic
CURRENCY: Rupee = 100 paisa

NEPAL

NEPAL LIES between India and China, on the shoulder of the southern Himalayan mountains. It is one of the world's poorest countries.

GEOGRAPHY
Mainly mountainous. Includes some of the highest mountains in the world, such as Mt. Everest. Flat, fertile river plains in the south.

CLIMATE
July–October warm monsoon. Rest of year dry, sunny, mild. Valley temperatures in Himalayas may average 14°F (−10°C).

PEOPLE AND SOCIETY
Few ethnic tensions, despite the variety of ethnic groups, including the Sherpas in the north, Terai peoples in the south, and the Newars, found mostly in the Kathmandu valley. Women's subordinate position enshrined in law. Hindu women are the most restricted. In 1991, first democratic elections for over 30 years ended period of absolute rule by the king.

THE ECONOMY
90% of the people work on the land. Crops include rice, corn and millet. Dependent on foreign aid. Tourism is growing. Great potential for hydroelectric power.

◆ INSIGHT: Southern Nepal was the birthplace of Buddha (Prince Siddhartha Gautama) in 563 B.C

FACT FILE

OFFICIAL NAME: Kingdom of Nepal
DATE OF FORMATION: 1769
CAPITAL: Kathmandu
POPULATION: 21.1 million
TOTAL AREA: 54,363 sq miles (140,800 sq km)
DENSITY: 388 people per sq mile

LANGUAGES: Nepali*, Maithilli, other
RELIGIONS: Hindu 90%, Buddhist 5%, Muslim 3%, other 2%
ETHNIC MIX: Nepalese 58%, Bihari 19%, Tamang 6%, other 17%
GOVERNMENT: Constitutional monarchy
CURRENCY: Rupee = 100 paisa

BHUTAN

PERCHED IN the eastern Himalayas between India and China, the landlocked kingdom of Bhutan is largely closed to the outside world.

GEOGRAPHY
Low, tropical southern strip rising through fertile central valleys to high Himalayas in the north. Two thirds of the land is forested.

CLIMATE
South is tropical, north is alpine, cold, and harsh. Central valleys warmer in east than west.

PEOPLE AND SOCIETY
The king is absolute monarch, head of both state and government. Most people originate from Tibet, and are devout Buddhists. 25% are Hindu Nepalese, who settled in the south. Bhutan has 20 languages. In 1988, Dzongkha (a Tibetan dialect) was made the official language and Nepali was banned. Many southerners deported as illegal immigrants, creating fierce ethnic tensions.

THE ECONOMY
Reliant upon aid from, and trade with, India. 80% of people farm their own plots of land and herd cattle and yaks. Development of cash crops for Asian markets.

◆INSIGHT: *TV is banned on the grounds that it might dilute Bhutanese values*

5000m/16405ft
4000m/13124ft
3000m/9843ft
2000m/6562ft
1000m/3281ft
500m/1640ft
200m/656ft
Sea Level

0   50 km
0   50 miles

CHINA

Himalayas

THIMPHU
Paro   Wangdi
International   Phodrang   Tashigang
Chhukha   Shemgang

Phuntsholing   Samdrup
                       Jonkhar
INDIA

FACT FILE

OFFICIAL NAME: Kingdom of Bhutan
DATE OF FORMATION: 1865
CAPITAL: Thimphu
POPULATION: 1.7 million
TOTAL AREA: 18,147 sq miles
(47,000 sq km)
DENSITY: 93 people per sq mile

LANGUAGES: Dzongkha*, Nepali, other
RELIGIONS: Mahayana Buddhist 70%,
Hindu 24%, Muslim 5%, other 1%
ETHNIC MIX: Bhutia 61%, Gurung
15%, Assamese 13%, other 11%
GOVERNMENT: Constitutional
monarchy
CURRENCY: Ngultrum = 100 chetrum

INDIA

SEPARATED FROM the rest of Asia by the Himalayan mountain range, India forms a subcontinent. It is the world's second most populous country.

GEOGRAPHY
Three main regions: Himalayan mountains; northern plain between Himalayas and Vindhya Mountains; southern Deccan plateau. The Ghats are smaller mountain ranges on the east and west coasts.

CLIMATE
Varies greatly according to latitude, altitude, and season. Most of India has three seasons: hot, wet, and cool. In summer, the north is usually hotter than the south, with temperatures often over 104°F (40°C).

PEOPLE AND SOCIETY
Cultural and religious pressures encourage large families. Today, nationwide awareness campaigns aim to promote the idea of smaller families. Most Indians are Hindu. Each Hindu is born into one of thousands of castes and subcastes, which determine their future status and occupation. Middle class enjoys a very comfortable lifestyle, but at least 30% of Indians live in extreme poverty. In Bombay alone, over 100,000 people live on the streets.

◆ INSIGHT *India's national animal, the tiger, was chosen by the Mohenjo-Daro civilization as its emblem, 4,000 years ago*

5000m/16405ft
4000m/13124ft
3000m/9843ft
2000m/6562ft
1000m/3281ft
500m/1640ft
200m/656ft
Sea Level

0   200 km
0   200 miles

PAKISTAN

Rann of Kachch

Gulf of Kachch

Ahmadābād

Jāmnagar   Rājkot

Gulf of Khambhāt

Arabian Sea

30°
70°
25°
20°
15°
10°

FACT FILE

OFFICIAL NAME: Republic of India
DATE OF FORMATION: 1947
CAPITAL: New Dehli
POPULATION: 896.6 million
TOTAL AREA: 1,269,338 sq miles (3,287,590 sq km)
DENSITY: 770 people per sq mile

LANGUAGES: Hindi*, English*, other
RELIGIONS: Hindu 83%, Muslim 11%, Christian 2%, Sikh 2%, other 2%
ETHNIC MIX: Indo-Aryan 72%, Dravidian 25%, Mongoloid and other 3%
GOVERNMENT: Multiparty republic
CURRENCY: Rupee = 100 paisa

THE ECONOMY

Undergoing radical changes from protectionist mixed economy to free market. Increasing foreign investment. New high-tech industries. Principal exports are clothing, jewelry, gems, and engineering products.

'line of control'
is agreed between
ndia and Pakistan
in 1972

*Aksai Chin -
occupied by China,
claimed by India*

*Demchok/Dêmqog -
claimed by
India and China*

Srinagar

Indus

Jammu &
Kashmir

aritsar,

Jalandhar

CHINA

udhiana

Chandigarh

H i m a l a y a s

Meerut

W DELHI

Delhi

Bareilly

NEPAL

Shiliguri

BHUTAN

Brahmaputra

MYANMAR

Agra

Lucknow

A s s a m

dhpur

Jaipur

Kanpur

Ganges

Patna

BANGLADESH

Imphal

Kota

Gwalior

Varanasi

Ganges

Dhanbad

Bhopal

Jabalpur

Ranchi

Haora

Calcutta

Indore

Narmada

Jamshedpur

*Mouths
of the Ganges*

adodara

Nagpur

Cuttack

rat

Mahanadi

Kalyan

Nanded

Godavari

ombay

D e c c a n

G
h
a
t
s

Pune

Solapur

Visakhapatnam

Krishna

Hyderabad

B a y
o f
B e n g a l

Hubli

anaji

Andaman Islands

North
Andaman

Eastern Ghats

Middle
Andaman

Madras

South
Andaman

Port Blair

Bangalore

I N D I A N

Little
Andaman

Mysore

O C E A N

Coimbatore

ikshadweep
accadive Is.)

Cochin

Madurai

Nicobar Islands

Great
Nicobar

75°

80°

85°

90°

95°

MALDIVES

THE MALDIVES is an archipelago of 1,190 small coral islands set in the Indian Ocean, southwest of Sri Lanka. Only 202 islands are inhabited.

GEOGRAPHY
Low-lying islands and coral atolls. The larger ones are covered in lush, tropical vegetation.

CLIMATE
Tropical. Rain in all months, but heaviest June–November, during monsoon. Violent storms occasionally hit northern islands.

PEOPLE AND SOCIETY
Maldivians are descended from Sinhalese, Dravidian, Arab, and black ancestors. About 25% of the population, who are all Sunni Muslim, live on Male'. Tourism has grown in recent years, but resort islands are separate from settler islands. Politics is restricted to a small group of influential families, and is based around family and clan loyalties rather than formal parties. New young elite is pressing for a more liberal political system.

THE ECONOMY
Too dependent on fluctuating tourist industry, which is the economic mainstay. Fish, especially bonito and tuna, are the leading exports.

◆ INSIGHT: Rising sea levels, brought about by global warming and climatic changes, are threatening to submerge the islands

Ihavandippolhu Atoll

Faadhippolhu Atoll

Horsburgh Atoll

Male' Atoll

Ari Atoll

MALE'

Felidhu Atoll

Mulaku Atoll

Kolhumadulu Atoll

Hadhdhunmathi Atoll

One and Half Degree Channel

North Huvadhu Atoll

South Huvadhu Atoll

INDIAN OCEAN

Equator

Addu Atoll

Gan

▢ 200m/656ft
Sea Level

0 100 km
0 100 miles

FACT FILE

OFFICIAL NAME: Republic of Maldives
DATE OF FORMATION: 1965
CAPITAL: Male'
POPULATION: 200,000
TOTAL AREA: 116 sq miles (300 sq km)

DENSITY: 1,734 people per sq mile
LANGUAGES: Dhivehi (Maldivian)*, Sinhala, Tamil
RELIGIONS: Sunni Muslim 100%
ETHNIC MIX: Maldivian 99%, Sinhalese and other South Asian 1%
GOVERNMENT: Republic
CURRENCY: Rufiyaa = 100 laari

SRI LANKA

India

SRILANKA

SEPARATED FROM India by the narrow Palk Strait, Sri Lanka comprises one large island and several coral islets to the northwest.

GEOGRAPHY
Main island is dominated by rugged central highlands. Fertile northern plains dissected by rivers. Much of the land is tropical jungle.

CLIMATE
Tropical, with breezes on the coast and cooler air in highlands. Northeast is driest and hottest.

PEOPLE AND SOCIETY
Majority Sinhalese are mostly Buddhist; minority Tamils are mostly Muslim or Hindu. Since independence from Britain in 1948, Tamils have felt sidelined, and support for secession has grown. Long-standing tensions between the groups erupted into civil war in 1983. Tamils demand an independent state in the north and east.

THE ECONOMY
World's largest tea exporter. Manufacturing now accounts for 60% of export earnings. Civil war is a drain on government funds and deters investors and tourists.

2000m/6562ft
1000m/3281ft
500m/1640ft
200m/656ft
Sea Level

0   50 km
0   50 miles

Palk Strait

Bay of Bengal

Jaffna

Gulf of Mannar

Trincomalee

Anuradhapura

Batticaloa

Negombo   Kandy

COLOMBO   INDIAN OCEAN

Moratuwa   Sri Jayawardenapura
Ratnapura

Galle

Matara

◆ INSIGHT: *Sri Lanka elected the world's first woman prime minister in 1960*

FACT FILE

OFFICIAL NAME: Democratic Socialist Republic of Sri Lanka
DATE OF FORMATION: 1948
CAPITAL: Colombo
POPULATION: 17.9 million
TOTAL AREA: 25,332 sq miles (65,610 sq km)

DENSITY: 710 people per sq mile
LANGUAGES: Sinhala*, Tamil, English
RELIGIONS: Buddhist 70%, Hindu 15%, Christian 8%, Muslim 7%
ETHNIC MIX: Sinhalese 74%, Tamil 18%, Sri Lankan Moor 7%, other 1%
GOVERNMENT: Multiparty republic
CURRENCY: Rupee = 100 cents

BANGLADESH

BANGLADESH LIES at the north of the Bay of Bengal. It seceded from Pakistan in 1971 and, after much political instability, returned to democracy in 1991.

GEOGRAPHY
Mostly flat alluvial plains and deltas of the Brahmaputra and Ganges rivers. Southeast coasts are fringed with mangrove forests.

CLIMATE
Hot and humid. During the monsoon, water level can rise 20 feet (six meters) above sea level, flooding two thirds of the country.

PEOPLE AND SOCIETY
Bangladesh has suffered from a cycle of floods, cyclones, famine, political corruption, and military coups. Although 55% of people still live below the poverty line, living standards have improved in past decade. By providing independent income, textile trade is a factor in growing emancipation of women.

◆ INSIGHT: Since 1960, there have been six cyclones with winds of over 100 mph

THE ECONOMY
Heavily dependent on foreign aid. Agriculture is vulnerable to unpredictable climate. Bangladesh accounts for 80% of world jute fiber exports. Expanding textile industry.

FACT FILE
OFFICIAL NAME: People's Republic of Bangladesh
DATE OF FORMATION: 1971
CAPITAL: Dhaka
POPULATION: 122.2 million
TOTAL AREA: 55,598 sq miles (143,998 sq km)

DENSITY: 2,317 people per sq mile
LANGUAGES: Bangla*, Urdu, Chakma, Marma (Margh), other
RELIGIONS: Muslim 83%, Hindu 16%, other (Buddhist, Christian) 1%
ETHNIC MIX: Bengali 98%, other 2%
GOVERNMENT: Multiparty republic
CURRENCY: Taka = 100 paisa

BURMA (MYANMAR)

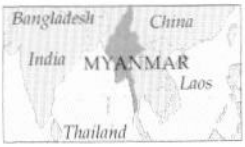
Bangladesh
China
India
MYANMAR
Laos
Thailand

BURMA FORMS the eastern shores of the Bay of Bengal and the Andaman Sea in Southeast Asia. It gained independence from Britain in 1948.

GEOGRAPHY

Fertile Irrawaddy basin in the center. Mountains to the west, Shan plateau to the east. Tropical rain forest covers much of the land.

CLIMATE

Tropical. Hot summers, with high humidity, and warm winters.

PEOPLE AND SOCIETY

Under socialist military rule since 1962, Burma has suffered widespread political repression and ethnic conflict. Minority groups maintain low-level guerrilla activity against the state. 1990 election was won by opposition democratic party. Its leader, Aung San Suu Kyi, was placed under house arrest. She was released in 1995.

◆ INSIGHT: *Burma is the world's biggest teak exporter, although reserves are diminishing rapidly*

THE ECONOMY

Under socialism, Burma has plunged from prosperity to poverty. Nationwide black market, on which prices are soaring. Main products are teak, rice, and gems.

INDIA
Myitkyina
CHINA
Irrawaddy
Monywa
Mandalay
Pakokku
Sagaing
Mekong
Sittwe
Taunggyi
Shan Plateau
LAOS
Toungoo
Sandoway
Prome
THAILAND
Bay of Bengal
Henzada
Pegu
Insein
Bassein
Thaton
RANGOON
Moulmein
Mouths of the Irrawaddy
Kyaikkami
Tavoy
Andaman Sea
Mergui
Mergui Archipelago
Isthmus of Kra
4000m/13124ft
2000m/6562ft
1000m/3281ft
500m/1640ft
200m/656ft
Sea Level
0 200 km
0 200 miles

FACT FILE

OFFICIAL NAME: Union of Myanmar
DATE OF FORMATION: 1948
CAPITAL: Rangoon (Yangon)
POPULATION: 44.6 million
TOTAL AREA: 261,200 sq miles (676,550 sq km)
DENSITY: 172 people per sq mile
LANGUAGES: Burmese*, Karen, Shan, Chin, Kachin, Mon, Palaung, Wa
RELIGIONS: Buddhist 89%, Muslim 4%, Baptist 3%, other 4%
ETHNIC MIX: Burman 68%, Shan 9%, Karen 6%, Rakhine 4%, other 13%
GOVERNMENT: Military regime
CURRENCY: Kyat = 100 pyas

THAILAND

THAILAND LIES at the heart of mainland Southeast Asia. Continuing rapid industrialization has resulted in massive congestion in the capital.

GEOGRAPHY
One third is occupied by a low plateau, drained by tributaries of the Mekong River. Fertile central plain. Mountains in the north.

CLIMATE
Tropical. Hot, humid March–May, monsoon rains May–October, cooler season November–March.

PEOPLE AND SOCIETY
The king is head of state. Criticism of him is not tolerated. Buddhism is national binding force. North and northeast are home to about 600,000 hill tribespeople, with their own languages and culture. Sex tourism is a problem. Women from the poor northeast enter prostitution in Bangkok and Pattaya.

◆ INSIGHT: Thailand, meaning "land of the free," is the only Southeast Asian nation never to have been colonized

THE ECONOMY
Rapid economic growth. Rise in manufacturing. Chief world exporter of rice and rubber. Gas reserves. Successful tourist industry.

MYANMAR
LAOS
Chiang Mai
Udon Thani
Khon Kaen
Nakhon Sawan
Phitsanulok
Ubon Ratchathani
Nakhon Ratchasima
BANGKOK
Thon Buri
Samut Prakan
Ratchaburi
Pattaya
CAMBODIA
Gulf of Thailand
Chumphon
Isthmus
Nakhon Si Thammarat
Phuket
Songkhla
Hat Yai
Malay Peninsula
Andaman Sea
MALAYSIA

2000m/6562ft
1000m/3281ft
500m/1640ft
200m/656ft
Sea Level

0   200 km
0   200 mls

FACT FILE

OFFICIAL NAME: Kingdom of Thailand
DATE OF FORMATION: 1882
CAPITAL: Bangkok
POPULATION: 56.9 million
TOTAL AREA: 198,116 sq miles (513,120 sq km)
DENSITY: 286 people per sq mile

LANGUAGES: Thai*, Chinese, Malay, Khmer, Mon, Karen, Miao, English
RELIGIONS: Buddhist 95%, Muslim 4%, other (inc. Hindu, Christian) 1%
ETHNIC MIX: Thai 75%, Chinese 14%, Malay 4%, Khmer 3%, other 4%
GOVERNMENT: Constitutional monarchy
CURRENCY: Baht = 100 stangs

LAOS

A FORMER French colony, independent in 1953, Laos lies landlocked in Southeast Asia. It has been under communist rule since 1975.

GEOGRAPHY
Largely forested mountains, broadening in the north to a plateau. Lowlands along Mekong valley.

CLIMATE
Monsoon rains September–May. Rest of the year is hot and dry.

PEOPLE AND SOCIETY
Over 60 ethnic groups. Lowland Laotians (*Lao Loum*), live along Mekong River and are wet-rice farmers. Upland Laotians (*Lao Theung*) and mountain top Laotians (*Lao Soung*) practice slash-and-burn farming. Government efforts to halt this traditional farming method, which can destroy forests and watersheds, have been resisted.

◆ INSIGHT: *In the early 1990s, Laos and Thailand built a "Friendship Bridge" across the Mekong at Vientiane*

THE ECONOMY
One of the world's 20 least-developed nations. Government began to introduce market-oriented reforms in 1986. Potential for timber, mining, garment manufacturing.

FACT FILE

OFFICIAL NAME: Lao People's Democratic Republic
DATE OF FORMATION: 1953
CAPITAL: Vientiane
POPULATION: 4.6 million
TOTAL AREA: 91,428 sq miles (236,800 sq km)

DENSITY: 52 people per sq mile
LANGUAGES: Lao*, Miao, Yao, other
RELIGIONS: Buddhist 85%, Christian 2%, Muslim 1%, other 12%
ETHNIC MIX: Lao Loum 56%, Lao Theung 34%, Lao Soung 10%
GOVERNMENT: Single-party republic
CURRENCY: Kip = 100 cents

CAMBODIA

LOCATED ON the Indochinese Peninsula in Southeast Asia, Cambodia has emerged from two decades of civil war and invasion from Vietnam.

GEOGRAPHY
Mostly low-lying basin. Tônlé Sap (Great Lake) drains into the Mekong River. Forested mountains and plateau east of the Mekong.

CLIMATE
Tropical. High temperatures throughout the year. Heavy rainfall during May–October monsoon.

PEOPLE AND SOCIETY
Under Pol Pot's Marxist Khmer Rouge regime between 1975 and 1979, over one million Cambodians died. Half a million more went into exile in Thailand. Effects of revolution and civil war are still felt and are reflected in the world's highest rate of orphans and widows. Free elections held under UN supervision in 1993 brought fragile stability, although the Khmer Rouge, still led by Pol Pot, continues its armed struggle.

THE ECONOMY
Economy is still recovering from civil war. Loss of skilled workers as result of Khmer Rouge anti-bourgeois atrocities in 1970s. Modest trade in rubber and timber.

◆ INSIGHT: Cambodia has many impressive temples, dating from when it was the center of the Khmer empire

FACT FILE

OFFICIAL NAME: State of Cambodia
DATE OF FORMATION: 1953
CAPITAL: Phnom Penh
POPULATION: 9 million
TOTAL AREA: 69,000 sq miles (181,040 sq km)
DENSITY: 130 people per sq mile

LANGUAGES: Khmer*, French, other
RELIGIONS: Buddhist 88%, Muslim 2%, Christian 1%, other 9%
ETHNIC MIX: Khmer 94%, Chinese 4%, Vietnamese 1%, other 1%
GOVERNMENT: Constitutional monarchy
CURRENCY: Riel = 100 sen

VIETNAM

SITUATED ON the eastern coast of the Indochinese Peninsula, the country is still rebuilding after the devastating 1962–1975 Vietnam War.

GEOGRAPHY
Heavily forested mountain range separates northern Red River delta lowlands from southern Mekong delta in the south.

CLIMATE
Cool winters in north; south is tropical, with even temperatures.

PEOPLE AND SOCIETY
Partitioned in 1954, the communist north reunited the nation after the Vietnam War, in which two million people died. Women outnumber men, largely because of war deaths. Resettling of lowlanders in mountain regions has put pressure on farming and forest resources. Family life is based on kinship groups within village clans.

◆ INSIGHT: *A new mammal species, the* Vu Quang Ox, *was recently discovered in the forests of north Vietnam*

THE ECONOMY
After years of stagnation, the economy is recovering. Government seeking transfer to market economy. Growing steel, oil, gas, car industries.

FACT FILE

OFFICIAL NAME: Socialist Republic of Viet-Nam

DATE OF FORMATION: 1976

CAPITAL: Hanoi

POPULATION: 70.9 million

TOTAL AREA: 127,243 sq miles (329,560 sq km)

DENSITY: 556 per sq mile

LANGUAGES: Vietnamese*, other

RELIGIONS: Buddhist 55%, Catholic 7%, Muslim 1%, other 37%

ETHNIC MIX: Vietnamese 88%, Chinese 4%, Thai 2%, other 6%

GOVERNMENT: Single-party republic

CURRENCY: Dong = 10 hao = 100 xu

MALAYSIA

MALAYSIA'S THREE separate territories stretch over 1,240 miles (2,000 km) from the Malay Peninsula to the northeastern area of the island of Borneo.

GEOGRAPHY
Peninsular Malaysia (Malaya) has mountain ranges along its axis. Almost three quarters of the land is tropical rain forest or swamp forest. Territories of Sabah and Sarawak in Borneo are rugged and forested.

CLIMATE
Equatorial. Warm, with year-round rainfall. Heaviest rain March–May and September–November.

◆ INSIGHT: *Malaysia accounts for almost half of world timber exports*

PEOPLE AND SOCIETY
Indigenous Malays are the largest ethnic group, but Chinese have traditionally controlled most economic activity. Malays favored in education and jobs since 1970s in order to address imbalance. Labor shortages attract many immigrants from other Southeast Asian states.

THE ECONOMY
Rapid growth since 1980s. Successful electronics, car industries. Leading producer of rubber, palm oil, pepper, tin, tropical hardwoods.

FACT FILE

OFFICIAL NAME: Malaysia
DATE OF FORMATION: 1965
CAPITAL: Kuala Lumpur
POPULATION: 19.2 million
TOTAL AREA: 127,317 sq miles
(329,750 sq km)
DENSITY: 148 people per sq mile

LANGUAGES: Malay*, Chinese*, Tamil
RELIGIONS: Muslim 53%, Buddhist and Confucian 30%, other 17%
ETHNIC MIX: Malay and aborigine 60%, Chinese 30%, Indian 8%, other 2%
GOVERNMENT: Federal constitutional monarchy
CURRENCY: Ringgit = 100 cents

INDONESIA

THE WORLD'S largest archipelago, Indonesia's 13,677 islands are scattered over 3,000 miles (5,000 km), from the Indian Ocean to the Pacific Ocean.

GEOGRAPHY
Mountains, tropical swamps, rain forests, and over 200 volcanoes, many still active. Most larger islands have coastal lowlands.

CLIMATE
Predominantly tropical monsoon. Hilly areas are cooler. June–September dry season.

◆ INSIGHT: *Indonesia is the fifth most populous country in the world; 40% of its people are aged under 15*

PEOPLE AND SOCIETY
A mosaic of different cultures and languages. Islam, urbanization, and national language, Bahasa Indonesia, are unifying factors. Papuans of Irian Jaya, East Timorese, and Aceh of north Sumatra, denied autonomy, are all in conflict with government.

THE ECONOMY
Varied resources, especially energy. Timber, minerals, fishing, are all important. Rice is the main cash crop for the rural population.

FACT FILE

OFFICIAL NAME: Republic of Indonesia
DATE OF FORMATION: 1949
CAPITAL: Jakarta
POPULATION: 194.6 million
TOTAL AREA: 735,555 sq miles
(1,904,570 sq km)
DENSITY: 276 people per sq mile

LANGUAGES: Bahasa Indonesia*, 250 (est.) languages or dialects
RELIGIONS: Muslim 87%, Christian 10%, Hindu 2%, Buddhist 1%
ETHNIC MIX: Javanese 45%, Sundanese 14%, Madurese 8%, other 33%
GOVERNMENT: Multiparty republic
CURRENCY: Rupiah = 100 sen

SINGAPORE

A CITY state linked to the southernmost tip of the Malay Peninsula by a causeway, Singapore is one of Asia's most important commercial centers.

GEOGRAPHY
Little remains of the original vegetation on Singapore island. The other 54 much smaller islands are swampy jungle.

CLIMATE
Equatorial. Hot and humid, with heavy rainfall all year round.

PEOPLE AND SOCIETY
Dominated by the Chinese, who make up three quarters of the community. English-speaking Straits Chinese and newer Mandarin-speakers are now well integrated. There is a significant foreign work force. Society is highly regulated and government campaigns to improve public behavior are frequent. Crime is limited and punishment can be severe.

THE ECONOMY
Highly successful financial, banking and manufacturing sectors. Produces 50% of the world's computer disk drives. All food and energy has to be imported.

◆ INSIGHT: *Singapore has full employment, and the world's highest rate of home ownership and national savings*

FACT FILE

OFFICIAL NAME: Republic of Singapore
DATE OF FORMATION: 1965
CAPITAL: Singapore City
POPULATION: 2.8 million
TOTAL AREA: 239 sq miles (620 sq km)

DENSITY: 11,715 people per sq mile
LANGUAGES: Malay*, Chinese*, other
RELIGIONS: Buddhist 30%, Christian 20%, Muslim 17%, other 33%
ETHNIC MIX: Chinese 76%, Malay 15%, South Asian 7%, other 2%
GOVERNMENT: Multiparty republic
CURRENCY: Singapore $ = 100 cents

BRUNEI

LYING ON the northwestern coast of the island of Borneo, Brunei is surrounded and divided in two by the Malaysian state of Sarawak.

GEOGRAPHY
Mostly dense lowland rain forest and mangrove swamps. Mountains in the southeast.

CLIMATE
Tropical. Six-month rainy season with very high humidity.

PEOPLE AND SOCIETY
Malays benefit from positive discrimination. Many in Chinese community are stateless. Independent from the UK since 1984, Brunei is ruled by decree of the Sultan. In 1990, "Malay Muslim Monarchy" was introduced, promoting Islamic values as state ideology. Women less restricted than in some Muslim states.

THE ECONOMY
Oil and natural gas reserves yield one of the world's highest standards of living. Massive overseas investments. Major consumer of high-tech audio equipment, VCRs, and Western designer clothes.

◆ INSIGHT: *The Sultan spent US $450 million building the world's largest palace at Bandar Seri Begawan*

FACT FILE

OFFICIAL NAME: The Sultanate of Brunei

DATE OF FORMATION: 1984

CAPITAL: Bandar Seri Begawan

POPULATION: 300,000

TOTAL AREA: 2,228 sq miles (5,770 sq km)

DENSITY: 134 people per sq mile

LANGUAGES: Malay*, English, Chinese

RELIGIONS: Muslim 63%, Buddhist 14%, Christian 10%, other 13%

ETHNIC MIX: Malay 69%, Chinese 18%, other 13%

GOVERNMENT: Absolute monarchy

CURRENCY: Brunei $ = 100 cents

PHILIPPINES

AN ARCHIPELAGO of 7,107 islands between the South China Sea and the Pacific. After 21 years of dictatorship, democracy was restored in 1986.

GEOGRAPHY
Larger islands are forested and mountainous. Over 20 active volcanoes. Frequent earthquakes.

CLIMATE
Tropical. Warm and humid all year round. Typhoons occur in rainy season, June–October.

PEOPLE AND SOCIETY
Over 100 ethnic groups. Most Filipinos are of Malay origin, and Christian. Catholic Church is the dominant cultural force. It opposes state-sponsored family planning programs designed to curb accelerating population growth. Women have traditionally played a prominent part in society. Many enter the professions. Half the population live on the poverty line.

◆ INSIGHT: *The Philippines is the only Christian state in Asia*

THE ECONOMY
Now open to outside investment. Agricultural productivity is rising. Power failures limit scope for expansion. Weak infrastructure.

FACT FILE

OFFICIAL NAME: Republic of the Philippines
DATE OF FORMATION: 1946
CAPITAL: Manila
POPULATION: 66.5 million
TOTAL AREA: 115,831 sq miles (300,000 sq km)

DENSITY: 569 people per sq mile
LANGUAGES: Pilipino*, English*, other
RELIGIONS: Catholic 83%, Protestant 9%, Muslim 5%, other 3%
ETHNIC MIX: Filipino 96%, Chinese 2%, other 2%
GOVERNMENT: Multiparty republic
CURRENCY: Peso = 100 centavos

TAIWAN

THE ISLAND republic of Taiwan lies 80 miles (130 km) off the southeast coast of mainland China. China considers it to be one of its provinces.

GEOGRAPHY
Mountain region covers two thirds of the island. Highly fertile lowlands and coastal plains.

CLIMATE
Tropical monsoon. Hot and humid. Typhoons July–September. Snow falls in mountains in winter.

PEOPLE AND SOCIETY
Most Taiwanese are Han Chinese, descendants of 17th-century settlers from the mainland. Taiwan came into existence in 1949, when the government was expelled from Beijing (then Peking) by the communists under Mao. 100,000 Nationalists arrived and established themselves as ruling class. Taiwan is diplomatically isolated and cannot gain representation at the UN.

THE ECONOMY
One of the world's most successful economies, based on small, adaptable manufacturing companies. Goods include televisions, calculators, footwear.

◆ INSIGHT: *Taiwan has the world's second largest foreign currency reserves*

FACT FILE

OFFICIAL NAME: Republic of China (Taiwan)
DATE OF FORMATION: 1949
CAPITAL: Taipei
POPULATION: 20.8 million
TOTAL AREA: 13,969 sq miles (36,179 sq km)

DENSITY: 1,489 people per sq mile
LANGUAGES: Mandarin*, other
RELIGIONS: Buddhist, Confucian, and Taoist 93%, Christian 5%, other 2%
ETHNIC MIX: Taiwanese 84%, mainland Chinese 14%, other 2%
GOVERNMENT: Multiparty republic
CURRENCY: New Taiwan $ = 100 cents

CHINA

CHINA COVERS a vast area of East Asia. From the founding of Communist China in 1949 until his death in 1976, Mao Zedong dominated the nation.

GEOGRAPHY
Huge physical diversity. Great mountain chains and world's highest plateau in west. Arid basin in north and northeast. Deserts in northwest. South is mountainous. Rolling hills and plains in east.

CLIMATE
North and west are semiarid or arid, with extreme temperature variations. South and east are warmer and more humid, with rain throughout the year. Winter temperatures vary with latitude. Summer temperatures are more uniform, rising above 21°C (70°F).

THE ECONOMY
Moving rapidly toward a market-oriented economy. Vast mineral reserves. Increasingly diversified industrial sector. Low wage costs. Self-sufficient in food.

◆ *INSIGHT: China has the world's oldest continuous civilization. Its recorded history began 4,000 years ago, with the Shang dynasty*

KAZAKHSTAN

Karamay
Yining
Ürümqi
KYRGYZSTAN
Tien Shan
XINJIANG
Kashi
Korla
TAJIKISTAN
Taklimakan Shamo
AFGHANISTAN
Altun Sh
PAKISTAN
Kunlun Sha
INDIA
YANG ZIZHIQU
(TIBET)
Lhasa
Himalaya
NEPAL
INDIA BHUTAN
90°

FACT FILE
OFFICIAL NAME: People's Republic of China
DATE OF FORMATION: 1912
CAPITAL: Beijing
POPULATION: 1.2 billion
TOTAL AREA: 3,628,166 sq miles (9,396,960 sq km)

DENSITY: 330 people per sq mile
LANGUAGES: Mandarin*, other
RELIGIONS: Confucian 20%, Buddhist 6%, Taoist 2%, other 72%
ETHNIC MIX: Han 93%, Zhaung 1%, Hui 1%, other 5%
GOVERNMENT: Single-party republic
CURRENCY: Yuan = 10 jiao = 100 fen

PEOPLE AND SOCIETY

Most people are Han Chinese. Rest of population belong to one of 55 minority nationalities, or recognized ethnic groups. Policy of resettling Han Chinese in remote regions is deeply resented and has led to uprisings. Government has relaxed one-child family policy for minorities after some small groups brought close to extinction. Han Chinese still face controls.

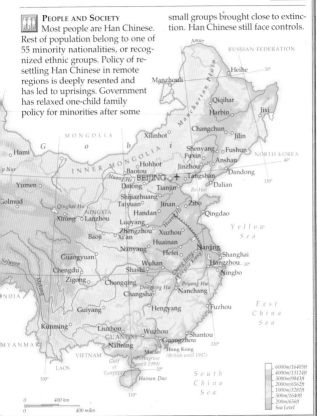

RUSSIAN FEDERATION

Amur

Heihe

Manzhouli

Qiqihar

Harbin

Jixi

Changchun

Jilin

MONGOLIA

Xilinhot

Shenyang

Fushun

Hami

Fuxin

Anshan

NORTH KOREA

INNER MONGOLIA

Hohhot

Jinzhou

Dandong

p Nur

Baotou

Huang He

BEIJING

Tangshan

Dalian

Yumen

Datong

Tianjin

Bo Hai

Golmud

Shijiazhuang

Qinghai Hu

Taiyuan

Jinan

Zibo

Qingdao

NINGXIA

Handan

Xining

Lanzhou

Luoyang

Huang He

Yellow Sea

Baoji

Zhengzhou

Xi'an

Xuzhou

Huainan

Nanjing

Guangyuan

Nanyang

Hefei

Shanghai

Chang Jiang (Yangtze Rang)

Chengdu

Wuhan

Hangzhou

Zigong

Shashi

Ningbo

Chongqing

Dongting Hu

Poyang Hu

Changsha

Nanchang

Guiyang

Hengyang

Fuzhou

East China Sea

Kunming

Liuzhou

Wuzhou

Shantou

GUANGXI

Guangzhou

MYANMAR

Nanning

VIETNAM

Macao (Portuguese until 1999)

Hong Kong (British until 1997)

LAOS

Gulf of Tongking

Hainan Dao

South China Sea

	6000m/16405ft
	4000m/13124ft
	3000m/8843ft
	2000m/6562ft
	1000m/3281ft
	500m/1640ft
	200m/656ft
	Sea Level

0   400 km

0   400 miles

NORTH KOREA

NORTH KOREA comprises the northern half of the Korean peninsula. A communist state since 1948, it is largely isolated from the outside world.

GEOGRAPHY
Mostly mountainous, with fertile plains in the southwest.

CLIMATE
Continental. Warm summers and cold winters, especially in the north, where snow is common.

PEOPLE AND SOCIETY
People live severely regulated lives. Divorce is nonexistent and extramarital sex highly frowned upon. Women form 57% of the work force, but are also expected to run the home. From an early age, children are looked after in state-run nurseries. Korean Workers' Party is only legal political party. Membership is essential for advancement. The political elite enjoy a privileged lifestyle.

◆ INSIGHT: *Private cars and telephones are forbidden in North Korea*

THE ECONOMY
Economy has suffered badly in 1990s, since end of aid from China and former Soviet Union. Manufacturing, agriculture, and mining all in decline. Electricity shortage is a problem.

FACT FILE

OFFICIAL NAME: Democratic People's Republic of Korea
DATE OF FORMATION: 1948
CAPITAL: Pyongyang
POPULATION: 23.1 million
TOTAL AREA: 46,540 sq miles (120,540 sq km)

DENSITY: 496 people per sq mile
LANGUAGES: Korean*, Chinese
RELIGIONS: Traditional beliefs 16%, Ch'ondogyo 14%, Buddhist 2%, unaffiliated 68%
ETHNIC MIX: Korean 99%, other 1%
GOVERNMENT: Single-party republic
CURRENCY: Won = 100 chon

SOUTH KOREA

SOUTH KOREA occupies the southern half of the Korean peninsula. Under US sponsorship, it was separated from the communist North in 1948.

GEOGRAPHY
Over 80% is mountainous and two thirds is forested. Flattest and most populous parts lie along west coast and in the extreme south.

CLIMATE
Four distinct seasons. Winters are dry, and bitterly cold. Summers are hot and humid.

PEOPLE AND SOCIETY
Inhabited by a single ethnic group for the last 2,000 years. Tiny Chinese community. Family life is a central and clearly defined part of Korean society. Women's role is traditional; it is not respectable for those who are married to have jobs. Since the inconclusive Korean War (1950–1953), North and South Korea have remained mutually hostile.

◆ INSIGHT: Over 60% of Koreans are named Kim, Lee, or Park

THE ECONOMY
World's biggest shipbuilder. High demand from China for Korean goods, especially cars. Electronics, household appliances also important.

FACT FILE

OFFICIAL NAME: Republic of Korea
DATE OF FORMATION: 1948
CAPITAL: Seoul
POPULATION: 44.5 million
TOTAL AREA: 38,232 sq miles
(99,020 sq km)
DENSITY: 1,163 people per sq mile

LANGUAGES: Korean*, Chinese
RELIGIONS: Mahayana Buddhist 47%, Protestant 38%, Catholic 11%, Confucian 3%, other 1%
ETHNIC MIX: Korean 99.9%, other (mainly Chinese) 0.1%
GOVERNMENT: Multiparty republic
CURRENCY: Won = 100 chon

JAPAN

JAPAN IS located off the East Asian coast and comprises four principal islands and over 3,000 smaller ones. A constitutional monarchy, with an emperor as head of state, it is the world's most powerful economy.

GEOGRAPHY

Predominantly mountainous, and generally heavily wooded, with small fertile areas. Lies on a fault line: earthquakes and volcanic eruptions are frequent. Pacific coast is vulnerable to *tsunamis* – tidal waves triggered by submarine earthquakes.

CLIMATE

Generally temperate oceanic. Spring is warm and sunny, summer hot and humid, with high rainfall. In western Hokkaidō and northwest Honshū, winters are very cold, with heavy snowfall.

PEOPLE AND SOCIETY

Racially homogenous society. Its sense of order is reflected in the phenomenon of the lifetime employer. People define themselves by the company they work for, not the job they do. Employers organize social activities and even approve marriages. Women mostly play a traditional role running the home. Respect for elders and social and business superiors is strong. Education system is highly pressurized.

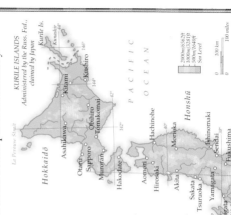

KURILE ISLANDS
*Administered by the Russ. Fed.,
claimed by Japan*

Kurile Is.

Kunashir

P A C I F I C

O C E A N

La Perouse Strait

Hokkaidō

Kitami

Asahikawa

Otaru

Sapporo

Muroran

Hakodate

Obihiro

Tomakomai

Kushiro

Honshū

Hachinohe

Morioka

Aomori

Hirosaki

Akita

Sakata

Tsuruoka

Yamagata

Sendai

Ishinomaki

Fukushima

Kōriyama

Aizu-Wakamatsu

Niigata

Sado

S e a
o f
J a p a n

2000m/6562ft
1000m/3281ft
500m/1640ft
Sea level

0   100 km
0   100 miles

◆ INSIGHT: *Japan is, in dollar terms, the world's second largest filmmaker after the USA. It is also Hollywood's major export market*

THE ECONOMY

World's most competitive producer of high-tech electronic products and cars. Commitment to long-term research and development. Revolutionary management and production methods lead the world. Most raw materials and energy are imported.

LANGUAGES: Japanese*, Korean, Chinese
RELIGIONS: Shinto and Buddhist 76%, Buddhist 16%, other (including Christian) 8%
ETHNIC MIX: Japanese 99.4%, other (mostly Korean) 0.6%
GOVERNMENT: Constitutional monarchy
CURRENCY: Yen = 100 sen

FACT FILE
OFFICIAL NAME: Japan
DATE OF FORMATION: 1868
CAPITAL: Toyko
POPULATION: 125 million
TOTAL AREA: 145,869 sq miles (377,800 sq km)
DENSITY: 861 people per sq mile

211

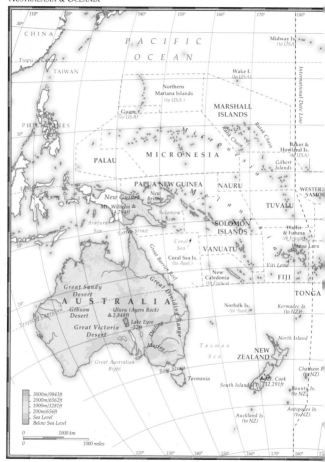

AUSTRALASIA & OCEANIA

THIS REGION includes the world's smallest, flattest continent, Australia; large island groups such as New Zealand, Papua New Guinea, and Fiji; and myriad volcanic and coral islands scattered across the Pacific Ocean, which comprise three main groups: Micronesia, Melanesia, and Polynesia. The peoples of Oceania colonized the Pacific by 1500 A.D. Their insular farming and fishing communities have developed distinctive cultures. Owing to its isolation from other continents, Australia's flora and fauna have evolved many unique species.

Hawaiian Islands

Johnston Atoll
(to USA)

Hawaii
(to USA)

Kingman Reef
(to USA)

Palmyra Atoll
(to USA)

Teraina
Tabuaeran

Jarvis I.
(to USA)

Kiritimati

KIRIBATI

Line Islands

Phoenix Islands

Polynesia

Equator

Tokelau
(to NZ)

Northern
Cook Is.

American
Samoa
(to USA)

Marquesas Is.

French Polynesia
(to France)

Cook Islands
(to NZ)

Niue
(to NZ)

Southern
Cook Is.

Tahiti

PACIFIC

10°

Society Islands

OCEAN

Pitcairn Islands
(to UK)

20°

CONTINENTAL FACTS

HIGHEST POINT:	LARGEST LAKE:
Mt. Wilhelm, Papua New Guinea 14,794 ft (4,509 m)	Lake Eyre, Australia 3,700 sq miles (9,583 sq km)
LOWEST POINT:	**LONGEST RIVER:**
Lake Eyre, Australia 52 ft (16 m) below sea level	Murray-Darling, Australia 2,330 miles (3,750 km)

AUSTRALIA

Papua
New
Guinea

Indonesia

AUSTRALIA

New
Zealand

AN ISLAND continent located between the Indian and Pacific oceans. European settlement, mainly from Britain and Ireland, began 200 years ago. Today, Australia's international focus has shifted away from Europe toward Asia.

GEOGRAPHY

Western half is mostly arid plateaus, ridges, and vast deserts. Central-eastern area comprises lowlands and river systems draining into Lake Eyre. To the east are the mountains of the Great Dividing Range. In the north are tropical rain forests.

CLIMATE

The interior, west, and south are arid and very hot in summer. Central desert areas can reach 120°F (50°C). The north is hot throughout the year, and humid during the summer monsoon. East, south-east, and southwest coastal areas are temperate.

PEOPLE AND SOCIETY

Immigration drives many immi-grants have been Asian. Aborigines, the first inhabi-tants, are sidelined economically and socially. They have made an increasingly organized stand over land rights in recent years. Wealth disparities are small, but 1990s recession increased gap between rich and poor.

THE ECONOMY

Efficient mining and agricultural industries. Successful tourist industry. Investor in booming Southeast Asian economies. High unemployment.

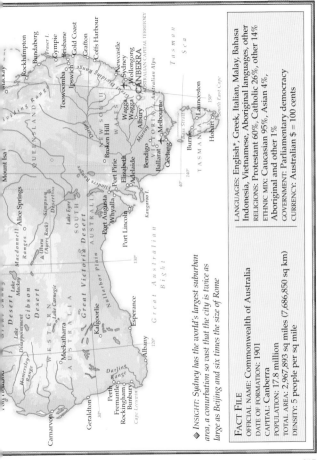

◆ INSIGHT: *Sydney has the world's largest suburban area, a conurbation so vast that the city is twice as large as Beijing and six times the size of Rome*

FACT FILE

OFFICIAL NAME: Commonwealth of Australia
DATE OF FORMATION: 1901
CAPITAL: Canberra
POPULATION: 17.8 million
TOTAL AREA: 2,967,893 sq miles (7,686,850 sq km)
DENSITY: 5 people per sq mile

LANGUAGES: English*, Greek, Italian, Malay, Bahasa
Indonesia, Vietnamese, Aboriginal languages, other
RELIGIONS: Protestant 60%, Catholic 26%, other 14%
ETHNIC MIX: Caucasian 95%, Asian 4%,
Aboriginal and other 1%
GOVERNMENT: Parliamentary democracy
CURRENCY: Australian $ = 100 cents

VANUATU

AN ARCHIPELAGO of 82 islands and islets in the Pacific Ocean, it was ruled jointly by Britain and France from 1906 until independence in 1980.

GEOGRAPHY
Mountainous and volcanic, with coral beaches and dense rain forest. Cultivated land along coasts.

CLIMATE
Tropical. Temperatures and rainfall decline from north to south.

PEOPLE AND SOCIETY
Indigenous Melanesians form a majority. 80% of the population live on 16 main islands. People are among the most traditional in the Pacific: local social and religious customs are strong, despite centuries of missionary influence. Subsistence farming and fishing are the main activities. Women have lower social status than men and payment of bride price is common.

◆ INSIGHT: *With 105 indigenous languages, Vanuatu has the world's highest per capita density of languages*

THE ECONOMY
Copra and cocoa are the largest exports. Recent upsurge in tourist industry. Offshore financial services are also important.

▨	1000m/3281ft
▨	500m/1640ft
▨	200m/656ft
	Sea Level

FACT FILE

OFFICIAL NAME: Republic of Vanuatu
DATE OF FORMATION: 1980
CAPITAL: Port-Vila
POPULATION: 155,000
TOTAL AREA: 4,706 sq miles (12,190 sq km)
DENSITY: 34 people per sq mile

LANGUAGES: Bislama (Melanesian pidgin)*, English*, French*, other
RELIGIONS: Protestant 77%, Catholic 15%, traditional beliefs 8%
ETHNIC MIX: Ni-Vanuatu 98%, European 1%, other 1%
GOVERNMENT: Multiparty republic
CURRENCY: Vatu = 100 centimes

FIJI

A VOLCANIC archipelago in the southern Pacific Ocean, Fiji comprises two large islands and 880 islets. From 1874 to 1970, it was a British colony.

GEOGRAPHY
Main islands are mountainous, fringed by coral reefs. Remainder are limestone and coral formations.

CLIMATE
Tropical. High temperatures year round. Cyclones are a hazard.

PEOPLE AND SOCIETY
The British introduced workers from India in the late 19th century, and by 1946 their descendants outnumbered the Native Fijian population. In 1987, the Indian-dominated government was overthrown by Native Fijians. Many Indo-Fijians left the country. Civilian rule returned in 1990, and a new constitution discriminating against Indo-Fijians was introduced.

◆ INSIGHT: *Both Fijians and Indians practice fire-walking; Indians walk on hot embers, Fijians on heated stones*

THE ECONOMY
Well-diversified economy based on sugar production, gold mining, timber, and commercial fishing. Tourists are returning after a drop in numbers after the coups.

1000m/3281ft	
200m/656ft	
Sea Level	

0   100 km
0   100 miles

FACT FILE
OFFICIAL NAME: Republic of Fiji
DATE OF FORMATION: 1970
CAPITAL: Suva
POPULATION: 700,000
TOTAL AREA: 7,054 sq miles (18,270 sq km)
DENSITY: 99 people per sq mile

LANGUAGES: English*, Fijian*, Hindi, Urdu, Tamil, Telugu
RELIGIONS: Christian 52%, Hindu 38%, Muslim 8%, other 2%
ETHNIC MIX: Native Fijian 49%, Indo-Fijian 46%, other 5%
GOVERNMENT: Multiparty republic
CURRENCY: Fiji $ = 100 cents

PAPUA NEW GUINEA

ACHIEVING INDEPENDENCE from Australia in 1975, PNG occupies the eastern section of the island of New Guinea and several other island groups.

GEOGRAPHY
Mountainous and forested mainland, with broad, swampy river valleys. 40 active volcanoes in the north. Around 600 outer islands.

CLIMATE
Hot and humid in lowlands, cooling toward highlands, where snow can fall on highest peaks.

PEOPLE AND SOCIETY
Around 750 language groups – the highest number in the world – and even more tribes. Main social distinction is between lowlanders, who have frequent contact with the outside world, and the very isolated, but increasingly threatened, highlanders who live by hunter-gathering. Great tensions exist between highland tribes: anyone who is not a *wontok* (of one's tribe) is seen as potentially hostile.

THE ECONOMY
Significant quantities of gold, copper, silver. Oil and natural gas reserves. Secessionist violence on Bougainville deters investors.

◆ *INSIGHT: PNG is home to the only known poisonous birds; contact with the feathers produces skin blisters*

Map

New Guinea — Lorengau, Aitape, Wewak, Admiralty Is., *Bismarck Sea*, New Ireland, *Bismarck Archipelago*, Rabaul, Madang, New Britain, Pomio, Mount Hagen, Goroka, Kandrian, Bougainville I., Kieta, Lae, *Solomon Sea*, Popondetta, Kiriwina Is., PORT MORESBY, *Louisiade Archipelago*, *Coral Sea*, PACIFIC OCEAN, INDONESIA, *Owen Stanley Range*

145°, 150°, 155°, 5°, 10°

3000m/9843ft
2000m/6562ft
1000m/3281ft
500m/1640ft
200m/656ft
Sea Level

0   200 km
0   200 miles

FACT FILE

OFFICIAL NAME: The Independent State of Papua New Guinea
DATE OF FORMATION: 1975
CAPITAL: Port Moresby
POPULATION: 4.1 million
TOTAL AREA: 178,700 sq miles (462,840 sq km)

DENSITY: 23 people per sq mile
LANGUAGES: Pidgin English*, Motu*, Papuan, 750 native languages
RELIGIONS: Christian 66%, other 34%
ETHNIC MIX: Papuan 85%, other 15%
GOVERNMENT: Parliamentary democracy
CURRENCY: Kina = 100 toea

SOLOMON ISLANDS

THE SOLOMONS archipelago comprises several hundred islands scattered in the southwestern Pacific. Independence from Britain came in 1978.

GEOGRAPHY
The six largest islands are volcanic, mountainous, and thickly forested. Flat coastal plains provide the only cultivable land.

CLIMATE
Northern islands are hot and humid all year round; farther south a cool season develops. November–April wet season brings cyclones.

PEOPLE AND SOCIETY
Most Solomon Islanders are Melanesian. Around 87 native languages are spoken, but Pidgin English is used as a contact language between tribes. Most people live on shifting, subsistence agriculture in small rural villages. Villagers work collectively on community projects and there is much sharing among clans. Animist beliefs are maintained alongside Christianity.

THE ECONOMY
Main products are palm oil, copra, cocoa, fish, and timber. Bauxite deposits found on Rennell Island, but islanders persuaded the government that exploiting them would destroy the island.

◆ *INSIGHT: The Solomons have no television service; the islanders oppose television as it might dilute their culture*

FACT FILE

OFFICIAL NAME: Solomon Islands
DATE OF FORMATION: 1978
CAPITAL: Honiara
POPULATION: 400,000
TOTAL AREA: 111,583 sq miles (289,000 sq km)
DENSITY: 29 people per sq mile

LANGUAGES: English*, Pidgin English, 87 (est.) native languages
RELIGIONS: Christian 91%, other 9%
ETHNIC MIX: Melanesian 94%, other (Polynesian, Chinese, European) 6%
GOVERNMENT: Parliamentary democracy
CURRENCY: Solomon Is. $ = 100 cents

PALAU

THE PALAU archipelago, a group of over 300 islands, lies in the western Pacific Ocean. In 1994, it became the world's newest independent state.

GEOGRAPHY
Terrain varies from thickly forested mountains to limestone and coral reefs. Babelthuap, the largest island, is volcanic, with many rivers and waterfalls.

CLIMATE
Hot and wet. Little variation in daily and seasonal temperatures. February–April is the dry season.

PEOPLE AND SOCIETY
Palau was the last remaining US-administered UN Trust Territory of the Pacific Islands, until 1994. Only nine islands are inhabited and two thirds of the population live in Koror. Society is matrilineal; women choose which males will be the clan chiefs. Local traditions remain strong, despite US influence.

◆ *INSIGHT: Palau's reefs contain 1,500 species of fish and 700 types of coral*

THE ECONOMY
Subsistence level. Main crops are coconuts and cassava. Revenue from fishing licenses and tourism. Heavily reliant on US aid.

FACT FILE

OFFICIAL NAME: Republic of Palau
DATE OF FORMATION: 1994
CAPITAL: Koror
POPULATION: 16,000
TOTAL AREA: 192 sq miles (497 sq km)
DENSITY: 78 people per sq mile

LANGUAGES: Palauan*, English*, Sonsorolese-Tobian, other
RELIGIONS: Christian (mainly Catholic) 70%, traditional beliefs 30%
ETHNIC MIX: Palaun 99%, other (mainly Filipino) 1%
GOVERNMENT: Multiparty republic
CURRENCY: US $ = 100 cents

MICRONESIA

THE FEDERATED States of Micronesia, situated in the western Pacific, comprise 607 islands and atolls grouped into four main island states.

GEOGRAPHY
Mixture of high volcanic islands with forested interiors, and low-lying coral atolls. Some islands have coastal mangrove swamps.

CLIMATE
Tropical, with high humidity. Very heavy rainfall outside the January–March dry season.

◆ INSIGHT: *A major Japanese naval base during World War II, Chuuk's lagoon contains the sunken wrecks of over 100 Japanese ships and 270 planes*

PEOPLE AND SOCIETY
Part of the US-administered UN Trust Territory of the Pacific Islands, until independence in 1979, but it still relies on US aid, which funds food stamps, schools, and hospitals. Most islanders live without electricity or running water. Society is traditionally matrilineal.

THE ECONOMY
Fishing and copra production are the mainstays. Construction industry is largest private-sector activity. High unemployment.

FACT FILE
OFFICIAL NAME: Federated States of Micronesia

DATE OF FORMATION: 1979

CAPITAL: Kolonia

POPULATION: 101,000

TOTAL AREA: 1,120 sq miles (2,900 sq km)

DENSITY: 374 people per sq mile

LANGUAGES: English*, Trukese, Pohnpeian, Mortlockese, other

RELIGIONS: Catholic 50%, Protestant 48%, other 2%

ETHNIC MIX: Micronesian 99%, other 1%

GOVERNMENT: Republic

CURRENCY: US $ = 100 cents

MARSHALL ISLANDS

UNDER US rule as part of the UN Trust Territory of the Pacific Islands until independence in 1986, the Marshall Islands comprise a group of 34 atolls.

GEOGRAPHY
Narrow coral rings with sandy beaches enclosing lagoons. Those in the south have thicker vegetation. Kwajalein is the world's largest atoll.

CLIMATE
Tropical oceanic, cooled year-round by northeast trade winds.

PEOPLE AND SOCIETY
Majuro, the capital and commercial center, is home to almost half the population. Tensions are high due to poor living conditions. Life on the outlying islands is still traditional, based around subsistence agriculture and fishing. Society is matrilineal: chiefly titles descend through the mother.

THE ECONOMY
Almost totally dependent on US aid and the rent paid by the US for its missile base on Kwajalein atoll. Revenue from Japan for use of Marshallese waters for tuna fishing. Copra and coconut oil are the only significant agricultural exports.

◆ INSIGHT: In 1954, Bikini atoll was the site for the testing of the largest US H-bomb – the 18–22 megaton Bravo

PACIFIC OCEAN

Bokak

Enewetak
Bikini
Rongelap

Ujelang

Likiep
Kwajalein
Wotje

Ratik Chain

Maloelap

164°

Ralik Chain
Jabat

MAJURO
Majuro

Jaluit

Narikrik

All land under 100m/328ft

0   200 km
0   200 miles

Ebon

170°

FACT FILE

OFFICIAL NAME: Republic of the Marshall Islands
DATE OF FORMATION: 1986
CAPITAL: Majuro
POPULATION: 48,000
TOTAL AREA: 70 sq miles (181 sq kms)

DENSITY: 689 people per sq mile
LANGUAGES: English*, Marshallese*
RELIGIONS: Protestant 80%, Catholic 15%, other 5%
ETHNIC MIX: Marshallese 90%, other Pacific islanders 10%
GOVERNMENT: Republic
CURRENCY: US $ = 100 cents

NAURU

NAURU LIES in the Pacific, 2,480 miles (4,000 km) northeast of Australia. Phosphate deposits have made its citizens among the richest in the world.

GEOGRAPHY
Low-lying coral atoll, with a fertile coastal belt. Coral cliffs encircle an elevated interior plateau.

CLIMATE
Equatorial, moderated by sea breezes. Occasional long droughts.

PEOPLE AND SOCIETY
Native Nauruans are of mixed Micronesian and Polynesian origin. Most live in simple, traditional houses and spend their money on luxury cars and consumer goods. Government provides free welfare and education. Diet of imported processed foods has caused widespread obesity and diabetes. Mining is left to an imported labor force, mainly from Kiribati. Many young attend boarding school in Australia.

◆ INSIGHT: Phosphate mining has left 80% of the island uninhabitable

THE ECONOMY
Phosphate, the only resource, is sold to Pacific Rim countries for use as a fertilizer. Deposits are near exhaustion. Huge investments in Australian and Hawaiian property. Possible future as a tax haven.

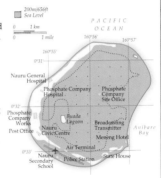

FACT FILE

OFFICIAL NAME: Republic of Nauru
DATE OF FORMATION: 1968
CAPITAL: No official capital
POPULATION: 10,000
TOTAL AREA: 8.2 sq miles (21.2 sq km)
DENSITY: 1,113 people per sq mile

LANGUAGES: Nauruan*, English, other
RELIGIONS: Christian 95%, other 5%
ETHNIC MIX: Nauruan 58%, other Pacific islanders 26%, Chinese 8%, European 8%
GOVERNMENT: Parliamentary democracy
CURRENCY: Australian $ = 100 cents

KIRIBATI

PART OF the British colony of the Gilbert and Ellice Islands until independence in 1979, Kiribati comprises 33 islands in the mid-Pacific Ocean.

 GEOGRAPHY
Three groups of tiny, very low-lying coral atolls scattered across 1,930,000 sq miles (5 million sq km) of ocean. Most have central lagoons.

CLIMATE
Central islands have maritime equatorial climate. Those to north and south are tropical, with constant high temperatures. Little rainfall.

PEOPLE AND SOCIETY
Locals still refer to themselves as Gilbertese. Apart from the inhabitants of Banaba, who employed anthropologists to establish their racial distinction, almost all people are Micronesian. Most are poor subsistence farmers. The islands are in effect ruled by traditional chiefs, though there is a party system based on the British model.

THE ECONOMY
Until 1980, when deposits ran out, phosphate from Banaba provided 80% of exports. Since then, coconuts, copra, fish, have become main exports, but the islands are heavily dependent on foreign aid.

◆ INSIGHT: *In 1981, the UK paid A$10 million in damages to Banabans for the destruction of their island by mining*

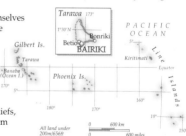

FACT FILE

OFFICIAL NAME: Republic of Kiribati
DATE OF FORMATION: 1979
CAPITAL: Bairiki
POPULATION: 7,500
TOTAL AREA: 274 sq miles (710 sq km)

DENSITY: 242 people per sq mile
LANGUAGES: English*, Kiribati, other
RELIGIONS: Catholic 53%, Protestant (mainly Congregational) 40%, other Christian 4%, other 3%
ETHNIC MIX: I-Kiribati 98%, other 2%
GOVERNMENT: Multiparty republic
CURRENCY: Australian $ = 100 cents

TUVALU

A TINY isolated state, linked to the Gilbert Islands as a British colony until independence in 1978, Tuvalu's nine islands lie in the central Pacific.

GEOGRAPHY
Coral atolls, none more than 15 feet (4.6 meters) above sea level. Poor soils restrict vegetation to bush, coconut palms, and breadfruit trees.

CLIMATE
Hot all year round. Heavy annual rainfall. Hurricane season brings many violent storms.

PEOPLE AND SOCIETY
People are mostly Polynesian, related to the Samoans and Tongans. Almost half the population live on Funafuti, where government jobs are centered. Life is communal and traditional. Most people live by sub-sistence farming, digging pits out of the coral to grow crops. Fresh water is precious due to frequent droughts.

◆ INSIGHT: *Tuvaluans have a reputation as excellent sailors. Many work overseas as merchant seamen on foreign ships*

THE ECONOMY
World's smallest economy. Fish stocks exploited mainly by foreign boats in return for licensing fees. Exports are few: copra, stamps, garments. Foreign aid is crucial.

FACT FILE

OFFICIAL NAME: Tuvalu
DATE OF FORMATION: 1978
CAPITAL: Fongafale
POPULATION: 9,000
TOTAL AREA: 10 sq miles
(26 sq km)
DENSITY: 900 people per sq mile

LANGUAGES: Tuvaluan, Kiribati, other (no official language)
RELIGIONS: Protestant 97%, other 3%
ETHNIC MIX: Tuvaluan 95%, other (inc. Micronesian, I-Kiribati) 5%
GOVERNMENT: Constitutional monarchy
CURRENCY: Australian $ = 100 cents

WESTERN SAMOA

THE SOUTHERN Pacific islands of Western Samoa gained independence from New Zealand in 1962. Four of the nine islands are inhabited.

GEOGRAPHY
Comprises two large islands and seven smaller ones. Two largest islands have rain forested, mountainous interiors surrounded by coastal lowlands and coral reefs.

CLIMATE
Tropical, with high humidity. Cooler May–November. Hurricane season December–March.

PEOPLE AND SOCIETY
Ethnic Samoans are world's second largest Polynesian group, after the Maoris. Way of life is communal and formalized. Extended family groups own 80% of the land. Each family has an elected chief, who looks after its political and social interests. Large-scale migration to the US and New Zealand reflects lack of jobs and attractions of Western lifestyle.

THE ECONOMY
Agricultural products include taro, coconut cream, cocoa, and copra. Growth of service sector since 1989 launch of offshore banking. Dependent on aid and expatriate remittances. Rain forests increasingly exploited for timber.

◆ INSIGHT: Samoa was named for the sacred (sa) chickens (moa) of Lu, son of Tagaloa, the god of creation

FACT FILE

OFFICIAL NAME: Independent State of Western Samoa
DATE OF FORMATION: 1962
CAPITAL: Apia
POPULATION: 162,000
TOTAL AREA: 1,027 sq miles (2,840 sq km)

DENSITY: 156 people per sq mile
LANGUAGES: Samoan*, English*
RELIGIONS: Protestant (mainly Congregational) 74%, Catholic 26%
ETHNIC MIX: Samoan 93%, mixed European and Polynesian 7%
GOVERNMENT: Parliamentary state
CURRENCY: Tala = 100 sene

TONGA

TONGA IS an archipelago of 170 islands, 45 of which are inhabited, in the South Pacific. Politics is in effect controlled by the king.

GEOGRAPHY
Easterly islands are generally low and fertile. Those in the west are higher and volcanic in origin.

CLIMATE
Tropical oceanic. Temperatures range between 68°F (20°C) and 86°F (30°C) all year round. Heavy rainfall, especially February–March.

PEOPLE AND SOCIETY
The last remaining Polynesian monarchy, and the only Pacific state never brought under foreign rule. All land is property of the crown, but is administered by nobles who allot it to the common people. Respect for traditional institutions and values remains high, although younger, Westernized Tongans are starting to question some attitudes.

◆ INSIGHT: *Tonga has the world's lowest annual death rate at one in 2,790*

THE ECONOMY
Most people are subsistence farmers. Commercial production of coconuts, cassava, and passion fruit. Tourism is increasing slowly.

FACT FILE

OFFICIAL NAME: Kingdom of Tonga
DATE OF FORMATION: 1970
CAPITAL: Nuku'alofa
POPULATION: 101,000
TOTAL AREA: 290 sq miles (750 sq km)

DENSITY: 341 people per sq mile
LANGUAGES: Tongan*, English
RELIGIONS: Protestant 82% (mainly Methodist), Catholic 18%
ETHNIC MIX: Tongan 98%, mixed European and Polynesian 2%
GOVERNMENT: Constitutional monarchy
CURRENCY: Pa'anga = 100 seniti

227

NEW ZEALAND

LYING SOUTHEAST of Australia, New Zealand comprises the North and South Islands, separated by the Cook Strait, and many smaller islands.

GEOGRAPHY
North Island has mountain ranges, valleys, and volcanic central plateau. South Island is mostly mountainous, with eastern lowlands.

CLIMATE
Generally temperate and damp. Extreme north is almost sub-tropical; southern winters are cold.

PEOPLE AND SOCIETY
Maoris were the first settlers, 1,200 years ago. Today's majority European population is descended mainly from British migrants who settled after 1840. Maoris' living and education standards are generally lower than average. Tense relations beween the two groups in recent years. Government now negotiating settlement of Maori land claims.

◆ INSIGHT: *New Zealand women were the first in the world to get the vote*

THE ECONOMY
Modern agricultural sector; world's biggest exporter of wool, cheese, butter, and meat. Growing manufacturing industry. Tourism.

| 2000m/6562ft |
| 1000m/3281ft |
| 500m/1640ft |
| 200m/656ft |
| Sea Level |

North Island

Auckland
Manurewa
Hamilton Cambridge
Rotorua
New   Taupo
Plymouth   Napier
           Hastings
           Palmerston
           North
Blenheim   Lower Hutt
           WELLINGTON
           Cook Strait

Tasman Sea

South Island

Southern Alps

Christchurch

Timaru

PACIFIC OCEAN

Dunedin

Invercargill
Stewart Island

0 100 km
0 100 miles

FACT FILE

OFFICIAL NAME: The Dominion of New Zealand
DATE OF FORMATION: 1947
CAPITAL: Wellington
POPULATION: 3.5 million
TOTAL AREA: 103,730 sq miles (268,680 sq km)

DENSITY: 34 people per sq mile
LANGUAGES: English*, Maori, other
RELIGIONS: Protestant 62%, Catholic 18%, other 20%
ETHNIC MIX: European 88%, Maori 9%, other (inc. Malay, Chinese) 3%
GOVERNMENT: Constitutional monarchy
CURRENCY: NZ $ = 100 cents

ANTARCTICA

THE CIRCUMPOLAR continent of Antarctica is almost entirely covered by ice over 1.2 miles (2 km) thick. It contains 90% of the Earth's fresh water reserves.

GEOGRAPHY & CLIMATE

The bulk of Antarctica's ice is contained in the Greater Antarctic Ice Sheet – a huge dome that rises steeply from the coast and flattens to a plateau in the interior. Powerful winds create a storm belt around the continent, which brings clouds, fog, and blizzards. Winter temperatures can fall to –112°F. (–80°C).

PEOPLE

No indigenous population. Scientists and logistical staff work at the 40 permanent, and as many as 100 temporary, research stations. A few Chilean settler families live on King George Island. Tourism is mostly by cruise ship to the Antarctic Peninsula. Tourist numbers increased by over 600% between 1985 and 1992.

TOTAL AREA:
5,366,790 sq miles
(13,900,000 sq km)

Ice Cap /
Permanent Ice

0   1000 km
0   1000 miles

Territorial Claims:

Chilean claim

Argentinian claim

Brazilian zone of interest

British claim

Norwegian undefined limit

Australian claim

French claim

New Zealand claim

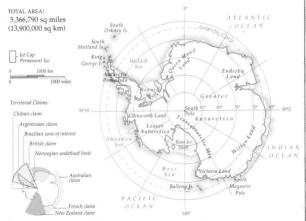

The Antarctic Treaty of 1959 holds all territorial claims in abeyance in the interest of international cooperation

◆ INSIGHT: *If Antarctica's ice sheets were to melt, the world's oceans would rise by as much as 200–210 ft (60–65 m)*

OVERSEAS TERRITORIES

DESPITE THE rapid process of decolonization since World War II, around 10 million people in 59 territories around the world continue to live under the protection of either France, Australia, Denmark, Norway, Portugal, New Zealand, the UK, the USA, or the Netherlands. These territories are administered in a wide variety of ways.

AUSTRALIA

Australia's overseas territories have not been an issue since Papua New Guinea became independent in 1975. Consequently, there is no overriding policy toward them. Norfolk Island is inhabited by descendants of the *HMS Bounty* mutineers and more recent Australian migrants. Phosphate is mined on Christmas Island.

ASHMORE & CARTIER ISLANDS (Indian Ocean)

STATUS: External territory
CLAIMED: 1978
AREA: 2 sq miles (5.2 sq km)

 ### CHRISTMAS ISLAND (Indian Ocean)

STATUS: External territory
CLAIMED: 1958
CAPITAL: Flying Fish Cove
POPULATION: 1,275
AREA: 52 sq miles (134.6 sq km)

COCOS ISLANDS (Indian Ocean)

STATUS: External territory
CLAIMED: 1955
CAPITAL: West Island
POPULATION: 647
AREA: 5.5 sq miles (14.24 sq km)

CORAL SEA ISLANDS (S. Pacific)

STATUS: External territory
CLAIMED: 1969
POPULATION: 3 (meteorologists)
AREA: Less than 1.16 sq miles (3 sq km)

HEARD & McDONALD ISLANDS (Indian Ocean)

STATUS: External territory
CLAIMED: 1947
AREA: 161 sq miles (417 sq km)

 ### NORFOLK ISLAND (S. Pacific)

STATUS: External territory
CLAIMED: 1913
CAPITAL: Kingston
POPULATION: 2,665
AREA: 13.3 sq miles (34.4 sq km)

DENMARK

The Faeroe Islands have been under Danish administration since Queen Margrethe I of Denmark inherited Norway in 1380. The Home Rule Act of 1948 gave the Faeroese control over all their internal affairs. Greenland first came under Danish rule in 1380. Today, Denmark remains responsible for the island's foreign affairs and defense.

FAEROE ISLANDS (N. Atlantic)

STATUS: External territory
CLAIMED: 1380
CAPITAL: Tórshavn
POPULATION: 48,065
AREA: 540 sq miles (1,399 sq km)

Strong sense of national identity. Voted against joining the EC with Denmark in 1973. Economy based on fishing, agriculture, Danish subsidies.

 ### GREENLAND (N. Atlantic)

STATUS: External territory
CLAIMED: 1380
CAPITAL: Nuuk
POPULATION: 55,385
AREA: 840,000 sq miles (2,175,516 sq km)

World's largest island. Much of the land is permanently ice-covered. Self-governing since 1979. Left the EU in 1985. Population is a mixture of Inuit and European in origin.

FRANCE

France has developed economic ties with its *Territoires d'Outre-Mer,* thereby stressing interdependence over independence. Overseas *départements,* officially part of France, have their own governments. Territorial *collectivités* and overseas *territoires* have varying degrees of autonomy.

CLIPPERTON ISLAND (E. Pacific)

STATUS: Dependency of French Polynesia
CLAIMED: 1930
AREA: 2.7 sq miles (7 sq km)

FRENCH GUIANA (S. America)

STATUS: Overseas department
CLAIMED: 1817
CAPITAL: Cayenne
POPULATION: 133,376
AREA: 35,135 sq miles (90,996 sq km)

The last colony in South America. Population is largely African and indigenous Indian. European Space Agency rocket launch facility.

 ### FRENCH POLYNESIA (S. Pacific)

STATUS: Overseas territory
CLAIMED: 1843
CAPITAL: Papeete
POPULATION: 210,333
AREA: 1,608 sq miles (4,165 sq km)

Most people live on Tahiti. Economy dependent on tourism and French military. Recent calls for autonomy.

GUADELOUPE (West Indies)

STATUS: Overseas department
CLAIMED: 1635
CAPITAL: Basse-Terre
POPULATION: 422,114
AREA: 687 sq miles (1,780 sq km)

Prospers from a strong infrastructure, plus French and EU aid. Indigenous population demands more autonomy.

MARTINIQUE (West Indies)

STATUS: Overseas department
CLAIMED: 1635
CAPITAL: Fort-de-France
POPULATION: 387,656
AREA: 425 sq miles (1,100 sq km)

Population largely of African origin. High living standards resulting from tourism and French subsidies.

MAYOTTE (Indian Ocean)

STATUS: Territorial collectivity
CLAIMED: 1843
CAPITAL: Mamoudzou
POPULATION: 89,938
AREA: 144 sq miles (374 sq km)

NEW CALEDONIA (S. Pacific)

STATUS: Overseas territory
CLAIMED: 1853
CAPITAL: Nouméa
POPULATION: 178,056
AREA: 7,374 sq miles (19,103 sq km)

Tensions between francophile expatriates and indigenous population
over wealth inequalities and independence. Large nickel deposits.

RÉUNION (Indian Ocean)

STATUS: Overseas department
CLAIMED: 1638
CAPITAL: Saint-Denis
POPULATION: 639,622
AREA: 970 sq miles (2,512 sq km)

Wealth disparities between white
and black communities. Ethnic
tensions erupted into rioting in
1991. Large French military base.

ST PIERRE & MIQUELON (N. America)

STATUS: Territorial collectivity
CLAIMED: 1604
CAPITAL: Saint Pierre
POPULATION: 6,652
AREA: 93.4 sq miles (242 sq km)

WALLIS & FUTUNA (Pacific)

STATUS: Overseas territory
CLAIMED: 1842
CAPITAL: Mata-Utu
POPULATION: 14,175
AREA: 106 sq miles (274 sq km)

NETHERLANDS

The country's two remaining territories were formerly part of the
Dutch West Indies. Both are now
self-governing, but the Netherlands
remains responsible for their defense.

ARUBA (West Indies)

STATUS: Autonomous part of
the Netherlands
CLAIMED: 1643
CAPITAL: Oranjestad
POPULATION: 62,365
AREA: 75 sq miles (194 sq km)

In 1990, Aruba requested and
received from the Netherlands
cancellation of the agreement to
automatically give independence
to the island in 1996.

NETHERLANDS ANTILLES (West Indies)

STATUS: Autonomous part of
the Netherlands
CLAIMED: 1816
CAPITAL: Willemstad
POPULATION: 191,311
AREA: 308 sq miles (800 sq km)

Economy based on tourism, oil
refining, and offshore finance.
Living standards are high. Political
instability and allegations of drug-
trafficking on smaller islands.

NEW ZEALAND

New Zealand's government has
no desire to retain any overseas
territories. However, the economic
weakness of Tokelau, Niue, and the
Cook Islands has forced it to remain
responsible for their foreign policy
and defense.

COOK ISLANDS (S. Pacific)

STATUS: Associated territory
CLAIMED: 1901
CAPITAL: Avarua
POPULATION: 18,903
AREA: 113 sq miles (293 sq km)

 NIUE (S. Pacific)

STATUS: Associated territory
CLAIMED: 1901
CAPITAL: Alofi
POPULATION: 1,977
AREA: 102 sq miles (264 sq km)

TOKELAU (S. Pacific)

STATUS: Dependent territory
CLAIMED: 1926
POPULATION: 1,544
AREA: 4 sq miles (10.4 sq km)

NORWAY

In 1920, 41 nations signed the Spitsbergen treaty recognizing Norwegian sovereignty over Svalbard. There is a Nato base on Jan Mayen. Bouvet Island is a nature reserve.

BOUVET ISLAND (S. Atlantic)

STATUS: Dependency
CLAIMED: 1928
AREA: 22 sq miles (58 sq km)

JAN MAYEN (N. Atlantic)

STATUS: Dependency
CLAIMED: 1929
AREA: 147 sq miles (381 sq km)

PETER I ISLAND (Southern Ocean)

STATUS: Dependency
CLAIMED: 1931
AREA: 69 sq miles (180 sq km)

SVALBARD (Arctic Ocean)

STATUS: Dependency
CLAIMED: 1920
CAPITAL: Longyearbyen
POPULATION: 3,209
AREA: 62,906 sq km (24,289 sq miles)

In accordance with 1920 Spitsbergen Treaty, nationals of the treaty powers have equal rights to exploit Svalbard's coal deposits, subject to Norwegian regulation. The only companies still mining are Russian and Norwegian.

PORTUGAL

After a coup in 1974, Portugal's overseas possessions were rapidly granted sovereignty. By 1976, Macao was the only one remaining.

MACAO (S. China)

STATUS: Special territory
CLAIMED: 1557
CAPITAL: Macao
POPULATION: 477,850
AREA: 7 sq miles (18 sq km)

By agreement with Beijing in 1974, Macao is a Chinese territory under Portuguese administration. It is to become a Special Administrative Region of China in 1999. Macanese born before 1981 can claim a Portuguese passport.

UNITED KINGDOM

The UK has the largest number of overseas territories. Locally governed by a mixture of elected representatives and appointed officials, they all enjoy a large measure of internal self-government, but certain powers, such as foreign affairs and defense, are reserved for Governors of the British Crown.

ANGUILLA (West Indies)

STATUS: Dependent territory
CLAIMED: 1650
CAPITAL: The Valley
POPULATION: 8,960
AREA: 37 sq miles (96 sq km)

ASCENSION (Atlantic)

STATUS: Dependency of St Helena
CLAIMED: 1673
POPULATION: 1,099
AREA: 34 sq miles (88 sq km)

 BERMUDA (N. Atlantic)

STATUS: Crown colony
CLAIMED: 1612
CAPITAL: Hamilton
POPULATION: 60,686
AREA: 20.5 sq miles (53 sq km)

Britain's oldest colony. People are of African or European descent. 74% voted against independence in 1995. One of the world's highest *per capita* incomes. Financial services and tourism are main currency earners.

 BRITISH INDIAN OCEAN TERRITORY

STATUS: Dependent territory
CLAIMED: 1814
CAPITAL: Diego Garcia
POPULATION: 3,400
AREA: 23 sq miles (60 sq km)

 BRITISH VIRGIN ISLANDS (West Indies)

STATUS: Dependent territory
CLAIMED: 1672
CAPITAL: Road Town
POPULATION: 16,644
AREA: 59 sq miles (153 sq km)

CAYMAN ISLANDS (West Indies)

STATUS: Dependent territory
CLAIMED: 1670
CAPITAL: George Town
POPULATION: 25,355
AREA: 100 sq km (259 sq km)

 FALKLAND ISLANDS (S. Atlantic)

STATUS: Dependent territory
CLAIMED: 1832
CAPITAL: Stanley
POPULATION: 2,121
AREA: 4,699 sq miles (12,173 sq km)

British sovereignty not recognized by Argentina, despite Falklands War in 1982. Economy based on sheep farming, sale of fishing licenses. Large oil reserves have been discovered.

GIBRALTAR (S.W. Europe)

STATUS: Crown colony
CLAIMED: 1713
CAPITAL: Gibraltar
POPULATION: 28,074
AREA: 2.5 sq miles (6.5 sq km)

Disputes over sovereignty between UK and Spain. The colony has traditionally survived on military and marine revenues, but cuts in defense spending by the UK have led to the development of an offshore banking industry.

 GUERNSEY (Channel Islands)

STATUS: Crown dependency
CLAIMED: 1066
CAPITAL: St Peter Port
POPULATION: 58,867
AREA: 25 sq miles (65 sq km)

HONG KONG (S. China)

STATUS: Crown colony
CLAIMED: 1842
CAPITAL: Victoria
POPULATION: 5.8 million
AREA: 415 sq miles (1,076 sq km)

One of the world's major trade and financial centers. Population is largely Han Chinese. Will revert to China in 1997, when the UK's 99-year lease on the New Territories expires. British and Chinese governments disagree about interpretation of the 1985 Sino-British agreement and the Basic Law (Hong Kong's post-1997 constitution). UK wants to push further toward elective democracy, China opposes changes to status quo.

ISLE OF MAN
(British Isles)

STATUS: Crown dependency
CLAIMED: 1765
CAPITAL: Douglas
POPULATION: 69,788
AREA: 221 sq miles (572 sq km)

JERSEY
(Channel Islands)

STATUS: Crown dependency
CLAIMED: 1066
CAPITAL: St Helier
POPULATION: 82,809
AREA: 45 sq miles (116 sq km)

MONTSERRAT
(West Indies)

STATUS: Dependent territory
CLAIMED: 1632
CAPITAL: Plymouth
POPULATION: 11,852
AREA: 40 sq miles (102 sq km)

PITCAIRN ISLANDS (S. Pacific)

STATUS: Dependent territory
CLAIMED: 1887
CAPITAL: Adamstown
POPULATION: 52
AREA: 1.35 sq miles (3.5 sq km)

ST HELENA
(Atlantic))

STATUS: Dependent territory
CLAIMED: 1673
CAPITAL: Jamestown
POPULATION: 6,720
AREA: 47 sq miles (122 sq km)

SOUTH GEORGIA & THE SANDWICH ISLANDS (S. Atlantic)

STATUS: Dependent territory
CLAIMED: 1775
POPULATION: No permanent residents
AREA: 1,387 sq miles (3,592 sq km)

TRISTAN DA CUNHA (S. Atlantic)

STATUS: Dependency of St Helena
CLAIMED: 1612
POPULATION: 297
AREA: 38 sq miles (98 sq km)

TURKS & CAICOS ISLANDS (West Indies)

STATUS: Dependent territory
CLAIMED: 1766
CAPITAL: Cockburn town
POPULATION: 12,350
AREA: 166 sq miles (430 sq km)

UNITED STATES OF AMERICA

US Commonwealth territories are self-governing incorporated territories that are an integral part of the US. Unincorporated territories have varying degrees of autonomy.

AMERICAN
SAMOA (S. Pacific)

STATUS: Unincorporated territory
CLAIMED: 1900
CAPITAL: Pago Pago
POPULATION: 50,923
AREA: 75 sq miles (195 sq km)

BAKER AND HOWLAND ISLANDS (S. Pacific)

STATUS: Unincorporated territory
CLAIMED: 1856
AREA: 0.54 sq miles (1.4 sq km)

 GUAM (W. Pacific)

STATUS: Unincorporated territory
CLAIMED: 1898
CAPITAL: Agaña
POPULATION: 133,152
AREA: 212 sq miles (549 sq km)

JARVIS ISLAND (Pacific)

STATUS: Unincorporated territory
CLAIMED: 1856
AREA: 1.7 sq miles (4.5 sq km)

JOHNSTON ATOLL (Pacific)

STATUS: Unincorporated territory
CLAIMED: 1858
POPULATION: 1,375
AREA: 2.8 sq miles (4.5 sq km)

KINGMAN REEF (Pacific)

STATUS: Administered territory
CLAIMED: 1856
AREA: 0.4 sq miles (1 sq km)

MIDWAY ISLANDS (Pacific)

STATUS: Administered territory
CLAIMED: 1867
POPULATION: 453
AREA: 2 sq miles (5.2 sq km)

NAVASSA ISLAND (West Indies)

STATUS: Unincorporated territory
CLAIMED: 1856
AREA: 2 sq miles (5.2 sq km)

 NORTHERN
MARIANA IS. (Pacific)

STATUS: Commonwealth territory
CLAIMED: 1947
CAPITAL: Saipan
POPULATION: 48,581
AREA: 177 sq miles (457 sq km)

PALMYRA ATOLL (Pacific)

STATUS: Unincorporated territory
CLAIMED: 1898
AREA: 5 sq miles (12 sq km)

 PUERTO
RICO (West Indies)

STATUS: Commonwealth territory
CLAIMED: 1898
CAPITAL: San Juan
POPULATION: 3.6 million
AREA: 3,458 sq km (8,959 sq km)

Population voted in 1993 to maintain
the current compromise between
statehood and independence.

 VIRGIN
ISLANDS (West Indies)

STATUS: Unincorporated territory
CLAIMED: 1917
CAPITAL: Charlotte Amalie
POPULATION: 101,809
AREA: 137 sq miles (355 sq km)

WAKE ISLAND (Pacific)

STATUS: Unincorporated territory
CLAIMED: 1898
POPULATION: 302
AREA: 2.5 sq miles (6.5 sq km)

INTERNATIONAL ORGANIZATIONS

THIS LISTING provides acronym definitions for the main international organizations concerned with economics, trade, and defense, plus an indication of membership.

AESAN
Association of Southeast Asian Nations
ESTABLISHED: 1989 MEMBERS: Brunei, Indonesia, Malaysia, Singapore, Thailand

CIS
Commonwealth of Independent States
ESTABLISHED: 1991 MEMBERS: Armenia, Belarus, Kazakhstan, Kyrgyzstan, Moldova, Russia, Tajikstan, Turkmenistan, Ukraine, Uzbekistan

COMM
The Commonwealth
ESTABLISHED: 1931; evolved out of the British Empire. Formerly known as the British Commonwealth of Nations. MEMBERS: 53

EU
European Union
ESTABLISHED: 1965; formerly known as EEC (European Economic Community) and EC (Economic Community) MEMBERS: Belgium, Denmark, France, Germany, Greece, Ireland, Italy, Luxembourg, Netherlands, Portugal, Spain, UK, Austria, Finland, Sweden

GATT
General Agreement on Tariffs and Trade
ESTABLISHED: 1947 MEMBERS: 104

G7
Group of 7
ESTABLISHED: 1985 MEMBERS: Canada, France, Germany, Italy, Japan, UK, USA

IMF
International Monetary Fund (UN agency)
ESTABLISHED: 1944 MEMBERS: 175

NAFTA
North American Free Trade Agreement
ESTABLISHED: 1994 MEMBERS: Canada, Mexico, USA

NATO
North Atlantic Treaty Organization
ESTABLISHED: 1949 MEMBERS: Belgium, Canada, Denmark, France, Germany, Greece, Iceland, Italy, Luxembourg, Netherlands, Norway, Spain, Turkey, UK, USA

OPEC
Organization of Petroleum Exporting Countries
ESTABLISHED: 1960 MEMBERS: Algeria, Gabon, Indonesia, Iran, Iraq, Kuwait, Libya, Nigeria, Qatar, Saudi Arabia, United Arab Emirates, Venezuela

UN
United Nations
ESTABLISHED: 1945 MEMBERS: 184; all nations are represented, except Palau, Kiribati, Nauru, Taiwan, Tonga, and Tuvalu. Switzerland and Vatican City have "observer status" only

KEY

━━━━━	International border
-----	Disputed border
....	Claimed border
......	Ceasefire line
	State/Province border
～	River
～	Lake
～	Canal
～	Seasonal river
～	Seasonal lake
─┤─	Waterfall
◇	Capital city
○	Other towns
✈	International airport
▲	Spot height - feet
•	Spot depth - feet

The asterisk in the Fact File denotes the country's official language(s)

DATE OF FORMATION in the Fact File denotes the country's date of independence or the date when its current borders were established

ABBREVIATIONS

Abbreviations used throughout this book are listed below:

abbrev. abbreviation
Afgh. Afghanistan
Arm. Armenia
Aus. Austria
Aust. Australia
Az. Azerbaijan

Bel. Belarus
Belg. Belgium
Bos. & Herz. Bosnia & Herzegovina
Bulg. Bulgaria

C. Central
C. Cape
Cam. Cambodia
CAR Central African Republic
Czech Rep. Czech Republic

D.C. District of Columbia
Dominican Rep. Dominican Republic

E. East
EQ. Equatorial
Est. Estonia
est. estimated

Fr. France
ft feet

Geo. Georgia
Ger. Germany

Hung. Hungary

I. Island
Is. Islands
inc. including

Kaz. Kazakhstan
km kilometers
Kyrgy. Kyrgyzstan

L. Lake, Lago
Lat. Latvia
Leb. Lebanon
Liech. Liechtenstein
Lith. Lithuania
Lux. Luxembourg

m meters
mi. miles
Mac. Macedonia
Med. Sea Mediterranean Sea
Mold. Moldova
Mt. Mount/Mountain
Mts. Mountains

N. North
N. Korea North Korea
Neth. Netherlands
NZ New Zealand

Peg. Pegunungan (Indonesian/Malay for mountain range)
Pol. Poland

R. River, Rio, Rio
Rep. Republic
Res. Reservoir
Rom. Romania
Russ. Fed. Russian Federation

S. South/Southern
S. Korea South Korea
SA South Africa
Slvka. Slovakia
Slvna. Slovenia
St. Saint
Str. Strait
Switz. Switzerland

Tajik. Tajikistan
Turkmen. Turkmenistan

UAE United Arab Emirates
UK United Kingdom
USA/US United States of America
Uzbek. Uzbekistan

Ven. Venezuela

W. West
W. Sahara Western Sahara

yds yards
Yugo. Yugoslavia

INDEX

KEY:
○ = Country
□ = Overseas territory